DATE DUE

APR 1 9 '89			
MAY 1 7 '96			
OCT 21			
DEC 4 '96			

GENERAL ROBERT E. LEE

From a Brady photograph

∗∗LEE∗∗

OF VIRGINIA

A Biography by

WILLIAM E. BROOKS

Illustrated

GREENWOOD PRESS, PUBLISHERS
WESTPORT, CONNECTICUT

Library of Congress Cataloging in Publication Data

Brooks, William Elizabeth, 1875–
    Lee of Virginia : a biography.

    Reprint of the ed. published by Bobbs-Merrill,
Indianapolis.
    Bibliography: p.
    Includes index.
    1. Lee, Robert Edward, 1807–1870. I. Title.
E467.1.L4B852   1975   973.7'3'0924 [B]   75–16842
ISBN 0–8371–8270–0

ACKNOWLEDGMENT

I WISH to acknowledge with grateful thanks the help that has been given me by many in the preparation of this book. Letters and diaries have been placed at my disposal by their owners, notably those of Bishop Peterkin. I have received many helpful suggestions from Dr. C. H. Ambler and Dr. O. P. Chitwood of the Department of History of West Virginia University, from Dr. John C. Fitzpatrick of Washington and from Dr. Thomas P. Martin of the Library of Congress. Especially am I grateful to Mr. C. G. Lee, Jr., of Washington, Historian of "The Lees of Virginia," who has aided me very much through placing at my disposal certain documents and letters not previously published. Also to my daughter, Jeanette Steele Brooks, who has helped in the preparation of the manuscript.

Grateful acknowledgment is also made of permission to use quotations from material copyrighted by them to the following: D. Appleton & Company, The Century Company, Dodd, Mead and Company, Doubleday, Doran & Company, Houghton Mifflin Company, Little, Brown & Company, The Macmillan Company, Charles Scribner's Sons and James C. Young.

WILLIAM E. BROOKS

Morgantown, West Virginia

CONTENTS

CONTENTS—*Concluded*

PART THREE
THE YEARS OF REBUILDING

ILLUSTRATIONS

FOREWORD

LEE of Virginia! There have been Lees before him and there will be Lees after, but Robert E. Lee is ever Lee of Virginia. Virginia mothered him, down in the Tidewater where the slow rivers run. To Virginia his heart ever turned in those days when he served in distant places, to Virginia and the white-pillared house on its northern border. It was at Virginia's call that he broke the old army ties and set aside the sober judgment which told him that secession was folly. It was on her fields that he won the fame that ranks him among the greatest of earth's captains. It was in her great Valley that he lived those last busy years when, with a war-weakened body, he strove unrestingly to fit her anew for the tasks of peace. And in her soil he sleeps. Virginia loves him as she does no other. Washington she reverences. Lee she adores.

Yet without in any way raping from Virginia that which she cherishes so greatly, it is time that we should think of him as the common heritage of us all, whether we come from north or south of that line which Mason and Dixon drew, which is only a line but which has been greater than the Chinese wall to our thinking. A past generation thought of him as one who would have destroyed America. It was difficult for that generation to think of him otherwise. They were partners in the event. Those who opposed him shut him out of their hearts because they feared him more than all the rest. Those who with him stood for the Lost Cause made him in their thinking the Hero of that Cause, the superman who emerges from every event, and whom humanity can not do without. So they built a legend about him and, as always is the way with legends, it has stifled the truth. It is the legend which has been responsible for most of the books about Lee. It painted the picture so familiar to many which hangs on the walls in the Memorial Chapel at Lexington—a plain attempt to apotheosize, to make him a sort of bearded Galahad. How he would have hated it all, did hate the beginnings of it while he lived, as Lincoln would have hated that white shrine they built for him at Washington!

Yet the truth is greater than the legend, for it is more human. And Lee is intensely human, with some human faults, but also with some great, supremely great, human qualities. Not least of these is the way he bore adversity. Compare him at Lexington, building quietly for a new day of peace, with Napoleon at St. Helena, fuming and scheming in little futile ways. And it is these qualities which are our common heritage. In them we may all exult. So those who opposed him, in shutting him out of their affections, have denied themselves and their children something which is rightly theirs. For "we are all of one blood and the triumph and the glory of one is the triumph and the glory of the other; the anguish and the tears of one is the anguish and the tears of the other; and the shame of one is the shame of the other."[1] This Lincoln saw. It rings through àll the Second Inaugural. It also rings through the many letters Lee wrote after the war to his old comrades-in-arms, bearing ever the same word: "The duty of its citizens then appears to me too plain to admit of doubt. All should unite in honest efforts to obliterate the effects of the war and to restore the blessings of peace."[2]

No dreaming of lost legions here, like Napoleon. He was

---

[1] Avary, p. 10.
[2] *R. and L.*, p. 163.

part of us all, by his own choice, directly after Appomattox.

So Virginia must give us the privilege of sharing in him, and we must exercise it. There is much to share. There is the glory of his achievements. What captain, other than Washington, ever did so much with the resources at his command? For four long years he carried the war on the bayonets of his ragged and steadily shrinking army. Campaign after campaign followed in which he defeated the best that the North had to send against him. True he was defeated at last. The marvel is that he was able to continue the battle as long as he did. Grant's strategy outwitted him, holding him as it did on the Petersburg line, while Sherman smashed in the back door of the Confederacy. Even there, there will always be the question of what might have happened had Davis permitted the evacuation of Richmond and the retreat to the Carolinas to join Johnston, which Lee urged weeks before Appomattox.[3] For four years he not only held off the northern hosts but he conquered the fears that began to grow in the hearts of his men that their victories might in the end avail them nothing. Very early those fears came, as we shall see. And although many of his men slipped away, what others among them thought of him can best be expressed in the words of a private soldier who had been sitting with the others about a camp-fire discussing the then new matter of evolution: "Well, boys, the rest of us may have developed from monkeys, but I tell you only God Almighty could make a man like Marse Robert."[4] That is why they charged as they did. To those ragged veterans he and the cause became identified. His military secretary, Colonel

---

[3] Long, p. 403.
[4] *Lee after Appomattox*, p. 103.

Marshall, bears testimony to this: "Such was the love and veneration of the men for him that they came to look upon the cause as General Lee's cause and they fought for it because they loved him. To them he represented cause, country, and all."[5] While the tale of these old wars is told men are not likely to forget the Captain who achieved so much with so little.

Then there is the glory of his personality. It has been pointed out again and again that in everything that was essential Lee resembled Washington. The stamp of it appears from his boyhood. He seems to have consciously set out to model his life on that of Washington, who had been his father's friend and into whose line he had married, until he made himself Washington's spiritual heir. He was, as has been already pointed out, hot-tempered, a bit hasty when he was denied, but so was Washington, as another Lee remembered after Monmouth. But he possessed that courtesy which was ready with apology when the moment of passion had passed. He was a little stately, perhaps, on most occasions, and not inclined to overmuch humor, but they raised stately men in Tidewater Virginia, and if this be an offense then Washington is equally guilty. But these are not the qualities that cause men to lay down their lives for a leader. There were other things in Lee. There was courage unquestionably. He had shown that in those reconnaissances in Mexico. He showed it often in the later war. His staff lived in constant fear of his needlessly exposing himself. And there is the well-known story of how at Spottsylvania soldiers making a charge seized the reins of Traveller when he had ridden too far into the battle lines and refused to go on with the charge until he had gone back to safety. But bravery

[5] R. and L., p. 138.

was not his highest quality. That was obedience to conscience. We can question his judgment at certain critical
moments and especially in *the* critical moment in April,
'61, when he made his great decision, but there is not a
shadow of a doubt but that all the time he did that which
his conscience told him was right. Men knew it. It went
far to create that trust in him which they had, that almost
blind trust which caused them to follow even when they
could not agree. This was shown in the way they received
his decision to surrender. Bradford quotes "one of the
coolest of the Confederate writers" in his account of the
surrender: "Other men fairly raved with indignation and
declared their desire to escape or die in the attempt. . . .
On the contrary, all expressed the greatest sympathy for
him and declared their willingness to submit at once, or to
fight to the last man, as he ordered."[6]

Least of all can we forget the way in which he met the
supreme test of the days after Appomattox. Fortune gone,
himself proscribed, the wife he loved an invalid, his own
health undermined by the strain and the hardships of the
war years, he threw himself with all his might into the
task of rebuilding the nation. Denying himself ease and
unearned wealth, refusing to sell his fame for his own
advantage, declining above all to run away from those
who demanded vengeance, he did the one thing he could
do to aid Virginia to her feet. He believed that as he
had led the young men of the South to battle so it was
his task to train them to do their duty in peace. He
spoke of this as a "self-imposed task which I must accomplish."[7] For this they needed training, not only in the
arts, but in the art of living. The story of those quiet

----

[6] Bradford, p. 122.
[7] *R. and L.*, p. 376.

difficult years, as he struggled to put a bankrupt college on its feet and reshape it into an instrument for rebuilding a war-wrecked land, is as greatly heroic as any tale ever told of an American. It has not the glamour of battle about it. It has an even greater, if more quiet, splendor.

We are accustomed to say that Lincoln grew with the war. So did Lee. And he rises to the full height of the heroic in those years at Lexington. It was my privilege to study one morning his letter-copy book containing one record of those crowded years. I discovered there that for him there was no detail too small so long as it would aid in the achievement of the task he had set himself. With failing strength he went on. Virginia must be fitted for the day that lay ahead. That record of those years is a proud record that we dare not forget, but we are apt to lose sight of it as we think of the tale of battle. I sometimes think that here his greatest value to his fellow-Americans is to be found. To be great after failure, quiet amid obloquy, steady when all around are shaken, that is great living. That that living was seen and understood of the boys who came to him in that little mountain college is proved by one of his old students who afterward wrote of the impressions that he made upon them: "He is an illustrious example of those whose moral judgments no glory can obscure; whose integrity no temptation can corrupt. He is an epistle written of God and designed by God to teach the people of this country that earthly success is not the criterion of merit nor the measure of true greatness."[8]

It was left for a British soldier, Viscount Wolseley, to point a generation ago a fact which Americans have not yet accepted, but which some day they will accept, that of

---

[8] *Lee after Appomattox*, p. 103.

all the men whom that stirring age produced Lincoln and Lee are the most worthy of remembrance. "To me," he wrote, "two figures stand out in that history towering above all others, both cast in hard metal that will be for ever proof against the belittling efforts of all future detractors. One, General Lee, the great soldier: the other, Mr. Lincoln, the far-seeing statesman of iron will, of unflinching determination. Each is a good representative of the genius that characterised his country. As I study the history of the Secession war, these seem to me the two men that influenced it most and who will be recognised as its greatest heroes when future generations of American historians record its stirring events with impartiality."[9] We can not pass by the great soldier's estimate, for it sifts out of all the figures of the war the two that most deserve our thought.

Strangely enough they were both Virginians, in a sense, these two. For while Lincoln was born in Kentucky, the place of his birth had been claimed by Virginia only a few years before and his forebears were Virginians. What strange contrasts they present! Lincoln was a poor white, born in a cabin in a clearing! (I think it can hardly be said that Doctor Barton has proved his case in the effort to make Lincoln a distant cousin of Lee.[10]) Lee, "the best representative of the aristocratic principle in all American history," was born in stately Stratford.[11] Lincoln opposed the War with Mexico.[12] In this war Lee won his first fame and the high opinion of Scott. Lee was opposed to slavery. But he was not opposed to it as was Lincoln. As early as 1856 he was writing from his post on the Rio Grande:

[9] *MacMillan's Magazine*, Vol. 55, p. 321.
[10] *Lineage of Lincoln*, pp. 209-10.
[11] *Lincoln or Lee*, p. 177.
[12] *Works of Abraham Lincoln*, Lapsley, Vol. II, p. 38,

"There are few, I believe, in this enlightened age, who will not acknowledge that slavery as an institution is a moral and political evil in any country. It is useless to expatiate on its disadvantages. I think it is a greater evil to the white than to the black race. While my *feelings are strongly enlisted on behalf of the latter, my sympathies are more strong for the former.*"[13] (Italics mine.) Contrast this with the speech Lincoln made in Philadelphia in Independence Hall on his way to his inauguration: "I have never had a feeling, politically, that did not spring from the Declaration of Independence. . . . It was not the mere matter of separation of the colonies from the motherland, but that sentiment in the Declaration of Independence which gave liberty not alone to the people of this country, but hope to all the world, for all future times, which gave promise that in due time the weights would be lifted from the shoulders of all men."[14] Perhaps in no way can the difference between the two men be set forth more clearly than in those two utterances.

Lifting the weights from the shoulders of *all* men. Lee, with all his greatness, never saw that. "This man," as the kindliest of his northern biographers puts it, "fighting as he believed for freedom, for independence, for democracy, was fighting also to rivet the shackles more firmly on millions of his fellow men. . . . And this it is that makes the tragedy of his career so large, so fatal, so commanding in its grandeur."[15] Yet both were singularly alike in that both followed their duty as they saw it, without any regard to selfish advantage. They both purposed purely, but Lincoln saw more clearly. And this it is that makes us put him first. Yet had Lincoln lived to address

---

[13] White, p. 50.
[14] Quoted *Lincoln or Lee,* p. 30.
[15] Bradford, pp. 43-44.

himself to the tasks of reconstruction he would have found Lee a helper. Ben Wade and Sumner could have plotted as they would in the Senate, and Stevens, of the twisted foot and far more badly twisted soul, threatened in the House, but Lincoln would have gone ahead. And Davis might have sneered in his exile, but Lee would have worked with Lincoln. Loyalty had been greater than logic in '61, it would have been greater than all the sneers in '65. The South would have been spared the bitter shame of that terrible decade, and there would be no sectionalism to-day. Booth's bullet deprived both men of their greatest chance.

So they stand, the two preeminent figures of the war, not Grant but Lincoln, not Davis but Lee, each representing what was best and highest in the causes which came into conflict. And we are all coming to see that it was best for us all that Lincoln won. Yet Lee also we must claim as part, and a great part, of our American heritage. Washington, Lincoln, Lee, each great in his own way, each cast of metal that rings true and that time can not tarnish.

So I, of whose family every one of the men old enough to bear arms fought with the North against him, have written this book about him, because I believe that those who regard Robert E. Lee with the old doubts are losing something we ought to cherish. Yet I have not sought to recreate the legend but to make live the man.

WILLIAM E. BROOKS

PART ONE

THE YEARS OF PREPARATION

Lee of Virginia

CHAPTER I

Ancestry

THE nearest approach to a hereditary aristocracy in America was that of Tidewater Virginia. And Robert E. Lee was its peculiar flower. Aristocracy among us is a system derided, and rightly so. But in our derision we must not forget that while as a system it promotes many things that we will not tolerate, it also promotes other things. There is an aristocracy of achievement which stimulates to fresh achievement for the honor of the family. And none more so than among the Lees. Stratford had been their home for generations, and in its great hall hung portraits whose story was an incentive to all who bore the name. There had been born Richard Henry Lee, member of the Continental Congress from Virginia, who on June 7, 1776, moved in that Congress that "these colonies are and of right ought to be free and independent states." There also his brother, Francis Lightfoot Lee, and the names of both appeared on the bottom of that Declaration which a month later followed the resolution. And Arthur Lee, who helped negotiate the treaty of alliance with France, and William Lee, who was the fiscal agent abroad of the Colonies during the Revolution, were also born there. And to this house Light Horse Harry Lee had come home after following Washington in the wars. It was an old house full of memories, far different from that cabin in Kentucky. It had been built in 1727

by Thomas Lee, President of the Council, Governor of the
Colony, and father of those sons whom President John
Adams (who did not always love Virginians) described
as "that band of brothers intrepid and unchangeable, who
like the Greeks at Thermopylæ stood in the gap in the
defense of their country from the first glimmering of
the Revolution on the horizon, through all its rising light,
to its perfect day."[1]   And its doors had opened to welcome
every one of worth in Virginia, from Washington down,
and its halls had echoed to their voices.   There were many
things for the young Lees to think of as they walked
through Stratford's great rooms.

But the Lees were older in America than Stratford.
The first settlements were but thirty-four years begun
and Charles I was on the throne, with his head still
securely on his shoulders, when the first Lee, Richard,
came to Virginia.   He was a man of no slight means, a
landholder of Stratford-Langton, in the English county
of Essex.[2]   The earliest Virginia land-grant recorded
in his name bears the date of August 10, 1642.   Charles II
made him governor of the Colony, his houses and lands
multiplied and when he died he left vast tracts of the sun-
smitten soil on both banks of the Potomac, described by
Captain John Smith as "lusty and very rich."[3]

His son Richard succeeded to the headship of the family on the death of the elder John, and he in time was
followed by Thomas.   We are interested in Thomas because he was the builder of Stratford.   Tradition says that
he built it with funds "contributed by certain London
merchants and the Queen who wanted the President of

---

[1] Letter of John Adams, August 11, 1819.
[2] White, p. 3.
[3] *Ibid.*, p. 4.

the Council to be fully housed."⁴ For a fire had destroyed
the house at Mt. Pleasant. Stratford is not the best of
colonial Virginia. It was massive but not beautiful, built
for the years, its walls enclosing two and a half feet of
English brick at the base and no less than two feet above
the first floor. Here is the way Robert E. Lee described
it, as he remembered it, years later.

"The approach to the house is on the south, along the
side of a lawn several hundred acres in extent, adorned
with cedars, oaks, and forest poplars. On ascending a hill,
not far from the gate, the traveler comes in full view of
the mansion, when the road turns to the right and leads
straight to a grove of sugar maples, around which it sweeps
to the house. The edifice is built in the form of an H,
and of bricks brought from England. The cross furnishes
a saloon of thirty feet cube, and in the center of each
wing rises a cluster of chimneys, which form the columns
of two pavilions connected by a balustrade. The owner,
who before the Revolution was a member of the King's
Council, lived here in great state and kept a band of musi-
cians to whose airs his daughters Matilda and Flora, with
their companions, danced in the saloon or promenaded on
the house-top."⁵

One does not gather from that that his memories of it
were very sweet, though he had long wished to own it.
It was a bit solid and a bit forbidding. There was not the
graciousness about it that Arlington had. The main floor
was too far above the ground. In the great central hall
hung the famous portraits, and they with the tall Corin-
thian pilasters in black walnut gave an air of austerity to
the place. Nor was this dispelled by the great fireplace one
usually found in such halls, whose glowing welcome gave

⁴Young, p. 11.
⁵Quoted by Young, p. 11.

the entering guest not only warmth but cheer, for the hall was heated only by charcoal braziers so that it was always chill and lacking in welcome. From the hall two drafty corridors led to the dining-room and the sleeping apartments. In the Virginia fashion the kitchen stood about fifty feet from the house, and its fireplace was twelve feet wide, six feet high and five feet deep, big enough to roast an ox. Beyond were the slave-quarters, the carriage house, the stables and all the array of out-buildings that made up the home of a Virginia gentleman. The woods cut off the view of the Potomac except when one climbed to the roof.

It seems strange that from this Stratford were to come Richard Henry and his patriot brothers, for Thomas Lee was a royalist and a churchman of whom we read "his voice was against the wide extension of the privileges of public worship to the religious Dissenters."[6] But no single house in America contributed so many members to the task of ending royalty for ever.

The second Richard had another son Henry. On his death in 1747 he handed on his estate to three sons and a daughter, the third also named Henry. He in turn had a son whom his soldiers later were to call "Light Horse Harry." As the father of Robert he deserves our particular attention. He would deserve it in any event. He came to this earth as stirring events were shaping themselves, at "Leeslyvania" in Prince William County, in 1755. He was a boy when Patrick Henry's voice began ringing through Virginia in opposition to the tyrannies of the King. His father seems early to have thrown in his lot with the revolutionary party, and when he came to choose a college for his son it was not to old William and Mary, stronghold

---

[6]Fitzhugh Lee, p. 7.

of the establishment, but to Princeton he sent him, where at the feet of Witherspoon he was to learn doctrines that George III considered dangerous.

Young Henry was graduated in 1773 and returned to Virginia to study law, but the books were soon laid aside in preparation for the coming conflict. As captain of a band of Light Horse, Henry Lee presented himself for orders at Washington's headquarters in Morristown, New Jersey, one hundred days after the battles of Trenton and Princeton. He entered at once on the arduous task of scouting and foraging for Washington's army, and he had not long to wait for the General's commendation for "gallant behavior." Perhaps there was another reason for Washington's interest in the young dragoon. Lucy Grymes was his mother and before Henry Lee had married her the tale was told that Washington loved her.[7] But whatever the beginnings of the friendship it continued and was strengthened by the qualities displayed by the young soldier.

Early in 1778 he was promoted to major and placed in command of a corps of Light Horse. Among its members was Peter Johnston, who joined the corps when only sixteen years old, and led the forlorn hope at the storming of Fort Watson. His son, Joseph E. Johnston, was to be heard from in a later war. It was Lee who suggested the capture of Stony Point, and he led the successful dash against Paulus Hook on the Jersey coast. For this later exploit Congress voted him a medal with warm commendation of "his remarkable prudence, address and bravery." In the campaign in the Carolinas he won his greatest measure of fame. As Washington sent him to join Greene he wrote to John Matthews, a member of

[7] *Ibid.*, p. 10.

Congress from South Carolina, informing him of the intended movement: "Lee's corps will go to the southward; it is an excellent one, and the officer at the head of it has great reserves of genius."[8]

In the campaign that followed Lee proved himself more than a match for Tarleton, the British cavalry leader. Long after the war was over men remembered him as the typical *beau sabreur*. He delighted in nothing so much as to lead a charge, himself at the head of his legion, with sabers flashing in the sun, straight into the British army. It is little wonder that Washington—a bit more dashing than his classical portraits would have us think— loved him.

The war over he retired to Stratford, of which he had become the master through his marriage with the daughter of Philip Ludwell Lee in 1782. Perhaps retired is a word that never should be spoken of him. He was for ever faring forth on some new venture. Washington, now president, commissioned him as major-general to lead the army he had raised to put down the Whisky Rebellion in western Pennsylvania growing out of the resistance of the settlers to the tax laid on distilled spirits. The President accompanied him on the march as far as Bedford. Again we learn his judgment of its commander from his words of farewell to the army: "In leaving the army I have less regret as I know I commit it to an able and faithful direction."[9]

After his bloodless victory over the Scotch-Irish malcontents Lee returned to Virginia. Twice he served as its governor, and as a Federalist was elected to the Sixth Congress where steadily he opposed the policies and the

[8] *Ibid.*, p. 9.
[9] *Ibid.*, p. 11.

rising power of Jefferson. On the election of the latter to the presidency he left politics behind and planned to spend his life as a country gentleman. A bewitching, bewildering figure, this Light Horse Harry, more fitted for the days of chivalry than for those troublous years of the young republic he had helped to establish. He liked swift horses, he liked gallant talk. His friends were the great men of his time, Washington, Hamilton, Madison, Patrick Henry. When his young wife, "the Divine Matilda," died he planned to resign his governorship and offer his sword to the revolutionary party in France. With the same recklessness he plunged into gambling in western lands. Reckless; yes, he had been that at the head of his Light Horse. And ever after!

It was in 1790 that the divine Matilda died and instead of offering his sword to France he offered his hand to Ann Hill Carter, daughter of Charles Carter of Shirley. He was only thirty-seven and she was twenty. The family from which she came was no less distinguished than the Lees. Her father was the fourth of the line in America. The most famous of it was "King" Carter, Speaker of the House of Burgesses, Rector of William and Mary College, and Governor of the Colony of Virginia. His memorial in Christ Church in Lancaster describes him thus: "An honorable man, who by noble endowments and pure morals gave lustre to his gentle birth."[10] He looms large in the chronicles of colonial Virginia.

And Ann Carter was of his blood. She bore herself greatly in the bleak days that followed. And it was during the bleak days, on January 19, 1807, that her fifth child was born. He was an unwanted child. His mother had many things to trouble her. Charles Carter had just

---

[10] White, p. 16.

died. Her husband's debts were accumulating. She was
grieving over the sickness of her sister Mildred. It is little
wonder that she did not look forward with eagerness to
the coming of another child. She writes to her sister-in-
law early in January in no uncertain tones: "That part of
your letter which relates to your expecting another son
shortly is so defaced by the seal that I cannot understand
it; I applied to your husband for an explanation and from
his answer I suppose he also had reason for such an ex-
pectation—you have my best wishes for your success my
dear and truest assurances that I do not envy your prospects
nor wish to share in them."[11]

But wishes can not stay such things, and when the boy
came they called him Robert Edward. He was born in
the same high-ceilinged bedroom at the southeast corner of
the house and on the same big four-poster bed in which
three generations of Lees had been born. January is cold
even in the Tidewater, and the shallow fireplace barely
took the chill off the room. There were many thoughts
in the mind of Ann Carter as she lay and looked out on
the winter fields. But it is not likely that she dreamed
of the glory that was to be hers through that son that had
been of her and that now lay at her side.

So in this old house, full of memories and portraits, the
life of Robert Lee began. Of course they told him later,
when he began to understand, whose the portraits were.
They were careful of such things in Virginia. It is not
hard to imagine Ann Carter, in the troubled days that
followed, when shame was her daily bread and the debtors
came clamoring to the door, taking her boy by the hand
and leading him up and down the hall and telling him
the tale of the Lees who had lived there before him, and

[11]Boyd, p. 286.

who, bewigged and powdered, watched him from the walls to see that he lived worthy of the name. It helped her pride; it would help her boy. An honorable line they were, empire builders, shapers of great fortunes, men of rectitude, given to hospitality, mighty in the thought of men. These were his forebears, and this was their home. And when Arlington was gone for ever and had become a place of sepulture, he wrote his wife from his camp in Georgia: ". . . it has always been the desire of my life to be able to purchase it. Now that we have no other home and the one we loved has been so foully polluted the desire is stronger with me than ever."[12] But it was a desire never to be realized.

It is little wonder that Robert E. Lee has been called "the best representative of the aristocratic spirit in America." Why should he not be with that background?

---

[12] *R. and L.*, p. 56.

CHAPTER II

Youth

WHEN the Revolution was over and peace was assured along the western border the young nation began to push westward. It did not know much about that western country, but it knew that destiny called it to go up and possess it. And the treaty that ended the war had not been signed before the pack-trains began to move beyond the mountains and the sound of axes was heard in the forests. There were those who, not going themselves, thought they could win fortune through the purchase of western lands, and the bottom-lands beyond the mountains were the scene of wild speculation. Among those who thus ventured was Henry Lee. A certain William McCleery, in Morgantown in western Virginia, was his agent in this speculation, and when the bottom dropped out of the movement in 1805 McCleery sued him for unpaid balances. Robert Morris, the Philadelphia banker, had owed him forty thousand dollars, and when Morris's tragic failure occurred Lee was left without the means to meet his own obligations. McCleery's suit was the signal for other creditors to fall upon him, and the days of young Robert's infancy found the house undergoing a constant siege by bailiffs. Night and day the great doors were chained and no doubtful person found admittance. The estate began to shrink in size and the buildings were badly in need of repair. At last McCleery got his man and he who had been Washington's dependence when he needed a stroke of daring in the perilous days was locked up as a common debtor in the Westmoreland County jail at Montross. It was evident that the Stratford days were nearly done. But before she left it, Ann Carter took her little son and went with him into the garden and planted a horse-chestnut tree, as though for the day they would return. And long afterward, in the midst of a great war, Robert was to remember it.[1]

While he was in jail the thoughts of the broken soldier returned to the days when he had ridden at the head of his swift-charging, green-jacketed Legion, and the South had echoed with his fame. So he began to write his narrative of the *War in the Southern Department,* and after Robert's years of fighting were over he was to prepare a new edition of it and write the Introduction, his only piece of literary work. Some time in the spring of 1810 the debts were settled and Henry Lee returned to Stratford. But shortly after Matilda's son, Henry, came of age and Stratford, which his mother had inherited from her father, became his. So the family moved in 1811 to Alexandria to a house on Cameron Street near Christ Church. There, in the old church where Washington had been pewholder, the family worshiped. Ann Carter found religion a stay on which she rested, and her boy found a friend in the rector of the church who profoundly impressed him and turned his life toward the way of faith it never left. It was fortunate for him that he did not stay in Stratford with that elder brother who was the new squire. For Henry Lee, the younger, was the blackest sheep that ever grew up in the Lee fold.

Compared with the lavish opulence of the Stratford days life in Alexandria was straitened. Yet there were enough

[1]Boyd, p. 292.

slaves to care for the house, and the family could keep two horses and a cow. Alexandria was a comfortable town, substantially built and just across the river from Washington. Although he had retired from politics, the Colonel could keep watch on the events which were shaping at the Capital where the grievances against England were finding champions in two young men from the South, John C. Calhoun and Henry Clay. The dying Federalist party was assaulting the policy of the Administration and opposing the war. And the Colonel was a Federalist, divided now in his sympathies, for the friend of Washington could not bestow his sympathies on England. Neither could the politician, who had retired from active participation in affairs, whole-heartedly support the party whose success had led to his retirement.

Then occurred an event which was to have a profound effect on his future. Hanson, the editor of a Federalist paper in Baltimore, had poured bitter words upon the Administration. Bitterness provoked bitterness, and his opponents attacked and burned his printing house. Lee among others rushed to his defense, the crusader again. With twenty of his friends about him Hanson turned his house into a fortress and defied his enemies. In the struggle that followed Lee was wounded. It was at first reported that he was dead of his wounds, but the slighting reference of the Democratic *National Intelligencer* to his supposed death gave the Federalist papers the opportunity to remind the country of his services in the Revolution. He was able at last to return to Alexandria, but for the remainder of his life he was an invalid. The doctors ordered his removal to a warmer land. From there on till his death he was "an aged ungirt Ulysses" wandering from one West Indian Island to another in search of health.[2] The letters that came back to his family are those of a weary man, full of longing for those he loved and anxious for their well-being. To one he writes: "You know how I love my children, and how dear Smith is to me. Give me a true description of his person, mind, temper & habits. Tell me of Ann; has she grown tall? And how is my last, in looks and understanding? Robert was always good, and will be confirmed in his happy turn of mind by his ever-watchful and affectionate mother; does he strengthen his native tendency?"[3] But to the younger of those children he soon became little more than a memory.

The years of suffering and exile were nearly ended. Wanting to see his family again before he died he turned his face homeward. But he got only as far as Cumberland Island off the coast of Georgia. There at the home of the old Commander under whom he had fought in the Carolinas, General Greene, "did he enter into rest March 25, 1818, and there do the magnolias still stand guard over his grave." Long years afterward his son, when in command in the Carolinas in '61, was to visit that grave for the first time. Very tender is his aide's description of the incident: "He went alone to the tomb, and after a few minutes of silence, plucked a flower and slowly retraced his steps."[4]

Charles Carter had left Ann's portion of his estate in trust, so that her husband's debts might not swallow it up. This was now the mainstay of the family. They were not easy years for the growing boy, Robert, left fatherless at eleven. The care-free days of youth were never his. The long troubles had told on Ann Carter, in

[2]*Ibid.*, p. 332.
[3]*Ibid.*, p. 335.
[4]Long, p. 23.

spite of her indomitable spirit, and her body began to break
under it. So the care of his mother and the direction of
the household became largely his responsibility. The elder
brother Carter was at Harvard, Smith had become a mid-
shipman in the navy, one sister was an invalid in Philadelphia, and the other was younger than he. So that he
became the actual head of the household. Among the
papers of his old schoolmaster was found a memorandum
speaking of him as "an exemplary student,"[5] and we have
had preserved for us a picture of him, hurrying home
from school, to take his mother driving in the family carriage, when he was careful to fasten the curtains and close
up the cracks to keep the drafts from her.[6] It is not
hard to trace the effect of this on his later years. We
know little more about his childhood and what few stories
we have sound apocryphal. He himself had little to say
about it. Longstreet records in his memory of him in
war-days: " 'Twas seldom that he allowed his mind to
wander to the days of his childhood and talk of his father
and his early associates, but when he did he was far more
charming than he thought."[7] And there is the story of
his visit to Alexandria only a little while before his death
when one who had been his neighbor years before found
him looking over the fence into the old garden. "I am
looking to see if the old snowball trees are there," he said.
"I should have been sorry to have missed them."[8]

At eighteen he received an appointment to West Point,
at the hands of Andrew Jackson himself. One of his class-
mates was the son of that Peter Johnston who had won
distinction in his father's legion. Let that Joseph E.

---

[5] Young, p. 24.
[6] Page, p. 10.
[7] Longstreet, p. 287.
[8] Mason, *Popular Life of Gen. R. E. Lee*, p. 24.

Johnston describe him in those cadet days as afterward he remembered him. "We had the same intimate associates who thought as I did that no other youth or man so united the qualities that win warm friendship and command high respect. For he was full of sympathy and kindness, genial and fond of gay conversation, and even of fun, while his correctness of demeanor and attention to all duties, personal and official, and a dignity as much a part of himself as the elegance of his person, gave him a superiority that everyone acknowledged in his heart."[9] He bore off the coveted cadet-adjutancy of the corps and was graduated second in his class of forty-six. He was assigned to the Engineers, the corps which was to produce, with the exception of Grant and Jackson, nearly all the officers who won high rank in the war. And with his commission in his hand and his new blue uniform he hurried back to his mother. She had lived to see the unwanted child become her best loved child and to see him start on his career. A few months later he journeyed to Stratford to lay her with the other Lees. Youth was over, what little youth he had, and the busy years came crowding on him.

---

[9]Quoted by Page, p. 15.

CHAPTER III

Marriage and Early Service

LIEUTENANT LEE began his army service as assistant to
Captain Andrew Talcott, the engineer in charge of the
building of the works at Fortress Monroe. Lieutenant
Joseph E. Johnston was also assigned to this duty and the
friendship of cadet days was further cemented. In a
letter written after he became famous a near relative of
his, who acknowledged that she "did not see anything in
him that prepared me for his so far outstripping all his
compeers," remembers him as "splendid looking—as full
of life, and particularly of teasing, as any of us."[1]

But the particular thing to him about this service was
that Fortress Monroe was not really very far from Washington. And that was important for him, for across the
river from Washington was Arlington, and Mary Custis.
Arlington will be much in this story. It would be well to
stop and take a glance at it. It stands on a hill, high above
the river, overlooking the Capital. It was built by Washington's adopted son, George Washington Parke Custis. It
was filled with the treasures of Mount Vernon, portraits of
Washington, the Cincinnati china, the famous punch-bowl
made for Washington when President, the silver service of
1789, his camp equipment, the great four-poster bed in
which he died, and many other things. It was the scene of
open hospitality, for Mr. Custis liked to play the part of a
lavish host. His only child, Mary Ann Randolph Custis,

---

[1]Long, p. 30.

38

was sought by many suitors. One can not help wondering how history might have been changed had she listened to the addresses of one of them, Sam Houston, then Representative Houston, Chairman of the Congressional Board of Visitors to West Point.[2] Houston was already famous, and many a belle in Washington would have said a trembling and joyful "yes" to his question, for it was already whispered around the Capital that Jackson had him in mind for the succession. But Mary had danced with a tall cadet in gray when he came home to Alexandria and not even fame could thrust him out of her heart. So Houston went in his glory to inspect West Point without Mary, and after the cadet had become a lieutenant Mary married him. On June 30, 1831, the right-hand drawing-room at Arlington was filled with a brilliant company when the service was read by Reverend William Meade, afterward Bishop of Virginia. There were six groomsmen, all army men but one, and six of Virginia's daughters fluttered in crinoline down the great stairs before the bride. It rained that night and the clergyman arrived thoroughly drenched for the ceremony. There were no clothes into which he could change save those of Mr. Custis, and Mr. Custis was short and stout and Mr. Meade was tall and thin. It was one of those occasions on which he was thankful for a surplice.[3] But not even a rain-soaked clergyman could dampen the merriment of that night.

Lee became the son of the house, and afterward the management of the estate passed largely into his hands, making it more valuable and remunerative than it had been before. The Custis estate included also the plantation of

[2] James, p. 55.
[3] Long, p. 32.

the White House on the Pamunkey River, where Washington had married the Widow Custis. The war brought tragedy to both places. The White House was burned to the ground, and Arlington became the National Cemetery. But for many years it was Lee's home, to which his thought turned when on his far service. And here he passed those seven weeks of question and indecision, before he resigned from the old army.

His service at Fortress Monroe lasted until 1834. Then for three years he served as assistant to the Chief Engineer in Washington, three happy years, with Arlington only a short horseback ride away. And there were army friends in Washington and all the gaiety and grace of Virginia before the war to entertain at Arlington. It was not a long ride from his office to his home and the exercise kept him fit. The story of one ride, which may have astonished some of his dignified friends and which shows that he was not always dignified, still remains. As he was about to start for Arlington one afternoon his friend, Lieutenant Macomb, appeared, and Lee hailed him with, "Come get up with me." To his surprise Macomb put his foot in the stirrup and mounted behind him. Lee, not to be outdone, rode off down Pennsylvania Avenue and as they passed the White House they met the Secretary of the Treasury, Honorable Levi Woodbury, to whom they both bowed with great dignity. A more astonished gentleman has not been seen before or since.[4]

This tour of duty being ended, he was assigned to the task of defining the border between Ohio and Michigan, and then in the summer of 1837 he was sent to St. Louis in response to a request of the city authorities for an engineer who would avert the peril which threatened the

---

[4] *Ibid.*, p. 37.

city, of the Mississippi's cutting a new channel through the Illinois bottom-lands, leaving St. Louis an inland city. It was in June, 1837, that he started westward with his aides for this last-named duty. They went by the way of the Pennsylvania Canal to Pittsburgh, where they took a steamer and descended to Louisville. Here they organized a party of river-men and proceeded with their chartered boat to the rapids above St. Louis, of which they made thorough surveys. The whole river was thoroughly mapped from the mouth of the Missouri to some distance below St. Louis before a plan was made. The plans he made were approved by Congress and were the basis of the appropriations made for the control of that difficult stream. And the Mississippi never threatened to desert St. Louis again.

In 1838 he received his captaincy, and for several summers he had charge of the work at St. Louis. But always there was Arlington to come back to. He was only thirty, married to a wife whom he adored, the father of growing children, the manager of a property that put him beyond the fear of want. Best of all he was making a name for himself in his profession. And he was learning to know the country and the people of its various sections as few of that day did. Surely he must have thought himself a favorite of fortune. Yet, if he did, he kept it to himself. General Meigs, who was one of his subordinates in the St. Louis operations, gives us this picture of him in this period: "A man then in the vigor of youthful strength, with a noble commanding presence, and an admirable, graceful and athletic figure. He was one with whom nobody ever wished or ventured to take a liberty, though kind and generous to his subordinates, admired by all women and respected by all men."[5]

---

[5] *Ibid.*, p. 44.

In 1841 he was placed in charge of the construction of fortifications at Fort Hamilton in New York harbor. Mrs. Lee and the children joined him here, and even though the officers' quarters in a fortress did not have the comfort of Arlington still it was home. There was New York near by with its social life, its theaters, the chance for many things which he enjoyed. The post itself held much outside of the usual round of duties. He was a vestryman in the little parish church of which the post chaplain was the rector, and he was as careful of his duties here as elsewhere.

An officer who was stationed with him at the Fort tells a story which shows his diplomacy. The Tractarian movement had reached America; Tract Number XC had been published. Puseyism was a bone of contention. The excitement invaded the little parish, and it created feeling, for the Low-Church members vehemently suspected the rector of High-Church views because of certain suspicious prayers that he used to which they had not been accustomed. From all this Captain Lee kept aloof, and, as he was altogether too important a member to make his views a matter of indifference, various were the efforts made to draw him out—each party hoping for his powerful support—but without success, for he always contrived in some pleasant way to avoid any expression of opinion that would commit him to either faction. One evening he came into the quarters of one of the younger officers, where a number of officers and one or two of the neighbors were assembled. Soon the inevitable subject came up and was discussed with considerable warmth, and, on the part of two or three, with some feeling. Captain Lee was quiet, but, to those who understood him, evidently amused at the efforts to draw him out. On some direct attempt to do so he turned to one of them and in his impressive grave manner said, "I am glad to see that you keep aloof from the dispute that is disturbing our little parish. That is right, and we must not get mixed up in it; we must support each other in that. But I must give you some advice about it, in order that we may understand each other: BEWARE OF PUSSYISM! PUSSYISM is always bad, and may lead to unchristian feeling; therefore beware of PUSSYISM!" The ludicrous turn given by his pronunciation, and its aptness to the feeling that one or two had displayed, ended the matter in a general burst of laughter, for the manner more than the words conveyed his meaning. It became rather a joke at the expense of the officer, however, for sometimes when several of them met Lee would look at him in a grave way, shake his head, and say, "Keep clear of this Pussyism!" And this was as near as they ever got to committing Captain Lee to a church quarrel.[6]

No stupid Galahad would be guilty of a pun like that. Nor of shocking a Cabinet minister in front of the President's house. This Captain Lee had manifestly many admirable qualities. Among them was a saving sense of humor.

---

[6] *Ibid.*, pp. 67-68.

Chapter IV

Mexico

MEN differed about the Mexican War when it was fought. They differ about it still. But we see more clearly than they did in 1846 whose hands were on the pieces and why the moves were made on the national chess-board, see this far more clearly than did James K. Polk, who was president. Poor Polk! He was the tool of abler men who knew exactly what they wanted, and got it. Or at least thought they had got it until gold was found at Sutter's Fort in California. That brought in a new factor they had not foreseen. One of those who did see things Polk had not seen was Abraham Lincoln and he had the courage to set forth what he saw in a speech delivered in 1847 while a member of Congress: "Let him [President Polk] remember he sits where Washington sat, and so remembering, answer as Washington would answer. As a nation should not, and as the Almighty will not, be evaded, so let him attempt no evasion—no equivocation. And if he can show that the soil was ours where the first blood [Mexican] of the war was shed—then I am with him for his justification. But if he can not do this I shall be fully convinced that he feels the blood of this war, like the blood of Abel, is crying to heaven against him."[1]

Lee does not seem to have been concerned with the politics behind the war or the motives of those who brought it on. We find him objecting to the Administration,[2] but

[1] Quoted *Lincoln or Lee*, p. 8.
[2] Jones, *Life*, p. 56.

44

his objection is based on the treatment of Scott and other of his brother officers in the distribution of rewards. His attitude toward the war itself was that of a professional soldier: "It is rather late in the day," he writes, "to discuss the origin of the war; that ought to have been understood before we engaged in it. It may have been produced by the acts of either party or the force of circumstances. Let the pedants of diplomacy determine. It is certain that we are the victors in a regular war, continued, if not brought on, by their obstinacy and ignorance, and they are whipped in a manner of which women might be ashamed. We have the right, by the laws of war, of dictating the terms of peace and requiring indemnity for our losses and expenses. Rather than forego that right, except through a spirit of magnanimity to a crushed foe, I would fight them ten years, but I would be generous in exercising it."[3]

This war was to have a very important part in the shaping of his future. It gave him his first taste of actual battle. He had been dealing with obdurate rivers, with stone and mortar, and the materials of defense. Now he was to ride at the head of men, in reconnaissance, in charge. He was to display bravery and initiative that were to mark him in the eyes of his superiors and to give him the opportunities that come only to the marked man. It was because Scott saw him in battle, in the planning and carrying out of the serious business of battle, there in Mexico, that he was to recommend him to Lincoln later for the command of the Federal army. And it shaped events for that other war which followed it in which he was to win his greater fame.

His entry into the war began with the column of Gen-

[3] *Ibid.*, p. 57.

eral Wool, ordered to invade the northern departments of
Mexico. Taylor's victory at Buena Vista virtually ended
operations in northern Mexico, and Lee was ordered to
join General Scott for the attack on Vera Cruz. Lieutenant Beauregard was his assistant in the arranging of the
batteries whose firing compelled the surrender of the city.
And one of the guns in this battery was commanded by
Lieutenant Smith Lee of the navy, his brother. "No
matter where I turned," Lee wrote in a letter home after
the battle, "my eyes reverted to him and I stood by his
gun whenever I was not wanted elsewhere. Oh! I felt
awfully, and am at a loss what I should have done had he
been cut down before me. I thank God he was saved.
He preserved his usual cheerfulness, and I could see his
white teeth through all the smoke and din of the fire."[4]

The campaign begun at Vera Cruz went forward until
the Mexican Capital had fallen and the flag of the con-
queror waved over the fortress of the Montezumas. A
study of the official documents reveals constant mention
of Lee's services in Scott's dispatches. Beginning with the
report on Vera Cruz there is favorable mention. After
Cerro Gordo: "I am compelled to make special mention
of Captain R. E. Lee, Engineer. This officer was again
indefatigable during these operations in reconnaissances
as daring as laborious, and of the utmost value. Nor was
he less conspicuous in planting batteries and in conducting columns to their stations under the heavy fire of the
enemy." "At Contreras," Scott testified in the Pillow Inquiry, "the gallant and indefatigable Captain Lee performed the greatest feat of physical and moral courage
performed by any individual in my knowledge pending the
campaign."[5] This was the feat that called forth the
praise of his commander.

The city of Mexico lies in an elliptical valley, seven thousand feet above the sea. During the winter the valley is often covered with water and the only approaches to the city are on seven high causeways. The causeways toward the east and the south were strongly fortified. That leading from San Augustin to the city was fortified at San Antonio. West of this, two parallel roads led to the city. Contreras, four miles west of San Augustin, was the key to these two roads. Lee was sent with Beauregard to reconnoiter this position, and their journey took them over a vast field of broken volcanic rock, called the Pedregal. Only a few trails lay over it, and its sharp cutting ridges made difficult going. Early the next morning Lee, at the head of a corps of pioneers, constructed a road over this lava field. By noon he was able to bring up the divisions of Pillow and Twiggs to attack Valencia's position at the edge of the lava. Darkness found them in a position of extreme danger, with the enemy unbeaten and with reenforcements arriving for Valencia, the Mexican commander.

Then Lee performed the feat that was to win him Scott's applause.

Through the darkness and under a furious storm he groped his way across that lava wilderness, with no guide but the wind as it drove the cold rain in torrents against his face, or an occasional flash of lightning to give him a glimpse of the country around. General Henry J. Hunt who was in the battle says of this wilderness that when his own company tried to pass over it, "after two hours of motion we had not moved four hundred yards." And he adds regarding Lee's passage to it: "I would not believe that it could have been made, that passage of the Pedregal, if he had not said he made it."[6] He secured

---

[6] Quoted by Long, p. 57.

the reenforcements, and returned in time to assist in the taking of the Mexican position, which opened the way to Cherubusco, Molino del Rey and Chapultepec, and the occupation of the city, bringing the active fighting to an end.

For gallantry at Chapultepec, where he was Scott's chief aide, and where he was wounded, he was advanced to the brevet rank of colonel. Cerro Gordo had already brought him his brevet majority, and the ride at Contreras and his share in winning that field his lieutenant-colonelcy. It is not difficult to understand why Scott came to think of him as he did, or to understand why he said to General Preston long before the outbreak of the Civil War: "If I were on my death-bed to-morrow and the President of the United States should tell me that a great battle were to be fought for the liberty or slavery of the country and asked my judgment as to the ability of a commander, I would say with my dying breath 'Let it be Robert E. Lee.' "[7] And we have the word of that distinguished Senator from Maryland, Reverdy Johnson, that he had heard General Scott more than once say "that his success in Mexico was largely due to the skill, valor and the undaunted energy of Robert E. Lee."[8]

In the pages of those old reports occur many names that the nation was afterward to know on more famous fields. They who had slept beneath the same blankets and drunk from the same canteen and whose swords were pointed against a common foe were to divide in opposite camps and to draw those swords against each other. And that War with Mexico was the school whose lessons were to serve them well in the bigger test that followed. Beauregard had served at

[7] Page, p. 19.
[8] Long, p. 61.

Vera Cruz and was to win mention in later dispatches; Joseph E. Johnston was lieutenant-colonel of voltigeurs, wounded twice and brevetted three times; and Captain Braxton Bragg was the first man to plant the colors on the ramparts of Chapultepec. Second-Lieutenant Thomas J. Jackson, for his work with Magruder's battery, was brevetted captain and major of the artillery. And Longstreet, and the Hills A. P. and D. H., and Albert Sidney Johnston, and R. S. Ewell, and Jubal Early, were in that army. And there was also Ulysses S. Grant, a first-lieutenant of infantry who won so little renown that he was forgotten when the other war began. George Gordon Meade served as topographical engineer on the staffs of General Taylor and General Patterson. George B. McClellan won two brevets for bravery in battle, and three others who were afterward to command the Army of the Potomac, McDowell and Burnside and Hooker, were here to be found.

Yet it is not only the winner of brevets, the man constantly in dispatches, that we see in those pages and in the yellowing letters of the time. There is the brother watching over the captain of the gun at Vera Cruz, the same boy who had learned to watch over an invalid mother in Alexandria. There is the father writing to his son, Custis, at school, after Contreras: "I wondered when the musket balls and grape were whistling over my head in a perfect shower, where I could put you, if with me, to be safe."[9] There is the man who remembered long after the battle "the plaintive tones of a little Mexican girl whom he found bending over a wounded drummer boy." And there is the story of the night that a company of officers were celebrating the fall of the City of Mexico in the President's palace,

[9] Quoted by White, p. 38.

and one of them rose to propound the health of that Captain of Engineers who had found a way for the army to enter the city. Then it was discovered that Captain Lee was absent. Captain Magruder was dispatched to find him and after a long search discovered him in a remote room busy in the preparation of a map. "But," said the impetuous Magruder, "this is mere drudgery. Let some one else do it and come along." "No," was the answer "this is my duty."

It was a glad welcome that they gave him when he got back to Arlington although he had had to ride out from Washington on a borrowed horse, having missed in some way the carriage that had been sent for him. He writes to his brother a few days after his arrival: "Here I am once again, my dear Smith, perfectly surrounded by Mary and her precious children, who seem to devote themselves to staring at the furrows in my face and the white hairs in my head. It is not surprising that I am hardly recognizable to some of the young eyes around me and perfectly unknown to the youngest. But some of the older ones gaze with astonishment and wonder at me, and seem at a loss to reconcile what they see and what was pictured in their imaginations. I find them, too, much grown, and all well, and I have much cause for thankfulness and gratitude to that good God who has once more united us."[10]

Of course Mary rejoiced in the fame he had won. For General Scott was talking of him in Washington as he had in the dispatches, and she hoped as he hoped in the letter he sent her just after he started for the Southwest "that this shall be the last time that I shall be absent from you in my life." Little did they then see what was coming. For in the land that was taken as spoil in that war gold

---

[10] *R. and L.,* p. 4.

was to be found. And that gold was to make vast changes in the country, not so much in the South as in the North. The steady stream of it pouring out of California was to build new towns and set new chimneys smoking and shape new industries and make possible new railroads. It was to fill the hearts of the slavery leaders with fear of the North's new might and to hasten their fatal decision that was to end in civil war.

But of this Mary knew nothing as she sat on the porch at Arlington and looked across the river at the white pile of the Capitol, with her husband beside her, brevetted colonel for gallantry at Chapultepec. It was a time of happiness.

Chapter V

The Years Between

THE years that immediately followed his return from Mexico were probably the happiest years of Lee's life. He was with the family that he loved, watching the children grow up. For a while they were all at home. And the doors of Arlington were wide for the old army friends that duty brought to Washington or for the older friends of the Tidewater who came in the great lumbering carriages with black coachmen in splendor on the box. There is a very charming picture which his youngest son gives of his father and their life together at this time. That father seems to have known how to mingle comradeship and discipline.

"From that early time I began to be impressed with my father's character, as compared with other men. Every member of the household respected, revered and loved him as a matter of course, but it began to dawn on me that everyone else with whom I was thrown held him high in their regard. At forty-five years of age he was active, strong and as handsome as he had ever been. I never remember his being ill. I presume he was indisposed at times; but no impression of that kind remains. He was always bright and gay with us little folk, romping, playing, and joking with us. With the older children he was just as companionable, and I have seen him join my elder brothers and their friends when they would try their powers at a high jump put up in our yard. The two younger children he petted a great deal, and our greatest treat was to get into his bed in the morning and lie close to him, listening while he talked to us in his bright entertaining way. This custom we kept up until I was ten years old and over. Although he was so joyous and familiar with us, he was very firm on all proper occasions, never indulged us in anything that was not good for us, and exacted the most implicit obedience. I always knew that it was impossible to disobey my father. I felt it in me, I never thought why, but was perfectly sure that when he gave us an order it was to be obeyed. . . . He would often tell us the most delightful stories. . . . When we were a little older, our elder sister told us one winter the ever delightful 'Lady of the Lake.' Of course she told it in prose and arranged it to suit our mental capacity. Our father was generally in his corner by the fire, and would come in at different points of the tale and repeat line after line of the poem— much to our disapproval—but to his great enjoyment."[1]

Great years! He was strong, vigorous, "the handsomest man in the army," so one of his brother officers declared. The fame he had won in the Mexican campaign was wide-spread. One of Cuba's periodic revolutions breaking out about this time, he was offered the command of their army by the Junta in charge, but he declined as he felt it was not the sort of service in which he ought to engage as an officer in the United States Army. Instead he was assigned to direct the construction of Fort Carroll at Baltimore. The family took a house there. Ann, his sister, had married a Baltimorean, and every door in Baltimore was opened to the famous officer and his equally distinguished wife. This was followed in 1852 by his assignment as the Superintendent of the Military Academy at West Point, one of the choice posts in the little army of that time and usually reserved for an older man. The record of these years is that of a successful administration,

[1] R. and L., pp. 8-10.

the strengthening of the courses of study, the building of the new riding hall, and a quiet family life. For Mary and the children were with him in the big stone house above the Hudson. His oldest son, Custis, was a cadet, and he won the coveted cadet adjutancy which his father had had before him. His youngest son remembers how his father was always punctual in his attendance at Chapel and how he calmly fell asleep during the sermon. "At that time this drowsiness of my father's was something awful to me, inexplicable. I knew it was very hard for me to keep awake, and frequently I did not; but why he, who to my mind could do everything that was right, without any effort, should sometimes be overcome, I could not understand and did not try to do so."[2]

In 1855 Jefferson Davis, Secretary of War, succeeded in getting through a reluctant Congress a bill authorizing the addition to the little regular army of two regiments of cavalry. Practically every officer Davis picked for these regiments was afterward to win distinction in the Civil War. As Colonel of the Second Cavalry he chose Albert Sidney Johnston and as Lieutenant-Colonel Robert E. Lee. Joseph E. Johnston held the same rank in the First. Lee left the engineers with regret, for he had gained a reputation in the corps. But the army was small and a promotion to lieutenant-colonel of engineers might not come for years, so taking the family home to Arlington he left for the West and that further training in the handling of men that was to fit him for '61.

Yet it must have been uncongenial service. The territory which his regiment was expected to protect ran from the Rio Grande on the south, to the Arkansas on the north, and extended from the western boundary of the Indian territory to the eastern one of New Mexico. It was largely

[2]*Ibid.*, p. 12.

wilderness, inhabited by wild animals and wilder men.
There were no railroads, and the only means of travel was
as primitive as the people. The mails were few and
far between, depending on the arrival of some post-rider.
The forts were surrounded on all sides by wide strips of
dreary waste, and few of them had more than a company
or two of cavalry for the territory the regiment had to
protect was large. It was not possible for him to have
his family with him. The children had to go to school,
and Mary was already suffering from that rheumatic
trouble which was to cause him so much anxiety. One
could hunt, or read, or play poker and drink too much
whisky—which was not in his line. Most of the work
was in dealing with small bands of hostile Indians or interfering with the activities of the brigands who found the
border convenient for their operations. It can not be
imagined that such petty border warfare would be con-
genial to Lee's tastes. He writes during this period:

"We are on the Comanche Reserve, with the Indian
camps below us on the river belonging to Catumseh's
band, whom the Government is endeavoring to humanize.
It will be uphill work, I fear. Catumseh has been to see
me, and we have had a talk, very tedious on his part, very
sententious on mine. I hailed him as a friend as long as
his conduct and that of the tribe deserved it, but would
meet him as an enemy the first moment he failed to keep his
word. The rest of the tribe (about a thousand, it is said)
live north of us, and are hostile. Yesterday I returned his
visit and remained a short time at his lodge. He informed
me that he had six wives. They were riding in and out
of camp all day, their paint and ornaments rendering
them more hideous than nature made them, and the whole
race is extremely uninteresting."[3]

_____
[3]Long, p. 79.

Yet it was not all dealing with the Indians. He carried a few books always with him. Among them was a volume dealing with the campaigns of Napoleon. He studied them until he knew them by heart and could demonstrate the plan of every battle for any fellow officer who would stay to listen. He hated the heat as much as he did the Indians. His letters are full of allusions to it and to what they were doing at home while he was chasing Indians and studying Napoleon. He writes to his wife:

"I hope your father continued well and enjoyed his usual celebration of the Fourth of July [when he made patriotic speeches, that sentimental man!]. Mine was spent, after a march of thirty miles on one of the branches of the Brazos, under my blanket elevated on four sticks driven in the ground as a sunshade. The air was fiery hot, the atmosphere like the blast from a hot-air furnace, the water salt."[4]

This is the way our empire has been won, but it was dreary work for those who had to do the winning. And it was worse when those who did it had been born at Stratford. Lee did his duty as a soldier these years but he never liked it. The narratives that remain of those who knew him then reveal him very much the aristocrat. "The face and figure of the Captain are eminently noble, high-bred, dignified; yet with the dignity there is just a suggestion of haughtiness, of remoteness."[5] It is little wonder that he looked forward eagerly to the furloughs at Arlington. And in October, 1859, while on one of these furloughs, he was called on to play a part in a dramatic event which was to shake the land.

---

[4] Young, p. 61.
[5] Bradford, p. 21.

CHAPTER VI

The Threatening Cloud

THE question of the right or wrong of slavery was settled long ago, and it took four years of war to settle it. But one can not follow the story of Lee without considering the conditions surrounding the question when he came home on furlough in 1859 to assume the administration of the Custis estate. An event occurred during that furlough which gave a new turn to the whole matter. Had John Brown not raided Harper's Ferry, Lee would possibly have been unknown to history, for that event made impossible the solution of the slavery question by any other means than civil war. And had the war not begun in '61 it is unlikely that it would have ever been fought. But John Brown made it inevitable. Nothing more diabolical in its effect than this raid can be imagined had the whole thing been planned by His Satanic Majesty himself.[1]

To us who remember the tragedies and tears of the World War that older War of the 'Sixties seems among the far-off, faint and half-forgotten things. We think of it as a piece of preventable folly. We are apt to overlook the fact that "there is no other instance in all the history of the world when the civilizations of two different ages, with their antagonistic principles and modes of thinking and feeling, have been so intricately interwoven as in the United States during the times of the slavery contest."[2] It is difficult now to understand that struggle

[1] Burgess, Vol. I, p. 36.
[2] Von Holst, p. 2.

and the things that underlay it. Most of the men of to-day knew some of the men who fought in its battles, and whose stories will not soon be forgotten. Tradition has often blinded them to fact, and legend has taken the place of truth. Prejudices have not been allowed to pass. In the destruction of campaigns many documents and letters that would have shed light on critical phases were lost. So it is little wonder that with all that has been written men are confused about some things pertaining to the war and the events that led up to it. This is especially true of slavery.

One of the things about which much confusion of thought exists is as to the number of people in the South who were slaveholders. Burgess declares that the most generous estimate that can be made will show that not over two millions of the eight millions of whites inhabiting the slaveholding commonwealths in the sixth decade of the century were directly interested in slave property.[3] He bases this on the statement of the census of 1850 that there were about three hundred and twenty-five thousand slave-owners in the South at the time of the taking of that census. Estimating each of these as the head of a family of five or six persons there is obtained the number above, surely a more generous estimate of those directly interested in the maintenance of the institution. This leaves of the southern whites about six million who had no direct interest in slavery, in fact whose every interest was opposed to its maintenance. For this great group, which is the back-bone of the nation, was in the South despised. There were practically no industries in that section and the presence of slaves caused work with the hands to be looked on as degrading. In consequence the "poor whites" led

[3] Burgess, Vol. I, p. 28.

a rather precarious existence, getting little chance for an education, having no place in political management, and no real importance in the economic structure. Indeed the more enterprising among them left the South for the Border States and the opening West. An interesting study might be made of how many of these filled the armies of Grant and Sherman, largely recruited in the West, men and the sons of men who had left the South behind because slavery gave them no chance.

But to the favored class, the men who held slaves, it was a very valuable institution. It gave them vast fortunes with little expenditure of energy. And what a delightful life! "Their way of life was beautiful in their eyes," says Lord Charnwood. "It rested upon slavery. Therefore slavery was a good thing." We have caught glimpses of that life at Stratford and Arlington. And white pillared mansions like Arlington stood upon the plantations from the Potomac to the Gulf. The children who were born there wandered through the great halls as young Robert Lee had done at Stratford and were told the tales of this grandfather who fought for King Charles at Naseby, of this grandmother who was the toast of the town in the days of Queen Anne, or of these others who wore the buff and blue in the armies of Washington. Old swords hung on the walls, old silver gleamed on the sideboards, china that had been borne across the seas from the kilns of Wedgwood or Sèvres was brought out to deck the board when guests came. And guests came often, and there were dinners that lasted late, and dances where the old black fiddlers nodded in the corner, and grace and beauty swept in stately measures down the long room. The daughters of these houses had that charm which comes only of blood and courtly race. The sons grew up conscious that they came from a breed born to command. Bold riders they were and daring huntsmen. Over the best of these old families, and the best were not a small class, there was spread a dignity and graciousness less artificial than that of Versailles, less conventional perhaps than that of Victorian England. But that glittering social order rested on slavery!

There were some who shut their eyes to the things found on the malarial plantations in the deep South, and who argued with Alexander Stephens that "what was called slavery among us was but the legal subordination of the African to the Caucasian race. This relation was so regulated by law as to promote, according to the intent and design of the system, the best interests of both races, the Black as well as the White, the Inferior as well as the Superior. Both had rights secured and both had duties imposed. It was the system of reciprocal service and mutual bonds."[4] But there were some in the South who were beginning to question the real worth of the system. In the country towns there was growing up a middle class of merchants and bankers and lawyers and teachers who had little property interest in the perpetuation of slavery,[5] and who resented the lordly ways of those who lived on the great plantations. Further, they saw the North advancing in wealth and industry, attracting great numbers of immigrants from abroad while the South repelled them.[6] Foreign commerce was also largely in northern hands. They were cognizant of increasing hostility on the part of Europe, particularly England and France, to their peculiar institution. Also, they were beginning to question the real economic worth of slavery to their own situation.

[4] Stephens, Vol. I, p. 539.
[5] Burgess, Vol. I, p. 29.
[6] Morse, *Parties and Party Leaders*, p. 137.

Left entirely to themselves this hostility to the class of large slave-owners would probably have developed into an attack on slavery itself. Even some of the plantation owners themselves were questioning it. John S. Wise tells of a long and earnest conversation, to which as a boy he listened, between his father, then governor of Virginia, his uncle and his brother, after they had witnessed a slave auction. "They all agreed that a system in which things like that were possible was monstrous; and the question was not whether it should be abolished and abolished quickly, but as to the manner of its abolition."[7] Robert E. Lee was of the number of those who were thinking about these things. In a letter written from Texas, December 27, 1856, we find a rather full discussion of his views:

"There are few, I believe, in this enlightened age, who will not acknowledge that slavery as an institution is a moral and political evil in any country. It is useless to expatiate on its disadvantages. I think it a greater evil to the white than to the black race. While my feelings are strongly enlisted in behalf of the latter, my sympathies are more strong for the former. The blacks are immeasurably better off here than in Africa, morally, physically, and socially. The painful discipline they are undergoing is necessary for their further instruction as a race, and I hope will prepare them for better things. How long their servitude is necessary is known and ordered by a merciful Providence. Their emancipation will sooner result from the mild and melting influences of Christianity than from the storms and tempests of fiery controversy. This influence, though slow, is sure. The doctrines and miracles of our Saviour have required nearly two thousand years to convert but a small portion of the human race, and even among Christian nations what gross errors still exist. While we see the course of the *final* abolition of human slavery

---
[7] Wise, p. 7.

is still onward, and give it the aid of our prayers, and all the justifiable means in our power, we must leave the progress as well as the results in His hands Who sees the end; Who chooses to work by slow influences; and with Whom two thousand years are but as a single day. Although the Abolitionist must know this, must know that he has neither the right nor the power of operating, except by moral means, and that, to benefit the slave, he must incite angry feelings in the master; that, although *he* may not approve the mode by which Providence accomplishes its purpose, the result will still be the same; that the reasons he gives for interference in what he has no concern with hold good with every kind of interference with our neighbors; still I feel he will persevere in his evil course. . . . Is it not strange that the descendants of those Pilgrim Fathers who crossed the Atlantic to preserve their freedom have always proved the most intolerant of the spiritual liberty of others?"[8]

These men whose tolerance Lee questions form a factor in the problem hard to estimate quietly. Perhaps the light is not yet clear enough for an impartial judgment of the Abolitionists. They were not a large group. We may even come to think they were not a very wise one. They regarded slavery as a purely moral question, refusing to yield one inch or compromise in the slightest degree with evil. Like all those who dare to speak for God they could not compromise. Slavery, they declared, must be destroyed and destroyed at once. They were not willing to wait for the slower way that they in the South, who also saw that slavery was wrong, were already beginning to take. And there were many in the South who thought they spoke for the whole of the North. They were matched in the South by another small group, equally reckless, and far more shrewdly led, a group who made slavery

---

[8] Quoted by White, p. 50.

their program for the winning and holding of political power. Not only were they shrewdly led, but desperately led, as events proved. Their leader for years was John C. Calhoun, of South Carolina, and after his death Jefferson Davis, of Mississippi. Both were Senators, both yearned for the power that the presidency gave to a daring man. One who held that power later estimates them thus: "I confess I am unable to see wherein any conscienceless financier of the present day is worse than these two slave owners who spent their years trying to feed their thirst for personal power by leading their followers to the destruction of the Union."[9] That judgment is not likely to be seriously altered. Then suddenly John Brown's raid startled the nation. Colonel Lee was in Arlington when the attack took place. From his "Memorandum-book" the following record is taken:

"Oct. 17, 1859. Received orders from the Secretary of War in person to repair in the evening train to Harper's Ferry. Reached Harper's Ferry at 11 P.M. . . . . Posted marines in the United States armory. Waited until daylight, as a number of citizens were held as hostages, whose lives were threatened. Tuesday about sunrise, with twelve marines, under Lieutenant Green, broke in the door of the engine house, secured the insurgents, and relieved the prisoners unhurt. All the insurgents killed or mortally wounded but four, John Brown, Stevens, Coppie and Shields. Had the prisoners removed to a place of safety and their wounds dressed."[10]

Plain, matter-of-fact, very much the soldier's record. But behind it there is another story more dramatic, dramatic as tragedy always is.

---

[9] Letter of Theodore Roosevelt to Owen Wister, April 27, 1906, in *Roosevelt: The Story of a Friendship*, Macmillan, 1930.
[10] *R. and L.*, pp. 21-22.

John Brown had taken a prominent part in the troubles in Kansas. As "Ossawattomie Brown" he had been a terror to the slavery party. Afterward he gathered a group, some of whom had been active in the struggle there and others whom he recruited far and wide, and sent them one by one to the neighborhood of Harper's Ferry, Virginia. Here he appeared under the assumed name of Smith with two sons and a son-in-law, and took a farm some five miles from the town on the Maryland side of the Potomac, and on this place he secretly collected his followers and the arms he planned to use in the surprising event that was to follow. He was plentifully supplied with money, and the arms he had were the best that could be procured. Harper's Ferry is a quiet little town where the railroad crosses the Potomac from Maryland into Virginia. There the United States Army had an arsenal. On the night of the sixteenth Brown and his band slipped into the sleeping town, seized the railroad bridge across the river, the engine house, the watch house, the arsenal and the rifle factory. They halted all trains at the bridge and spent the night visiting the homes of prominent citizens, whom they seized as hostages, and whose slaves they forced into their ranks. Among the hostages taken was Colonel Lewis Washington, the grand-nephew of George Washington, and as John Brown entered his house he "appropriated" (to use his own word) the sword which Frederick the Great had given to George Washington. This he preserved for his own use in the rôle he essayed as liberator of the slaves. For Harper's Ferry was but the entering wedge he proposed to drive into the "slave kingdom." With the arms captured at the arsenal he planned to equip the host of black men whom he saw rising at his word to cast off the chains of their oppressors.

LIEUTENANT-COLONEL ROBERT E. LEE, U. S. A.

When the news of this attack reached Washington the government took active measures to capture the assailants. General Scott was absent at the time, but the Secretary of War summoned Colonel Lee to take command of the battalion of marines from the Navy-Yard and proceed with them to Harper's Ferry, together with the militia from the neighboring counties that had been hastily summoned. Lee's memorandum tells the story of what followed except in one important particular. There was a young preacher who had just begun his ministry in a little church outside Harper's Ferry. He hurried into the town to see the excitement and arrived in time to see the surrender. He records in a brief narrative, which he wrote years later when he was a minister of considerable standing in his denomination, this fact which he learned at that time. "About this time Colonel Robert E. Lee got within range of Captain Coppie's rifle. Prisoners say that Mr. Graham (one of the hostages) knocked the muzzle aside. Lee's life was saved."[11] That raid of John Brown's would have had greater significance for the South had that ball sped true!

Governor Wise, who arrived next day, has recorded his impression of Brown: "He was the gamest man I ever saw . . . like a broken-winged hawk, lying on his back, with a fearless eye and his talons set for further fight, if need be." Fearlessly he told them as he lay there wounded: "I claim to be here in carrying out a measure which I believe to be perfectly justifiable, and not to act the part of an incendiary or a ruffian—but on the contrary to aid those suffering of a great wrong. I wish to say, further, that you had better, all you people of the South, prepare yourself for a settlement of this question. . . . You may dispose of me very easily: I am nearly disposed of now, but

---

[11] Leech, p. 10.

this question is still to be settled—this negro question I mean. The end is not yet."[12]

The news of the raid aroused both North and South. It was not the firing on Sumter that cut the nation in two but the firing of John Brown's rifles. Governor Wise lost his head, which was a habit with him, and chose to make political capital out of the affair with the result that many in the North believed Brown to be a martyr when his execution was ordered. "The new saint will make the gallows glorious like the Cross" was the sentiment of Emerson that set a vast audience in Boston wild.[13] On the day of his execution there were the tolling of funeral bells and the firing of minute guns in many places in New England. In the Senate Douglas declared that the responsibility for John Brown's attack must be laid upon Lincoln's doctrine that the Union could not endure half-slave and half-free and upon Seward's theory of "irrepressible conflict" between North and South. And while Douglas knew that this was not true there were many in the South who believed him. The party in the South that planned and hoped for gradual abolition began to lose rapidly. The more radical took command. A wave of hysterical emotion swept all slaveholding states. A slave insurrection was the most hideous danger southern women had to fear. They still remembered Nat Turner's attempt in Virginia, and now in Virginia again there had been another attempt, this time led by a northern man, a pronounced Abolitionist, armed with weapons supplied by northern money. Although at the trial it was proved that this money had been furnished for the struggle in Kansas, yet the impression got abroad in the South that the whole violent business

---

[12]Thomason, p. 56.
[13]Quoted by White, p. 82.

had the virtual support of the northern opponents of slavery. It is scarcely to be wondered at that this had an immediate political effect. The slavery group in Congress, under the control of the extremists, determined to achieve their purpose at whatever cost, to enact laws further protecting slaves as property, permitting territorial expansion of the institution, and some went so far as to insist on the repeal of the laws forbidding the slave trade.[14] No single event of those frantic years did as much as this raid to make that coming conflict inevitable. Nor did its influence pass when the conflict began. When the hosts in blue gathered at Lincoln's call they came singing

"John Brown's body lies a-mouldering in the grave
And his soul goes marching on."

When Thomas Wentworth Higginson came to her little Adirondack home to explain to Mary Brown that there was little hope for John Brown she answered: "Does it seem as if freedom were to gain or lose by this?" I wonder if Lee asked himself the same question as he stood commanding the troops the day they hanged John Brown. We can answer the question now. Everything lost! Disaster is ever consequent when they whose zeal overrides their wisdom impatiently hurry events.

The threatening cloud was growing larger than a man's hand. And before Lee returned to his command in Texas by direction of the War Department, whose secretary was a Virginian, and at the request of a legislative committee, he went in January, 1860, to Richmond to throw the light of his experience on the matter of organizing and arming the Virginia militia, although he had written "my limited

---

[14]Wilson, pp. 203-4.

knowledge can be of little avail."[15] On February tenth he left Arlington for the West, having been made commander of the Military Department of Texas. The early part of the next year was spent in an effort to capture the Mexican brigand Cortinas. And when he was not chasing brigands he was pushing forward the building of the Episcopal Church at San Antonio. But of what he thought concerning what he had seen in Virginia and its consequences there remains little record.

[15] White, p. 96.

CHAPTER VII

Secession

WHEN the committee of which Alexander H. H. Stuart was chairman presented its report on the John Brown raid to the General Assembly of Virginia on January 26, 1860, it contained these significant words, "We have no desire to rupture the political, commercial or social ties which bind us to the North so long as our rights are respected, but, admonished by the past, it is our duty to prepare for the future by placing ourselves in an attitude of defense and thereby adopting such measures as may be necessary for our security and welfare."[1]

"Admonished by the past"! In these words we find the key to secession and the Civil War. It is a popular notion that the war was fought over slavery. The fact is that the armies of the North could have been counted by corporal's guards had Lincoln called them to free the slaves. And we have seen that in the South itself there was a great majority whose every interest was opposed to it, and a growing group among the slaveholders themselves who were awakening to the necessity of some plan of abolition. Yet if the war was not over slavery, slavery made it possible. Or rather it made it impossible that it should not be fought. It created a state of mind in the men of the South that would not listen to reason and would brook no further compromise. They had tasted the fears of servile insurrection and they, in consequence, followed the political

---

[1] Robertson, p. 176.

leaders who were anxious for the preservation of slavery as an institution and as the basis of their own political power. For the pro-slavery element in the Democratic party had secured control and they were governing the South and through the South the nation. When the campaign of 1860 began they were prepared to receive an unconditional surrender of their Free-Soil opponents, but not to yield a single concession on the great matter.[2]

Perhaps the South was more united in this spirit of no compromise than the North, but there also sectionalism was growing every day. William L. Yancey, of Alabama, was not the only fire-eater in the country. Wendell Phillips and William Lloyd Garrison were setting the North on fire, attacking slavery and the slave states so bitterly that they were creating a sectional spirit in the North that was beginning to equal that of the South. Just as it is difficult for the men of to-day to think of the Civil War as any other than a very old thing so it is difficult to realize the character of the years that preceded it—how very evil they were! The gospel of hate was silencing every other evangel. Led by the extremists there were gradually shaped two countries where had been the old Union. No man could serve the South without winning the hatred of the North or of the North without winning that of the South. For him who dared place the Union first there was the peril of being hated by his own section. That was Webster's fate. He had virtually said in his seventh of March speech, "I care more for the Union than for either section," and the result was repudiation by the North and distrust by the South. And many a man of lesser fame suffered the same fate. This thing entered into the lives of men and turned them so into creatures of bitterness that all judg-

[2] Smith, p. 48.

ment was destroyed. It made John Brown, who might have been a crusader, the organizer of the most horrible thing history knows—a servile insurrection. It made Stonewall Jackson, in whom religion and military genius were blended as in Cromwell, "eager to unfurl the black flag."[3]

The doctrine upon which the political leaders of the South relied to plead their cause with those of their followers who were hesitant in going to the lengths they planned to go was that the Union was a confederation of sovereign states each of which surrendered no essential part of its sovereignty when it entered that Confederation. If the state's rights were impugned it had the privilege of withdrawal. These rights the southern leaders sought to have their followers believe were impugned in the growing tide of opposition to their peculiar institution in the North, in the spirit which they declared they found in a people that were responsible for John Brown. "Their very love for the Union," Wise set forth, "influenced them against men, who, as they viewed it, were making union impossible except on terms rivaling humiliating surrender to the Abolitionists."[4]

The election of Lincoln brought the matter out of the realm of theory into that of action. It is true that the platform on which Lincoln ran declared that while slavery was not to be extended to any new territories no constitutional action was intended against those states where it was established. But the South believed that the triumph of the Republican party meant the destruction of the southern system and the defeat of southern interests, even to the point of countenancing and assisting servile insur-

---

[3] Morse, *Parties and Party Leaders*, p. 150.
[4] Wise, p. 117.

rection. Senator Benjamin declared that the Republicans did not mean to cut down the tree of slavery but they meant to gird it about and so cause it to die.[5] There seemed to be good reason why such views should be held, for a number of Northern States under Republican leadership had passed laws nullifying the Fugitive Slave Law. We know to-day that the judgment of the South was wrong, that no party which Lincoln led would have interfered with the constitutional existence of slavery in its borders, but the South could not see that then. It knew only that the party that was hotly intolerant of the peculiar southern institution and interest had triumphed in the election and was about to take possession of the government, and that it was morally impossible to preserve the Union any longer. "If you who represent the stronger portion," Calhoun had said in 1850, in words which perfectly convey this feeling in their quiet cadence, "cannot agree to settle the great questions at issue on the broad principles of justice and duty, say so; and let the States we both represent agree to separate and depart in peace."[6]

H. A. L. Fisher, of Oxford, in his Massachusetts Tercentenary speech says of "an earlier rebellion" what might be said of this: "We are accustomed to think of the severance of the colonists from the Mother country as inevitable, and given the political cultivation of the two parties to the dispute, inevitable it was. Inventions in the sphere of politics are not like inventions in electrical science. It is only by a long process of trial and error, only after the human race has paid in blood and treasure for the mistakes which arise from human pride and human blindness, that eventually some happy formula, some reconciling compro-

---

[5] Wilson, p. 208.
[6] *Ibid.*, p. 210.

mise, which all the time was lying ready at hand, if there had been eyes to see it, leaps to light and solves the difficulty."[7] But angry eyes can not see a "happy formula" no matter how close at hand it be. And in those last days of '60 and '61 those eyes were red with anger. Hate had done its work. Lincoln was right. His early conviction that slavery could not be peacefully ended was confirmed at last. On August 18, 1855, he had written to Judge Robertson at Lexington, "There is no peaceful extinction of slavery in prospect for us. The signal failure of Henry Clay and other good and great men in 1849 to effect anything in favor of gradual emancipation in Kentucky . . . extinguished that hope forever."[8]

This is not the place to follow the course of secession from its beginnings in South Carolina until the last of the eleven states had gone. Few of those responsible for it dreamed of what was to follow, and certainly none of the political leaders saw what Lee saw, that the war would be long and bloody. Jones was to write in his Diary in April '61: "It is too late to dream of peace—in or out of the Union. Submission will be dishonor. Secession can only be death, which is preferable."[9] But in none of the diaries of the politicians do we find such words.

We are interested, however, in the story of Virginia's action, because on it depended upon which side of the struggle would be found the sword of Lee. The situation there was not the same as in the Cotton States. The great planters of the Tidewater did not control the state politically as they did those farther south. John Letcher was elected governor in 1859 owing to the lack of sympathy

---

[7] Tercentenary Address, Boston Common, July 15, 1930.

[8] *Complete Works of Abraham Lincoln*, F. Tandy Co., N. Y., 1905, Vol. II, p. 278.

[9] Jones, Vol. I, p. 18.

in western Virginia for the pro-southern program. East
of the Blue Ridge the total majority was against him, but
west thereof he carried every Congressional district but
one.[10] The *Richmond Whig* declared: "Letcher owes his
election to the tremendous majority he received in the
Northwest Free Soil counties and in these counties to his
anti-slavery record." Remembering this one can not help
feeling that the tragedy of the war—at least on the grand
scale—might have been avoided if there had arisen in Virginia at that time a leader with vision, patience and that
other quality which Stephens saw in Lincoln: "The Union
with him arose to the sublimity of a religious mysti-
cism."[11] For with Virginia remaining in the Union everything would have been different. How many Confederate
military leaders of consequence came from Virginia—Lee,
Johnston, Jackson, Early, Ewell, A. P. Hill, Stuart! What
a different story had they not worn the gray!

The Unionist party in the Virginia Legislature succeeded in holding in check the movement for secession in
the early weeks of 1861. But it provided for the holding
of a Constitutional Convention on February thirteenth.
Of the one hundred and fifty-two delegates only thirty
were classified as outright Secessionists.[12] Most of these
came from the southern Tidewater. The Valley and the
trans-mountain sections sent delegations for the Union.
The election of these delegates took place on February
fourth, and the large majority for the Union did much to
halt the movement for secession in other Border States.[13]
It also stopped the plans for the seizure of Washington

---

[10] Ambler, *American Historical Review*, Vol. XV, p. 776.

[11] Stephens, Vol. II, p. 448.

[12] Smith, p. 109.

[13] *Ibid.*, p. 110.

and allowed the new Administration to assume office quietly. When the Convention met the Union men had complete control, and John Janney, of Loudoun County, was elected president. But their victory ended there. And the reason it did was that they lacked leadership. There were some great men in the Convention, who had held high office. But either they were filled with the uncertainty of the times or they had not the ability to commend their convictions to their fellow members. Or perhaps they did not know. What they should have done was to pass resolutions favoring the preservation of the Union and then adjourn. In contrast the Secessionists presented a solid front. There were no differences in policy or methods among them. They had the tremendous advantage always possessed by a minority with a definite purpose when the majority is tolerant, badly led and lacking a definite program.

The weeks dragged on in futile debate. The idea which seemed to possess the minds of the majority may perhaps be expressed in a single phrase of one of its members, that "he would neither be driven by the North nor dragged by the Cotton States."[14] The Convention was falling more and more under the influence of the radical group willing to use any means to accomplish its end. Then came the firing on Fort Sumter. Lincoln had given notice to the authorities at Charleston of his intention to provision the fort, and they, compelled by the war spirit throughout the seceded states, determined to reduce the garrison before that relief should come. But the impasse in the Richmond Convention had something to do with that decision. Roger A. Pryor, a member of Congress, was sent by the Secessionist group in Richmond to Charles-

---

[14] Nicolay and Hay, Vol. III, p. 422.

ton to urge action, assuring them that if they would strike a blow "Virginia would be in the Southern Confederacy within an hour by Shrewsbury clock. The very moment blood is shed Virginia will make common cause with her sisters of the South."[15] Governor Letcher, who had been swung over to the side of secession, answered the call of Lincoln for Virginia's quota of the seventy-five thousand militia with the defiant words: "You have chosen to inaugurate Civil War." The next day he called out the militia, ostensibly to protect the state against invasion, but really to use them in such a way as to force the Convention to action. Orders were issued for the seizure of Harper's Ferry, the Navy-Yard at Gosport, and Fortress Monroe. The Convention was swept off its feet, and the Ordinance of Secession was carried by eighty-eight to fifty-five. The war was to be on the Potomac. Virginia had been "admonished by the past"!

Back of the tragic irresolution of that Unionist majority stands the sinister figure of John Brown!

---

[15] Smith, p. 163.

CHAPTER VIII

The Weeks of Indecision

THERE is in the life of all men, as there was in the ancient Temple, a holiest of all where no feet may tread. There the great decisions are made. We stand outside and view the shrine and wonder. Did this happen there or that? And what were the factors that forced the issue, that caused his feet to take this road when he might have taken that? And often there is only silence in answer to our questions, and we must fall back on surmise. That hidden place in Lee's life is those weeks in Arlington while he was weighing his duty as to his part in the coming conflict. We have some very frank letters to those he loved, written when the decision was finally made. But none have come to light which tell of those days of great perplexity as he walked the broad-pillared veranda of his noble Arlington house, his eyes glancing across the river at the flag of his country waving above the dome of the Capitol and then returning to rest on the soil of his native Virginia. Probably no man in the state followed the halting course of the Richmond Convention with more eagerness than he. For none had more to gain or lose than he. But of what he thought meanwhile we know nothing.

But first the facts about those weeks so far as we know them. During the heated campaign, which eventuated in Lincoln's election, Lee was at Fort Mason, Texas. In a letter to Major van Horn, written from San Antonio July 3, 1860, we have one of his few references to it: "The papers will give you news of the Baltimore Convention. If Judge Douglas would now withdraw and join himself and party to aid in the election of Breckinridge he might retrieve himself before the country and Lincoln be defeated. Politicians I fear are too selfish to become martyrs."[1]

It seems evident that something must have been known about his views on secession for the Secession party in Texas were doubtful about him. In the quiet movement that was going on with the connivance of Floyd, Buchanan's secretary of war, for the placing of officers at important posts who would be in sympathy with their program, Lee was replaced by General D. E. Twiggs, who promptly turned over his stores to the Texas Committee on Public Safety.[2] George H. Thomas, then Major of the Second Cavalry, on returning to Washington November, 1860, reported to General Scott that he was convinced that Twiggs and Joseph E. Johnston "meditated treachery." It is significant that he did not mention his Lieutenant-Colonel.[3] It would seem by this order that Floyd, who was a Virginian, was doubtful himself whether Lee could be counted on in the movement for Virginia's secession which he was aiding and for which he was shortly to resign from Buchanan's Cabinet. At any rate the order was issued from the Headquarters of the Department of Texas February 4, 1861: "In compliance with instructions from the headquarters of the Army, Bvt. Colonel Robert E. Lee, Second Cavalry, is relieved from duty in this department and will repair forthwith to Washington and report in

---

[1] Library of Congress Manuscripts.

[2] James, p. 408.

[3] Van Horne, *Life of Thomas*, p. 20.

person to the General-in-Chief."[4]   As he left San Antonio
he saw the troops march out of the place[5] and as the evening shadows fell on the broad lawns of Arlington on
March first, four days before Lincoln's inauguration, he
alighted at the gate from the carriage which had brought
him from Alexandria.

That he had been thinking of these matters that every
one else was thinking about we know from a letter he had
written to his son Custis from Texas, where secession was
in full tide.

"The South in my opinion has been aggrieved by the
acts of the North, as you say. I feel the aggression, and
am willing to take every proper step for redress. It is the
principle I contend for, not individual or private benefit.
As an American citizen I take great pride in my country,
her prosperity, and her institutions, and would defend any
State if her rights were invaded. But I can anticipate no
greater calamity for the country than a dissolution of the
Union. It would be an accumulation of all the evils we
complain of, and I am willing to sacrifice everything but
honor for its preservation. I hope therefore, that all constitutional means will be exhausted before there is a resort
to force. Secession is nothing but revolution. The framers
of our constitution never exhausted so much labor, wisdom
and forebearance in its formation, and surrounded it with
so many guards and securities, if it was intended to be
broken by every member of the Confederacy at will. It
is intended for 'perpetual Union,' so expressed in the preamble,[6] and for the establishment of a government, not
a compact, which can only be dissolved by revolution, or

---

[4]O. R., Vol. I, p. 586.

[5]White, p. 99.

[6]Lee was mistaken in this statement. The term "perpetual Union" does not
occur in the preamble to the Constitution nor anywhere in the Constitution itself.
It did occur in the Articles of the Confederation.

the consent of all the people in the Convention assembled. It is idle to talk of secession; anarchy would (otherwise?) have been established, and not a government, by Washington, Hamilton, Jefferson, Madison, and all the other patriots of the Revolution. . . . Still, a Union that can only be maintained by swords and bayonets and in which strife and civil war are to take the place of brotherly love and kindness, has no charm for me. I shall mourn for my country and for the welfare and progress of mankind. If the Union is dissolved and the Government disrupted, I shall return to my native State and share the miseries of my people, and save in defense will draw my sword on none."[7]

Some further light on his thinking may be had from a letter written by Mrs. Lee to her friend, Mrs. Stires, February 9, 1861. They thought along the same lines, this husband and wife, and doubtless many letters passed between them in this period of which we have no knowledge. Mrs. Lee writes:

"Has all love for and pride in their country died at the South, that they are willing to tear her in pieces and even exult to see her glorious flag trailing in the dust? It should rather have drawn tears from their eyes. We have lived and fought and prospered under this flag for so many years, and though the South has suffered much from the meddling of the Northern fanatics, yet do they expect to fare better now? Are there no rights and privileges but those of negro slavery? . . . and yet after all these wrongs I would lay down my life could I save our Union. What is the use of a Government combined as ours is of so many parts, the Union of which forms its strength and power, if any one part has the right for any wrong, real or imaginary, of withdrawing its aid and throwing the whole into confusion, as Carolina, who refuses all overtures for peace and imagines the world will admire her independence, whereas they

[7] Jones, *Life*, p. 137.

laugh at her folly which is perfectly suicidal. You know my feelings are all linked with the South and you will bear with me in the expression of my opinion, but while there are many of the Northern politicians who deserve no better fate than to be hung as high as Haman, believe me that those who have been foremost in this revolution will deserve and meet with the reprobation of the world, whether North or South, for having destroyed the most glorious Confederacy that ever existed."[8]

Not even Lincoln could have put it in stronger words! There are certain other things that we know about the events of these weeks. Lee reported to Scott on his arrival and was ordered by him to remain in Arlington or Washington until further orders. On March sixteenth Lincoln promoted him to Colonel of the First Cavalry. Before he accepted this appointment he received the following letter:

"War Department
"Montgomery, March 15, 1861
"Brig. General Robert E. Lee:
"Sir: You are hereby informed that the President, by and with the advice of Congress has appointed you a brigadier-general in the Army of the Confederate States. You are requested to signify your acceptance or non-acceptance of said appointment, and should you accept you will sign before a magistrate the oath of office herewith and forward the same, with your letter of acceptance, to this Department.

"L. P. WALKER
"Secretary of War."[9]

The issue was now before him. Which should he do? Which way did duty lie? The way seemed clear, for the

[8] Young, p. 75.
[9] O. R., Vol. CXXVII, p. 65.

Richmond Convention was still standing by its original decision for the Union. But the matter must have been weighed carefully, for although he was still at or near Arlington it was not until two weeks after the appointment that he accepted the commission as colonel and took again the required oath of allegiance. There is no record that he ever answered the letter from Montgomery. Later his name was the first of four which Scott sent to Lincoln as officers qualified to fill the place of Brigadier-General made vacant by the death of Jessup.[10] There must have been frequent interviews between Lee and his old commander Scott, who had told Lincoln that Lee "would be worth fifty thousand men to the Union." Long, later Lee's military secretary, records that "the veteran commander earnestly sought to persuade the younger officer not to throw up his commission, telling him it would be the greatest mistake of his life."[11] Long must have got this information from his chief. Scott was a Virginian and so his words had extra weight for this Virginian passing through his agony while the Convention at Richmond hesitated.

But Scott had greater honors planned for him than the commission as brigadier. He had "selected him in his own mind as the most capable and promising officer in the service to become the principal commander in the field, and of this intention he spoke to many without reserve."[12] On April eighteenth, the third day after Lincoln's call for troops, Francis P. Blair invited Lee to a conference at his home in Washington. That evening Lee rode over to Washington, tied his horse in front of Blair's

[10] Snow, p. 35.
[11] Long, p. 94.
[12] Nicolay and Hay, Vol. IV, pp. 97-98.

house and there was held the memorable interview with him in which Blair "sounded him to know whether his feelings would justify him in taking command of our army."

This is one of the events concerning which historians will probably always differ. There is plenty of evidence as to the historicity of it. The difficulty is as to the details and their meaning. Cameron, then secretary of war, said afterward when senator, in a debate on the floor, that Lee accepted the offer: "General Lee called on a gentleman who had my entire confidence, and intimated that he would like to have the command of the army. He assured that gentleman, who was a man in the confidence of the administration, of his entire loyalty and devotion to the interests of the administration and of the country. The place was offered to him unofficially with my approbation and with the approbation of General Scott. It was settled by him verbally, with the promise that he would go into Virginia and settle his business and then come back to take command."[13]

Lee's own comment on the interview we have in a letter to Senator Reverdy Johnson written February 25, 1868. This letter followed Cameron's speech in the Senate and is one of the few times Lee broke his self-imposed rule of silence as to the events of the war. "I never intimated to anyone that I desired the command of the United States Army, nor did I ever have a conversation with but one gentleman, Mr. Francis Preston Blair, on the subject, which was at his invitation, and as I understood at the instance of President Lincoln. After listening to his remarks I declined the offer he made me, to take command of the army that was to be brought into the field, stating as candidly and as courteously as I could, that though opposed to

---

[13] Speech in Senate, February 19, 1868, *Globe*, p. 1290.

secession and deprecating war, I could take no part in an invasion of the Southern States."[14]

Mr. Blair's own account of the occasion is as follows: "In the beginning of the war Secretary Cameron asked me to sound General Robert E. Lee, to know whether his feelings would justify him in taking command of our army. His cousin, John Lee, sent him a note at my suggestion. Lee came. I told him what President Lincoln wanted him to do. He wanted him to take command of the army. Lee said that he was devoted to the Union. He said, among other things, that he would do everything in his power to save it, and that if he owned all the negroes in the South, he would be willing to give them up and make the sacrifice of the value of everyone of them to save the Union. We talked several hours on the political question in that vein. Lee said that he did not know how he could draw his sword upon his native State. We discussed the matter at some length, and had some hours of conversation. He said he could not decide without seeing his friend General Scott. He said he could not, under any circumstances, consent to supersede his old commander. He asked me if I supposed the President would consider that proper. I said yes. Then we had a long conversation on that subject. He left the house and was soon after met by a committee from Richmond. He went with them, as I understood from some friends afterwards, to consult the Virginia Convention as to some mode of settling the difficulty. I never saw him afterwards."[15]

Montgomery Blair, son of Francis P. Blair, and postmaster-general in Lincoln's Cabinet, wrote an earlier account as follows: "General Lee said to my father when

[14] R. and L., p. 27.
[15] Rhodes, Vol. III, p. 252.

he was sounded by him, at the request of President Lincoln, about taking command of our army against the rebellion, then hanging upon the decision of the Virginia Convention, 'Mr. Blair, I look upon secession as anarchy. If I owned the four million slaves of the South I would sacrifice them all to the Union, but how can I draw my sword upon Virginia, my native State?' He could not determine then; said he would consult his friend General Scott, and went on the same day to Richmond, probably to arbitrate difficulties, and we see the result."[16]

Out of these narratives has come the legend accepted in many sections and repeated by one of Lee's biographers after another that Lincoln offered Lee the command of the Union army. This story was even embroidered to the point where Lincoln was made to walk over in carpet slippers from the White House to Mr. Blair's residence to take part in the conference. I think that a careful reading of the narratives in the light of what we know about Lincoln's handling of certain matters will enable it to be said that Lincoln never in any sense *offered* the command of the Union army to Lee and never intended to do so. There are certain very definite suppositions against it. There is, to begin with, Lee's very positive statement that he had a "conversation with only one gentleman on the subject." This precludes any possibility of a direct contact with the President, and Lincoln had a way in the great matters of dealing with things himself, as Seward was to find out after his unfortunate assumption of power in dealing with the Southern Commission about Fort Sumter, and as all his Cabinet found out about Emancipation. And the general-in-chiefship of the army he was raising was one of the great matters. Then, anxious as he was to win

[16] *National Intelligencer*, Washington, August 9, 1866, Letter to W. C. Bryant.

the Border States, he was enough of a politician to know that the North would never have permitted the appointment of a southerner to this high post. When Secretary Welles of the navy picked Farragut to command a squadron indignant protests came from many in influential positions. The Chairman of the Senate Naval Committee, John P. Hale, thundered at Welles: "Do you know that he is a Southern man, lives in the South and has a Southern wife?" Only the fact that Welles was not easily swayed saved Farragut his command. But to put the defense of Washington in Lee's hands would have aroused a greater storm than even Lincoln was ready for.

Perhaps the final item in the matter is a letter which Lincoln wrote on July 12, 1863, to some citizens of Albany in which he makes this statement as to what was in his mind about a number of men who afterward gave distinguished service to the Confederacy: "Of how little value the constitutional provisions I have quoted [he is discussing his constitutional right to suspend the writ of habeas corpus] will be rendered if arrests shall never be made until defined crimes shall have been committed may be illustrated by a few notable examples. General John C. Breckenridge, General Robert E. Lee, General Joseph E. Johnston, General John B. Magruder, General William Preston, General Simon B. Buckner, and Commodore Franklin Buchanan, now occupying the very highest places in the rebel war service, were all within the power of the Government since the rebellion began and *were nearly as well known to be traitors now as then.*" (Italics mine.) [17] That last sentence indicates a doubt in Lincoln's mind about Lee. Is it likely he would have given him the command? Unquestionably he knew all that there was to be

[17] *O. R.,* Vol. CXIX, p. 6.

known about Lee, for he had the habit of going to the bottom of things, and he knew that he could never tempt Lee to go against what he thought was his duty by any high command even though that duty to Lincoln's mind was "traitorous."

How then shall we account for the impression that Lee received from Blair that he had approached him "at the instance of President Lincoln"? Was Blair misstating the facts? By no means. To understand the situation one has to take into account a method Lincoln had of dealing with those who thought they had a solution for a problem by which he retained their loyalty and at the same time permitted them to demonstrate to themselves that their solution was wrong. John Hay, who knew him better than most, said he was a man of "intellectual arrogance," but in spite of this he was ever ready to let anybody try anything in which they believed, however impossible he knew it to be, provided it did not hurt the cause for which he was struggling. He sent Greeley to Canada as commissioner to treat with the Confederates after Greeley had demanded again and again that he send some one. He probably smiled as he sent him for he knew what would happen to Greeley when he got there, but he sent him nevertheless. And when Francis P. Blair insisted in '64 that Davis was ready to end the war he sent him to Richmond as Blair suggested he should. There Blair found out what Lincoln knew. This method he had of dealing with men is the explanation of what happened on April 17, 1861.

Blair had been a figure of importance in Washington since Jackson's time. He may have thought, as Seward did, that he knew more about how to handle things than this unknown lawyer from Illinois who suddenly found himself president. It is not to his discredit if he did. Many others thought so. And he proved his loyalty to Lincoln in many ways afterward and so we can overlook any temporary idea of his superiority that he may have held. Also he thought that he knew Lee. His daughter had married Captain Phillips Lee of the navy, a cousin of Robert. Perhaps he had told his father-in-law of a dinner he had attended at Cassius Lee's in Alexandria along with Robert and Smith Lee shortly before this. Phillips Lee had then decided to retain his commission and Smith to resign his. And as they sat at dinner Smith threatened to plant a battery on the Virginia shore and blow Phillips' ship out of the water. And Phillips answered, "No, you won't, for I will invite you on board to have a drink." But Robert had sat silent through it all, deep in thought, taking no part.[18] When Blair heard this he probably thought from it that Robert had not yet settled the question and might yet be held for the Union. So he had gone to Lincoln with the proposition that he "sound Lee out." At least Lincoln did not forbid the inquiry, and Blair went ahead.

Cameron's story to the Senate is preposterous. Lee never asked any man for the command of the Union army. He would not have done so in any event. He simply did not do that sort of thing. Cameron's story bears every evidence of having been shaped after the event. There are only two persons whose accounts have any value in this case, and only one who was in a position to say what lay back of the offer. That was Blair and it is to be noted that he does not say that Lincoln stood back of the offer. So the story as it is usually told, that Lincoln offered the command to Lee, has about as much authenticity as that

---

[18] Told to author by C. G. Lee, Jr., grandson of Cassius Lee.

concerning Lincoln and the brand of Grant's whisky. It was an age when myths grew.

The long period of uncertainty came to an end when on the morning of April twentieth Lee sent his resignation to Scott. His letter to the Commanding General lifts the curtain for a moment and gives a glimpse of the agony of soul through which he had passed in the weeks that had just gone.

"Arlington, Washington City, D. C.
"20 April 1861

"Lt. General Winfield Scott.

"Comm. the Army.

"General:

"Since my interview with you on the 18th inst. I have felt that I ought not longer to retain my commission in the Army. I therefore tender my resignation, which I request you will recommend for acceptance.

"It would have been presented at once, but for the struggle it has cost me to separate myself from a service to which I have devoted all the best years of my life, and all the ability I possessed.

"During the whole of that time, more than 30 years, I have experienced nothing but kindness from my superiors and the most cordial friendship from my companions. To no one, General, have I been so indebted as to yourself for uniform kindness and consideration and it has always been my ardent desire to merit your approbation.

"I shall carry with me to the grave the most grateful recollections of your kind consideration and your name and fame will always be dear to me. Save in the defense of my native state, I never desire again to draw my sword.

"Be pleased to accept my most earnest wishes for the continuance of your happiness, prosperity and believe me most truly yours,

"R. E. LEE."[19]

---

[19] Library of Congress Manuscripts.

Another letter written on the same day to his dearly loved sister Ann, whose son was to fight in the Union army, gives a further glimpse:

> "Arlington, Virginia
> "April 20, 1861.

"My Dear Sister: I am grieved at my inability to see you. . . . I have been waiting for a 'more convenient season,' which has brought to many before me deep and lasting regret. Now we are in a state of war which will yield to nothing. The whole South is in a state of revolution, into which Virginia, after a long struggle, has been drawn; and though I recognize no necessity for this state of things, and would have forborne and pleaded to the end for redress of grievances, real or supposed, yet in my own person I had to meet the question whether I should take part against my native State.

"With all my devotion to the Union and the feeling of loyalty and duty of an American citizen, I have not been able to make up my mind to raise my hand against my relatives, my children, my home. I have therefore resigned my commission in the Army, and save in defense of my native State, with the sincere hope that my services may never be needed, I hope I may never be called on to draw my sword. I know you will blame me; but you must think as kindly of me as you can, and believe that I have endeavoured to do what I thought right.

"To show you the feeling and struggle it has cost me, I send you a copy of my letter of resignation. I have no time for more. May God guard and protect you and yours, and shower upon you everlasting blessings, is the prayer of your devoted brother,

> "R. E. LEE."[20]

There is one other letter, of which the original is preserved in the Library of Congress, to a young cousin who

---

[20] *R. and L.,* pp. 25-26.

was also an officer in the United States Army which must have been written in the same sitting. I have wondered much what he meant by the last sentence.

"Arlington, 20 April, 1861
"My dear Cousin Roger,
"I only received today your letter of the 17th. Sympathizing with you in the troubles that are pressing so heavily on our beloved country, I entirely agree with you in your notions of allegiance. I have been unable to make up my mind to raise my hand against my native State, my relatives, my children, my home. I have therefore resigned my commission in the army. I never desire again to draw any sword save in the defense of my State. I consider it useless to go into the reasons that influenced me. I can give you no advice. I merely tell you what I have done that you may do better.
"Wishing you every happiness and prosperity,
"I remain faithfully
"your kinsman
"R. E. LEE.
"Lt. R. Jones
"U. S. Army."

On the twenty-second he went to Richmond, and on the twenty-third he was publicly commissioned as major-general before the Convention and invested with the command of the troops of the State of Virginia. It is interesting to note, as indicating the state of mind of the day, that while Lee remained for two days at Arlington after his resignation no effort was made to arrest him and thus deprive the Confederacy of his valuable services.

CHAPTER IX

Loyalty or Logic?

WHEN Robert E. Lee surrendered the commission that Abraham Lincoln had given him three weeks before there were those that called him a rebel and a traitor. And yet feeling as he did about his native state of Virginia he could do nothing else. Much has been written about that event which was to mean so much to him and to the struggle just beginning. Perhaps the nearest approach to what lay at the back of his thoughts is to be found in the words John Drinkwater puts in his mouth on that night in Arlington when he reached his decision to resign. One of his guests says to him, speaking of the action of the Convention in passing the Ordinance of Secession: "They oughtn't to have done it." And he answers: "It's gone beyond that now. There's nothing left for each of us now but the last decision, and then to forget that it ought not to have been done, that somebody was foolish. We shall all have to believe that we were wise and just. That's the way with these things. Argument is over and faith begins."[1]

There can be little question that then and long afterward he thought that "somebody was foolish." That he was opposed to secession with all his heart is evident from the letters written during this time, and from every other evidence. And after the struggle was over and he had surrendered the broken fragments of his army there is the

---

[1]Drinkwater, *Robert E. Lee*, Scene 2.

letter Charles A. Dana, Assistant Secretary of War, wrote officially to his chief, Stanton, from City Point April 12, 1865: "General Grant had a long interview with Lee, who said that he should devote his whole efforts to pacifying the country and bringing the people back to the Union. He had always been for the Union in his heart and could find no justification for the politicians who had brought on the war, whose origin he believed to have been in the folly of the extremists on both sides."[2] It seems impossible that Dana could have twisted his words in what was an official report of the surrender and the events that followed.

And as he was opposed to secession so also had he little love for the institution of slavery, which he, in common with every one who saw clearly, recognized as the basis of all the trouble. We have already seen what he told Mr. Blair about this. In the letter from Texas written on December 27, 1856, he expressed himself even more strongly, showing that he had held the opinion for some years before the war: "There are few I believe, in this enlightened age, who will not acknowledge that slavery as an institution is a moral and political evil. It is idle to expatiate on its disadvantages. I think it is a greater evil to the white than to the colored race."[3] Every record that we have of those years points clearly to the fact that he did not resign from the army because he believed in secession or the thing that led to secession—slavery. On the contrary every instinct within him rose up in protest against the destruction of the nation that the other Lees before him had helped to found.

There were many reasons which led him to this earnestly

[2] O. R., Vol. XCVII, p. 716.
[3] Long, p. 83.

held opinion of the unwisdom of the course that the southern leaders were taking other than his undoubted devotion to the country he had so ably served and which had honored that service. He knew, as did few of those who were leading the clamor for secession, the practical impossibility of its success. They were parochial in their view-point. He knew the nation, for he had served at widely scattered points in it, and his was never a closed mind. St. Louis, the upper Missouri, Baltimore, New York, West Point, the Great Plains,—in all these places he had lived and served. He had traveled back and forth over many states in his army service, states that were afterward to supply Grant with his armies. Captain John Hampden Chamberlayne, who had fought under him and who knew him, saw this in him: "His mind was bounded by no lines of neighborhood or of states. He knew the men of the North as well as of the South; he had maturely weighed the wealth of one and the poverty of the other. Few knew so well as he, none better, the devotion we could apply to any one cause, but he knew likewise the stubborn, deep-resting strength of the Northern will that we took for a passing whim."[4] He knew that vast numbers of men had filled up the prairie lands, coming from the South, because slavery gave them no chance at home. They hated slavery and they loved the Union. In the one state of Iowa alone, the census of 1850 showed only fifty-five hundred from the six states of New England whereas there were eight thousand Virginians and nine thousand Kentuckians and a total of thirty thousand southerners. The same census showed only ten thousand New Englanders in Indiana but one hundred and seventy-nine thousand southerners. More or less the same proportions held for Ohio and Illinois.

---

[4]Address delivered in Richmond on Lee's birthday 1876.

These men, Lee knew, would never listen to Greeley and let "the erring sisters go in peace." The Union was their great passion. They thought as Lincoln thought.

He knew also the vast resources of the North for war. Yancey and his confrères might sneer at the North as a nation of shopkeepers, but Lee knew they had shops that could turn out rifles and cannon and clothing and all the vast machinery of war, and that the South did not have these things. He further knew that if Virginia seceded the war would be fought in her territory. Washington was the prize for which both forces would contend, and about it, his own country, the battle would be joined. He had no illusions about the result. The great houses by the slow flowing rivers would lie in ashes. The fields would be untilled, the civilization of Old Virginia, which his fathers had helped fashion, would be ended for ever.

Then too there would be his personal loss. Arlington, where he had won his bride and where his children had been born, whose walls sheltered the priceless relics of Washington, and to which his heart had ever turned in the days of march and weary bivouac, and where he had planned to spend the last years after his retirement, would be gone for ever. And with it the service that had been his pride. Now he had been offered, as he thought, the highest prize in the reach of an American soldier, the supreme command of that army. He was not blind to the fame that would follow. While Lee was in no sense an egoist he was, like every other man who achieves greatly, confident of his powers. With the resources at his command and with his ability he could have crushed secession in a very much shorter time than they did who had to meet him and Virginia. The command of a victorious army in America had always meant high political place. Washington, Jackson, Harrison, Taylor,—he remembered them all. And he came of a race that was rightly not without ambition. Everything in him, his personal fortunes, his ambitions, his clear understanding of all the factors involved in the problem, led him to oppose secession. But Virginia had chosen, and he was a son of Virginia. That is the whole story. The first call upon him, thinking as he did, was to follow the call of Virginia. Hers was his sword. Logic called him one way, loyalty called him another. And for him loyalty was greater than logic. And who will question him for that? Argument was over and faith began! How well he kept that faith those four memorable years when his ragged troops of the Army of Northern Virginia "carried the rebellion on their bayonets" history has told.

And yet there remains and apparently will remain, the mystery as to why he did not use the knowledge he had, the influence he undoubtedly possessed, to persuade the Richmond Convention from the path that led to Appomattox. He was afterward to testify before the Committee on Reconstruction: "I may have said that I may have believed that the positions of the two sections which they held to each other was brought about by the politicians of the country; that the great masses of the people if they understood the real question would have avoided it. . . . I did believe at the time that it was an unnecessary condition of affairs and might have been avoided, if forbearance and wisdom had been practiced on both sides." Why did he not express that belief in words loud enough for the Richmond Convention to hear? He was at Arlington for seven weeks before the Convention passed the Ordinance of Secession. It seems hardly credible that he was not in touch with some of its leaders during that time.

There were undoubtedly those outside the Convention who urged him to act. Even after his resignation his cousin, Cassius Lee, forwarded to him on April twenty-third a letter written by Doctor May of the Theological Seminary at Alexandria urging him as a Christian to use his influence to bring about peace, because "great respect would be shown to the judgment and Christian Spirit of one so distinguished as he." Cassius Lee wrote in forwarding it: "The enclosed letter was written to me, as you will see, in consequence of a remark I made to Dr. Sparrow, which he reported to the writer, Dr. May, that I hoped your connection with the Virginia forces, if you concluded to accept the command, might lead to some peaceful settlement of our difficulties. I hoped this from the friendship between yourself and General Scott. I have only time now to enclose you Dr. May's letter, and to offer my earnest prayer that God may make you instrumental in saving our land from this dreadful strife." To this letter Lee replied: "I am much obliged to you for Dr. May's letter. Express to him my gratitude for his sentiments and tell him that no earthly act would give me so much pleasure as to restore peace to my country. But I fear it is now out of the power of man and in God alone must be our trust."[5] But there is no record that he moved in any way to use his influence. It is difficult to understand.

It has been argued by some that as an army officer he felt that he should take no part in politics. But this was more than mere politics. And he did not come of a race prone to silence. Those famous Lees, whose portraits hung on the walls of Sherwood, were famous because they had refused to hold their peace when grave events impended.

---

[5] Letter in possession of C. G. Lee, Jr.

Nor was he without influence in his state. The great Tidewater leaders who were forcing the issue for secession were known to him and to his house. That the Convention held him in the highest honor is evidenced by the fact that immediately on his resignation becoming known he was its unanimous choice for the leadership of its armies. And there were other famous soldiers in Virginia. Yet as Fitzhugh Lee describes it "when the question of his nomination was put to that body there was immediate and ardent response, which attested the cordial and unbounded confidence in the man to whom Virginia committed her fortunes."[6] And in the speech with which President Janney welcomed him to the Convention he applies terms to him which clearly imply that they thought of him as a second Washington. After alluding to the fact that Lee was born in Westmoreland, Washington's old county, he went on, "Sir, we have by unanimous vote expressed our conviction that you are, among the living citizens of Virginia, 'first in war.' We pray to God most fervently that you may conduct the operations committed to your charge that it will soon be said of you that you are 'first in peace,' and when the time comes you will have earned the proud distinction of being 'first in the hearts of your countrymen.' "[7] And Mrs. Tyler, the wife of the ex-President who had been the leader of the secession forces in the Convention, wrote to her friend, Mrs. Alexander Gardiner, immediately after his appointment: "Colonel Lee, a splendid man every inch of him, is in command of the Virginia forces. . . . He can only lead to victory."

And the most amazing bit of evidence as to his influence

---

[6]Fitzhugh Lee, p. 89.

[7]*Ibid.*, p. 91.

with the Convention is to be found in Alexander H. Stephens' account of the next day when Lee's appointment as commander-in-chief of the Virginia forces seemed likely to block the way to the treaty of alliance with the Confederacy which he had come to Richmond to negotiate: "Feeling the deepest solicitude in the result I barely referred all parties approaching me in relation to it to General Lee himself. I advised them to consult him and to submit the whole matter to him, as he was the party immediately interested, and assured them that I believed that he would cordially approve what they had done; and if he did I thought the Convention ought to be satisfied. He was thoroughly sounded by several of his most devoted friends in the Convention, who left him feeling as fully assured as I did that he was perfectly satisfied with the Articles as they stood, and that there was no affectation on his part in this matter. *The truth is, a look, or even an intonation of voice, at this time, which would have indicated that his professed satisfaction was not the real and unaffected feeling of his heart, would have defeated that measure.*"[8]   (Italics mine.)

Surmise of course it is, but it seems like a reasonable surmise, that had Lee gone to that Convention before it had passed the Ordinance, with his knowledge of what the impending struggle would be like and the scanty chances for the southern success, with his magnetic personality, his great reputation as a soldier, the prestige of his family name and his wide connection with the group that had always led Virginia, he might have rallied the uncertain Union forces and saved Virginia for the Union and its fields from dreadful battle. But he stayed at Arlington for seven weeks while the secession leaders

---
[8]Stephens, Vol. II, p. 386.

worked their will with the Convention. Then of course it was, as he had written to his cousin, "out of the power of man."

Among those who have praised him as among the greatest of soldiers is the famous English Field-Marshal Wolseley, who was with him in Virginia as an observer. His words about him have often been quoted, "I have met many of the great men of my time, but Lee alone impressed me with the feeling that I was in the presence of a man who was cast in a grander mould and made of different and of finer metal than are other men."[9] In the same article in which occur these words he wrote this also: "Like all men Lee had his faults: like all the greatest of generals he sometimes made mistakes. His nature shrank with such horror from the dread of wounding the feelings of others, that upon occasions he left men in positions of responsibility to which their abilities were not equal. This softness of heart, amiable as that quality may be, amounts to a crime in a man entrusted with the direction of public affairs at critical moments. Lee's devotion to duty and great respect for obedience seems to have made him at times too subservient to those charged with the civil government of his country."

I think those words need to be kept in mind when we seek to understand these events. To be sure he was not "entrusted with the direction of public affairs" directly. But he was an officer of the army holding a commission which bound him "to bear true faith and allegiance to the United States of America, to serve honestly and faithfully against all enemies whatsoever." Were not Wise and those who with him were seeking to force Virginia to secede among those enemies? It was a "critical mo-

---

[9] *MacMillan's Magazine*, Vol. 55, p. 321.

ment" and one can not help feeling that this was one of the times when he was "too subservient to those charged with the civil government of his country."

Gamaliel Bradford is right when he speaks of Lee as "one of the most striking, one of the noblest tragic figures the world has ever produced."[10] Yet might not his own hand have averted the tragedy if he had helped the Convention to face "the real question" in the light of the facts as he knew them? It is not for us who know nothing of the agony of those years to blame him. Yet as one studies the events of that spring of '61 there are times that one thinks of Hamlet!

---

[10] Bradford, p. 43.

Chapter X

Arlington Farewell!

That last evening that Lee spent in Arlington is one about which the imagination plays. It was spring—and spring in Virginia! The air was soft and full of the scent that only April knows. That morning he had gone as was his habit to the service in Christ Church in Alexandria and then for a walk along the canal with his cousin Cassius with whom he talked about the proffered command of the Virginia forces, and Cassius had advised him to wait until the ordinance was ratified by the people of Virginia, but he had answered that he did not see how that would be possible.[1] The robins were singing their evening songs. Quietly he paced the wide porches and looked down the hill, where the slow river ran, across to the city where the white mass of the Capitol gleamed in the setting sun. This was home! Here his heart had turned so often in the old days, on the march or in the forlorn frontier posts, perhaps as he groped his way through the midnight darkness of the Pedregal. No matter what danger or discomfort he had had to face always he could think of this place of quiet that waited for him after his warring was done.

Here he and Mary would grow old together, and the sun would sink always behind the hills and its last rays would light up the Capitol and he would be content. What happy years they had had together here since that

[1] Mss. "Recollections of Mrs. Harriotte Lee Taliaferro." In possession C. G. Lee, Jr.

stormy night when Bishop Meade had married them, his surplice covering the borrowed and ill-fitting clothes that replaced his wet ones. Here the children had grown up, Custis and Mary and Fitzhugh and Annie and Robert and Mildred. How they had swarmed over him when he came into the great hall returning for his furloughs, and after their noisy welcome there were the household servants bobbing and smiling in the background to greet him also. This had been home for them as it had been for him, and his decision involved them. That was the worst about war, its victims were more than they who fell in the screaming charge. And Mary was ill now so often, her rheumatism was growing worse. It would be especially hard on her to miss the familiar things, the familiar places, to build another home in another place. And what hosts of friends had found shelter here! Among the thoughts that comforted him in those arid days in Texas was the one that when his duty there was done he could gather many around him here on many a happy night for better fare than army fare and better beds than a blanket spread on the grass. Those old army friends! How much that army had meant to him.

His daughter had that day told her cousin who had rushed wildly to express her gratification that "Cousin Robert had sent in his resignation": "It is no gratification to us, it is like a death in the house. Since my father went to West Point, the army has been his home and his life, he expected to live and die belonging to it, and only his sense of duty made him leave it."[2] They knew something of what it meant, those children who were so close to him, so they thought of it as like "a death in the house." But they did not know all! There was no doubt that it was

_____
[2] *Ibid.*

his duty to leave that army, but never in all his life had duty been harder.

Even though the army he was to lead were successful in the war that impended there was little chance that Arlington would escape. He had no illusion as to what the war would do to it. They might be gently courteous now, over there in Washington, and refuse to arrest him and the other Virginians who like him had resigned their commissions, but courtesy would not last when the dreadful business of battle began. And that dreadful business would last long he knew. He saw what few men saw in those excited days: "While the politicians and indeed the vast majority of the people anticipated but a very short decisive struggle General Lee took a different view, and stands alone, of all those known to me whose opinions were entitled to consideration, as having expressed his most serious apprehension of a prolonged and bloody war; he in an especial degree seemed to appreciate the magnitude of the impending conflict." So later his aide was to write about him.[3]

So of course Virginia would be invaded. He would invade it if he were in Scott's place. There was nothing else for the North to do if it followed Lincoln's demand that the Union must be preserved. And that meant the end of Arlington for him, at least until the war was done, and perhaps for ever. We can follow him as he went through the rooms for a last sight of them. Then in the morning the carriage came to take him to Alexandria for the Richmond train. Arlington was gone for ever.

He writes his wife from Richmond on April thirteenth that he is "glad to hear that all is well and as yet peaceful. I fear the latter state will not continue long. I think,

---

[3] Taylor, p. 12.

therefore you had better prepare all things for removal from Arlington—that is plate, pictures, etc., and be prepared to move at any moment. Where to go is the difficulty. When the war commences no place will be exempt; in my opinion, indeed, all the avenues into the state will be the scene of military operations. . . . The war may last ten years. Where are our ranks to be filled from then?"[4]

Again he writes on May eighth: "I received yesterday your letter of the 5th. I grieve at the anxiety that drives you from your home. I can appreciate your feelings on the occasion and pray that you may receive comfort and strength in the difficulties that surround you. When I reflect upon the calamity pending over the country my own sorrows sink into insignificance."[5]

Those sorrows of his country! It had not been easy for him to take off that blue coat! He writes in another letter to Mrs. Lee on May thirteenth: "Tell Custis (then a lieutenant in the U. S. Army) he may consult his own judgment, reason and conscience as to the course he may take. I do not wish him to be guided by my example or wishes. *If I have done wrong let him do better.*"[6]   (Italics mine.) And after long months of war when his fame was at its height, when the army he had shaped had pierced its farthest into northern territory and victory seemed nearest at hand, on that second day of Gettysburg, he was to lie on the grass for a few minutes, while his aides mounted the tower of the Seminary for an observation of the battle, and talk to a wounded prisoner in blue, a mere boy. And he was to tell him that he for years had belonged to that

[4] Fitzhugh Lee, p. 93.

[5] *Ibid.,* p. 95.

[6] *Ibid.,* p. 94.

army of which he was a part. And when the boy asked him in surprise why he left it, he was to lie silent for a minute and then to say, "Ah, my boy, when you are older you will understand!"[7]

Yet again and again one finds a note of courtesy—old-fashioned courtesy shall we call it?—amid all the confusion and sorrow of those days. Thus this letter which Mrs. Lee sent to General Scott in Washington, on May fifth:

"My dear General: Hearing that you desire to see the account of my husband's reception in Richmond, I have sent it to you. No honors can reconcile us to that fratricidal war which we would have laid down our lives freely to avert. Whatever may happen I feel that I may expect from your kindness all the protection you can in honor afford. Nothing can ever make me forget your kind appreciation of Mr. Lee. If you knew all you would not think so hardly of me. Were it not that I would not add one feather to his load of care nothing would induce me to abandon my home. Oh, that you could command peace to our distracted country.

"Yours in sadness and sorrow,
"M. C. LEE."[8]

In spite of all Lee's warnings she stayed on at Arlington. Some woman's hope perhaps that the war might pass around her and leave her undisturbed! But courtesy had to yield to stern necessity. The hills of Arlington were too fair a place for batteries. The word came to her, perhaps from Scott, that Arlington must be occupied. She left hurriedly, taking her daughters, a few devoted ser-

---

[7] Told by James M. Hill, 150 Pa. Volunteers, Company H, to Dr. J. S. Duncan, of Mercer, Pa.

[8] Fitzhugh Lee, pp. 93-94.

vants, and little else besides. Many of the treasures about which Lee had been anxious were left behind. Before her departure she wrote a letter to an army officer in charge of the Washington defenses asking his protection for the things she prized. One cherishes the answer that General Irvin McDowell sent in reply: "I assure you it will be my earnest endeavour to have all things so ordered that on your return you will find things as little disturbed as possible."

On your return! How little they saw! It is good to read that letter when one thinks of the March to the Sea! Of Sheridan riding with torch in hand through the Valley!

But there was to be no return. Arlington was only a memory for Robert E. Lee, an exile for a cause which he condemned, and for the preservation of an institution which he deplored—because Virginia demanded it!

PART TWO

THE YEARS OF BATTLE

Chapter XI

Jefferson Davis

THE stage was now set for the greatest and bloodiest war the American continent has ever seen. The slogans of the hour—State's Rights, the Union—were not to be the final battle-cries. Slavery was not a secondary issue as many suppose, but the main issue, confronted by a new world order, the culture of the Industrial Revolution.[1] It was a contest between what had been and what should be. The leader of one side had eyes that saw far into the future. His name was Abraham Lincoln. The leader of the other side had eyes turned toward the past. His name was Jefferson Davis. We can not go on with our story of Lee without pausing to look at this man who more than any other made it impossible for Lee to win the victory which would have established the Confederacy. For he could never see things as Lee saw them and in the critical moments he did not give Lee the support he should have given.[2] This may have been due to the fact that "he could never make up his mind to take risks for a great end."[3] Perhaps in turn this was because, unlike Lee, he could not see one thing at a time and concentrate on that. He saw too many things at once and allowed his mind to be diverted through them from the great issue of the moment. Consequently he was never prepared to press the great

---

[1]Fuller, p. 18.

[2]Maurice, *Statesmen and Soldiers*, p. 40.

[3]*Ibid.*, p. 27.

moment to the last advantage. Gettysburg is an illustration of this. Or it may be due to his thinking that he was a greater soldier than Lee. He too was a West Pointer. He had served with distinction in Mexico. He had been secretary of war. He resigned from the United States Senate when Mississippi seceded with the confident hope that he would command the army of the new nation, if nation it was to be, a hope which was seconded by the Mississippi Convention.[4] We have the word of his wife that before Gettysburg, again and again he said, "If I could take one wing and Lee the other, I think we could between us wrest the victory from those people."[5] He never got over the idea that for this he was supremely fitted. Lincoln learned to leave the campaigns to his captains. Davis never did. He held Richmond long after Lee advised its evacuation. And when that folly had worn out Lee's army on the impossible Petersburg line and he had to surrender, Davis gathered what remnants of government he could about him and fled from Richmond to carry on the war in the West. "His indomitable will, his obstinacy and lack of political sense both sustained and ruined his cause."[6]

He was fully six feet tall and carried himself well. He had rather irregular features, with large gray eyes; his limbs were long and loosely joined together, reminding one of his fellow Kentuckian who led the forces opposed to him. But unlike Lincoln he carried himself erectly, as do most West Pointers. "Every inch an aristocrat" thought Carl Schurz.[7] Mrs. Davis declared that he was keenly susceptible to the atmosphere about him and that

[4] Dodd, *Davis*, p. 220.
[5] Mrs. J. Davis, *Davis*, Vol. II, p. 392.
[6] Fuller, p. 30.
[7] Dodd, *Statesmen*, p. 194.

this sensitiveness and acute feeling of being misjudged made him reserved and unapproachable. Altogether he was "one of those subtle, fine, high-wrought, nervous organisms which America breeds, a trifle too fine, consuming in self-control too much of what ought to be active, practical, beneficent energy."[8] Like another great southerner in the time of another war he had the faults of pride, obstinacy, intolerance of opposition and even of advice. He was decided even to imperiousness, and he recognized as an intellectual equal only him whose ideas agreed with his. As a seeming consequence he was apt to suspect those who differed from him of being swayed by unworthy motives. He never won the heart of the people he led and apparently he never knew how to win it. They have tried to love him since, and failed. Lee has the love he might have won. Yet withal he was noble, kindly, generous in feeling if not in mind, self-sacrificing and greatly devoted to what he thought his duty.[9] In religion he was a southern Baptist, with all that meant of a rigid deterministic theology. Had he lived later he would have agreed with Mr. Bryan about evolution—but not about politics! There were times when his opponents in Richmond thought he left too much to Providence. It is true that Sam Houston dismissed him as "cold as a lizard and ambitious as Lucifer."[10] We can not dismiss him so easily. But it is not in Davis and the statesmen who surrounded him in Richmond that we find the glory and dignity of the southern cause. That is in Lee, in Jackson, in Jeb Stuart, and the men who fought with them. They it is whose story thrills even those whose grandsires fought on the other side.

---

[8] Bradford, p. 51.
[9] Burgess, Vol. I, p. 17.
[10] James, p. 378.

Davis, like Lincoln, was born on the Kentucky frontier, near the Green River Valley. His family were Georgians, and they did not sojourn long in Kentucky. His father, hearing of the great new wealth to be made in Mississippi in the growing of cotton, moved on there when Davis was two years old. Pioneers, of course, but not the sort of shiftless Tom Lincoln. No rail-splitting for him in youth, but college. He went to Transylvania University, the greatest institution of learning in the West, whose patron was Henry Clay. His record there was not extraordinary, nor was it at West Point which followed. In fact it has been thought that his failure to support Joseph E. Johnston later at the critical moments was due to a dislike which originated at West Point, when Johnston was a model and Davis an indifferent cadet.[11] All his life he had "the West Point manner."[12]

He soon left the army for the more profitable business of cotton-growing. The rigors of life at an army post in Wisconsin, followed by the fevers bred in the Mississippi swamps, had undermined his health. Never afterward was he a well man. In moments of most serious import during the war he was often confined to a sick-bed. That resolute will was all that held him steady. His brother had been among those who were piling up great fortunes on the rich bottom-lands of Mississippi with slave labor. He followed him in the same profitable business, and then, the beginnings of his fortune made, entered politics. It was not long until he became one of the leaders of the slavery party and, after Calhoun's death, its dominant figure. Before his appointment to the Senate, which followed the honors won in the Mexican War, he had been

[11] Maurice, *Statesmen and Soldiers*, p. 28.
[12] Dodd, *Statesmen*, p. 177.

a member of "The Mississippi Coterie," that little band of determined politicians who were so dominant in Polk's Administration, and in large measure responsible for the Mexican War. The group of which he was a member, economically and politically, not only dominated a president, but as well came to control the thought of southern men.

It is impossible here more than to glance at the achievements of those years immediately preceding the Civil War in which Davis passed from the Cabinet to the leadership of the Senate when the South waged its great struggle for the continued control of the nation. During those years he spoke for the South, and all Washington official life, from the President down, deferred to him. He was consulted on all important questions; he read and amended presidential messages to meet his ideas; he dictated most of the foreign policy of the country; and devised measures for the further aggrandizement of the South, confident that his section and his great interest, slavery, would not be thrust from the seat of the mighty for years to come.[13]

When the crisis came in '61 he was chosen provisional president of the Confederacy, and that in spite of the fact that he had been opposed to secession to the last, publishing a letter to that effect in the *Charleston Mercury*, November 10, 1860. He thought property rights and slavery would fare much better under the national government. That the tests and strains of the war-days would be hard on such a man, so that he might not always be wise, we can readily see. Of his quarrels with Joseph E. Johnston, one of the outstanding military men of the South, the record is full. It seriously affected the cause for which he was responsible and deprived the Confederacy of John-

[13] *Ibid.*, p. 211.

ston's services at a critical time. What Lee thought of
Johnston and of Davis's attitude toward him can best be
understood not by anything Lee said but by the fact that
one of his first acts, when he was made commander-in-
chief in the winter of '64-'65, was to call back Johnston
to command. It is quite probable that Johnston was not
very diplomatic with the President, any more than Mc-
Clellan was with Lincoln. Johnston undoubtedly had the
professional soldier's attitude toward "the damned politician." But the chief responsibility was Davis's and he
must bear the larger blame.

When we come to his relations with Lee we have another
story. Lee seems to have had all the confidence that he
was capable of giving any man. Mrs. Davis writes that
"he had possessed the confidence of the President always."[14] There is plenty of evidence that Lee was more
tactful with him than was Johnston. He invariably
treated the President with the utmost courtesy and respect, placed in his hands all the necessary information he
possessed, and being himself completely devoid of personal
ambition or of any trace of self-seeking, he never aroused
in his chief the faintest suspicion that he coveted powers
which should belong to the President. His letters to
Davis are full of the utmost deference. He consulted
him about his plans and Davis's decisions were final. The
English students of his campaigns think he carried this
too far. Colonel Henderson declares: "A true estimate of
Lee's genius is impossible, for it can never be known to
what extent his designs were thwarted by the Confederate
government."[15] Maurice is less circumspect: "The greatest
soldier of modern times could not do more than win vic-

---

[14] Mrs. J. Davis, *Davis*, Vol. II, p. 320.
[15] Henderson, *Jackson*, Vol. II, p. 601.

tories in the field. He needed, in the circumstances of the time, the aid of a great statesman to make victory decisive and the great statesman was in Washington not in Richmond."[16] Lee must have known this. Yet how his perfect courtesy shines out in that incident of which his son tells: "General Lee after the war was asked by a lady his opinion of the position and part Mr. Davis had taken and acted during the war. He replied:

" 'If my opinion is worth anything, you can *always* say that few people could have done better than Mr. Davis. I knew of none that could have done as well.' "[17] "An extraordinary man, by instinct a tyrant, by fate a politician; and through combining these two without taking the field, the most magnificent failure in the history of his country."[18]

Let this be said in extenuation. No modern president with a Senate on his hands had a harder task than he with the representatives of the people in Congress assembled. Although they must have known in the Confederacy that they had to work together if they were to win, yet the men chosen to the Congress never pulled together from the start of the struggle. Rather that Congress contained all the elements of discord and disagreement it was possible to assemble under one roof in the South at this time.[19] And this lasted and grew worse until the end.

It was evident whom the gods intended to destroy.

---

[16] Maurice, *Statesmen and Soldiers*, p. 56.
[17] *R. and L.*, p. 287.
[18] Fuller, p. 31.
[19] Dodd, *Davis*, p. 257.

Chapter XII

Organizing an Army

"Last summer at the White Sulphur were Rooney Lee and his wife, that sweet little Charlotte Wickham, and I spoke of Rooney with great praise. Mr. Izard said: 'Don't waste your admiration on him; wait till you see his father. He is the nearest to a perfect man I ever saw.' 'How?' 'In every way—handsome, clever, agreeable, high-bred.' "[1] So reads the diary of a South Carolina woman in the spring of '61. Those who saw General Lee that spring when he took command speak of his physical beauty, of his vigor, of the air of a soldier that was his. "A figure tall, graceful, erect, whilst a muscular square-built frame bespoke great activity of body."[2] Well might they call him handsome, with his deep dark eyes, that had a way of seeming darker when in the field, a well-shaped nose, a mouth indicative of an iron will, a voice that was calm and yet commanding. There was about him the power of charming those with whom he was associated. Somehow an impression has grown that he was over-serious, lacking a sense of humor. Yet a cousin tells of a "teasing letter" he had written to her telling her that she "was too young to get married,"[3] and his youthful aides record his laughing remarks about the dangers of the Richmond belles on their return from furloughs. To a lady who, dining that same summer at

---

[1] Chesnut, p. 94.

[2] *MacMillan's Magazine*, Vol. 55, p. 321.

[3] Taliaferro Mss.

White Sulphur before the war, accused him of being ambitious, he replied that his tastes were of the simplest. He "only wanted a Virginia farm, no end of cream and fresh butter and fried chicken—not one fried chicken, or two, but unlimited fried chicken."[4] Nor was he above "a mild sneer at the wise civilians in Congress who refrained from trying the battlefield in person, but from afar dictated the movements of armies."[5] And is not scorn humor in a more acid form? A vigorous healthy man, with charm and breeding, and the dignity that they knew in the Tidewater. So he was when the war began. It was to leave him an old man at its end.

His popularity came later. In that spring there were some who did not trust him. Perhaps they remembered that he had been opposed to secession. A South Carolina notable declared on the street: "At heart Robert E. Lee is against us."[6] And the *Richmond Examiner* on April thirtieth had a sneering editorial about those who "are set to inspect and rule over them [the troops] who were bitterly opposed to the act of secession and who now abhor that just war which is one of its inevitable consequences." On the other hand, the *Richmond Whig* assured its readers that it had never "ceased to be grateful that this prodigious humbug Winfield Scott prefers the command of the Northern Army to loyalty and good faith to Virginia. The consequence is that the North gets the benefit of his imbecility, arrogance, and bad temper, while Virginia has at the head of her army that gentleman of real merit, whose modesty is as great as his merit, Robert E. Lee." There was more than differences in view-point in all this. There was

---

[4]Chesnut, p. 94.

[5]*Ibid.*, p. 292.

[6]*Ibid.*, p. 63.

the man himself. A very clever woman who knew every one worth knowing of that time wrote this in her Diary about him: "I know Smith Lee well. Can anybody say they know his brother? I doubt it. He looks so cold, quiet and grand."[7]

His service as major-general commanding the troops of Virginia was short-lived. Alexander H. Stephens was sent to Richmond to negotiate for the entrance of Virginia into the Confederacy. He arrived on the day that Lee had been received by the Convention. That Convention was as uncertain about Virginia's course as it had been about secession and Stephens knew that on its decision hung the action of North Carolina. He saw that the appointment of Lee might be a serious bar to the negotiations he had come to conduct, for the highest grade in the army of the Confederacy was that of brigadier-general, and if Virginia entered into an alliance with the Confederate States her commander-in-chief, because he held only a state commission, would necessarily be subordinate to officers of lower rank in the Confederate army. And Stephens could make no promises of a commission in the Confederate forces, for that was Davis's prerogative. At his invitation Lee met him privately at his hotel. Stephens told him the nature of his mission, the alliance of Virginia with the Confederacy that he was proposing, and the effect it would be likely to have on his official position and rank. Lee understood the situation perfectly and declared himself for the alliance. The Convention discovered quickly when Stephens presented his plan that no provision had been made in it for Lee, and thereupon he was approached by some of his friends as to what attitude they should take in the circumstance. He assured them

<hr />

[7] *Ibid.*, p. 94.

that he was perfectly satisfied with the Articles as they stood and that he was not to be considered in the matter. "The truth is," said Stephens afterward, "a look, or an intonation of his voice even, at this time, which would have indicated that his professed satisfaction was not the real and unaffected feeling of his heart, would have defeated that measure."[8] This left him uncertain as to his future. Even on June ninth he writes to Mrs. Lee: "I do not know what my position will be. I should like to retire to private life, so that I could be with you and the children, but if I can be of service to the State or her cause, I must continue."[9]

But Davis, who knew him of old, had no intention of letting him go and directed him to carry on the work he had been doing in the preparation of the raw levies that were pouring into Richmond for the struggle that lay ahead, making him practically the drill-master of the Confederacy. It was not until August thirty-first that Congress acted to settle the matter of his rank. On that day it named five full generals, ranking in this order—Samuel Cooper, Albert Sidney Johnston, Robert E. Lee, Joseph E. Johnston and Pierre G. T. Beauregard. Of those who outranked him General Cooper had been adjutant-general of the old army and was to be adjutant-general of the Confederate army through the war. Albert Sidney Johnston had been his colonel in the First Cavalry. But he had not waited for this question of rank to be settled before proceeding with his task. We are accustomed to think of Lee as the master of troop movements, whose tactics prolonged the war for many years, outwitting the able soldiers who were sent against him. We have not always recog-

---

[8] Stephens, Vol. II, p. 386.

[9] Fitzhugh Lee, p. 98.

nized the great service he conferred upon the Confederate cause, in these months before the battles began, in creating an army.

Far more clearly than most he seems to have sensed the military situation that confronted the South. That situation briefly was this: It was out of the question to think of winning the war by the conquest of the North. Its resources both in men and material were too great to make that thinkable. The South's chances of success lay either through European intervention or through the breaking of the will to war of the North. That European intervention was not a dream can be easily seen by a glance at the political situation there. The forces of reaction were in control of the governments. The wave of republicanism that almost swept away autocracy in '49 had not been forgotten by the grim men who ruled in the chancelleries. And America was the home of republicanism. Every interest of reaction in Europe was against a strong America. Bismarck was to see this later and to admit that the failure to intervene on behalf of the Confederacy and so to destroy the great Republic of the West was the mistake of the age. And that the will to war of the North came pretty near being broken by Lee's defensive operations in the Wilderness and on the Petersburg line in '64 any one familiar with the presidential campaign of that summer will remember. Lee had to shape his campaign accordingly. Knowing the North as did few of the southern leaders, he knew that will would not soon be broken. And European intervention might be long deferred. France had hesitated a long while in the Revolution. Therefore his task was to prepare for the long war which he knew was ahead.

In June he went by train to Manassas. As the stop was made at Orange Court House the crowd demanded a speech. The car window was thronged and a number boisterously demanded that the General show himself and address the people from the platform. Thus surrounded, General Lee, without rising from his seat, turned his head toward the window and said: "We have entered upon a tremendous conflict. It will tax our resources to the utmost. We shall need them all. My friends, there is a great deal too much excitement in the country. I am sorry to see it; a little cool determination is worth a great deal of noise." His words were uttered in a way that quieted the uproar.[10] There was need for sober counsel such as that.

From the time Virginia seceded until the evacuation of Richmond a clerk named Jones in the war office at Richmond kept a diary. It is full of many trivialities, but it has also preserved for us many things which would have been forgotten which enable us to understand the great conflict better. And among these things he preserves a speech of Wise, the Governor who hanged John Brown: "Let brave men advance with flint locks and old-fashioned bayonets on the popinjays of the Northern cities—advance on and on, under the fire, reckless of the slain, and he would answer for it with his life, that the Yankees would break and run."[11] That was a sample of the speeches being made all over the South. The war would be a picnic. There would be a few casualties of course, but how tenderly would youth and beauty keep for ever green the graves of its fallen heroes. All was enthusiasm and excitement, and songs of Dixie and the South were borne upon the balmy air. Men formed their opinions of the coming war from their experiences in the recent clash with Mexico, where southern volunteers were largely in the majority,

[10] Newspaper clipping, Old Scrap-Book.
[11] Jones, Vol. I, p. 18.

and imagined that in military qualifications the northern army would be about equal to that of Mexico. This madness was not confined to the South. A speech was made in Chicago in which the orator assured his hearers that he did not endorse the President's call for troops: "He should have called on Illinois alone; this is an Illinois war. Let the President recall his troops, and let this State fight the slave-holders' rebellion and I'll stake my life and all that is dear to me that Illinois unaided and alone can conquer the South before the year is out."[12]

It is little wonder, in such a state of febrile excitement, that they planned for only a year in calling for volunteers in the Confederacy. That was an amazingly long time. Lincoln had called for only ninety days. No attention was paid to Lee's suggestion, based on his accurate knowledge of what was ahead, that all enlistments should be for the war. He contended that as soon as the war was over the troops could be at once disbanded, but that if it were to last longer than a year there would be a more urgent need than at the beginning. They were to see the wisdom of this council in that spring of '62 when McClellan was advancing on Richmond and the enlistments of their veteran regiments expired as the blue army drew close, but they would not listen in '61.

This mistake was to involve Davis in difficulty that lasted as long as did the Confederacy. The situation in '62 made necessary the law which Davis recommended conscripting all able-bodied men between the ages of eighteen and thirty-five for the war. The one-year men, whose enlistments were expiring when it was passed, felt that they had been treated badly by a law which compelled their immediate reenlistment. Stephens, who had already begun

---

[12] Hunter, p. 35.

his attack on Davis, used this action as a basis of vigorous
opposition to Davis's "tyranny" and in this he was joined
by Brown, the Governor of Georgia, and others of influence. All this might have been avoided had they listened
to Lee.

But they were not in a mood to listen to reason that
spring, either north or south of the line that Mason and
Dixon drew. The bands were playing, and the boys were
marching off to war, with garlands of roses about their
necks. And bright eyes were dancing and gleaming and
sweet voices were calling "good-by"—as their heroes
marched off to the war that was to be over when the
Yankees saw them and took to their heels. The bonnie
blue flag was brightly waving, and as the trains pulled out
or the boats from their landings they who were left behind
heard the strains of *The Girl I Left behind Me*. And as
they went northward they who watched them pass heard
them singing *Lorena*, tenor and bass joining in the plaintive words that were to be often on their lips before they
came back—if they did come back!

"The years creep slowly by, Lorena,
　　The snow is on the grass again,
The sun's low down the sky, Lorena,
　　The frost gleams where the flowers have been.
But the heart throbs on as warmly now
　　As when the summer days were nigh,
The sun can never dip so low
　　As down affliction's clouded sky.

"A hundred months have passed, Lorena,
　　Since last I held that hand in mine,
And felt its pulse beat fast, Lorena,
　　But mine beat faster far than thine.

A hundred months, 'twas flow'ring May,
  When up the hilly slope we climbed,
To watch the dying of the day
  And hear the distant church bells chime."[13]

Roses, dancing feet and wild impossible bombast,—was this the background for an army? Yet Lee made an army out of the men who came out of that land of excitement, an army of incredible valor. Swinton, who told the story of the host that long opposed it on the Potomac, writes: "Who that ever looked upon it can forget that army of tattered uniforms and bright muskets—that body of incomparable infantry which for four years carried the revolt upon its bayonets, opposing a constant front to the mighty concentration of power brought against it; which, receiving terrible blows, did not fail to give the like; and which, vital in all its parts, died only with its annihilation?"[14]

It was not an easy task to change that host of enthusiastic youth into the disciplined veterans that Swinton describes. It was much like the task that the trainer of blooded horses has before him. He must shape the colt to the bridle and the dreary drill of the work-out without breaking his spirit. Lee knew this fully. So he told his staff at the mess-table: "There is a great difference between mercenary armies and volunteer armies, and consequently there must be a difference in the mode of discipline. The volunteer army is more easily disciplined by encouraging a patriotic spirit than by a strict enforcement of the Articles of War."[15] By encouraging a patriotic spirit! He

---

[13] War Diary of G. W. Peterkin, in possession of W. G. Peterkin, Parkersburg, W. Va.

[14] Quoted by Long, p. 495.

[15] Long, p. 166.

took that effervescent enthusiasm with which they entered the war and he made it a solid enduring spirit which not even the furies of the long years, when Chancellorsville and Fredericksburg had become memories, could shake. We sometimes think the height of southern valor was displayed in Pickett's charge. Rather was it in those weary months in the works at Petersburg, when, half-starved, with the faint-hearted slipping away, that growing northern host watching every move, and victory appearing more remote with every day, they yet held on. Who made that possible? Robert E. Lee!

And one who followed him shook an empty sleeve and said: "I did it for Marse Robert and, by God, I'd do it again."

Not only did he have to build in them the spirit that would stand up through many campaigns but he had to provide them with the tools of war. The arsenals belonging to the national government in the South had been seized by the states as they seceded, and many thousand stands of arms and a great deal of ammunition had been taken with them. These stores had been replenished within recent months, for when General Scott, in 1860 asked permission of the Secretary of War to station troops in the South to prevent secession, Secretary Floyd sent arms, but no soldiers.[16] But the total amounts seized were not sufficient to equip the first troops sent into the field, and the South was notoriously deficient in manufacturing plants that could be turned into ordnance works. The blockade by the naval forces of the North, which began at once, tightened as the months passed, making difficult the importation of materials from Europe. Not until the war was half over had the necessary factories been built and

[16] Wilson, p. 245.

equipped for the manufacture of the required supplies.[17] Yet in spite of these handicaps he had an army ready when Bull Run was fought.

Much has been made of the greater fitness of the southern soldiers for warfare, but a dispassionate study of the facts reveals that the men on both sides were well-matched in courage and endurance. Colonel Henderson, the biographer of Stonewall Jackson, who, as a professor of the British Staff College, helped to prepare every one of the British leaders in the World War, settles this matter: "I am of the opinion, however, that in order to discover the secret of the Confederate successes there is no need either to search for nice distinctions in races closely akin, or to appeal to the fact that Lee and his great lieutenant, Jackson, were a head and shoulders above any Union leader who had appeared. It was not only the genius of its commanders that won the laurels of the Virginian army. Many of its victories were achieved by sheer hard fighting, they were the work of the soldiers themselves, and that the Confederates were able to wrest success from opponents of equal vigor was due to their superior organization, more accurate shooting, and above all their stronger discipline."[18]

It was these things that Lee was shaping those summer months in '61 in the camps about Richmond.

---

[17] *Ibid.*, p. 246.

[18] Henderson, *Science of War*, p. 198.

CHAPTER XIII

The Battles Begin

WHILE Lee was shaping things in Richmond there was pretty nearly a panic in Washington. Even the stout heart of Lincoln seemed to waver for a while. On April twenty-fourth John Hay was writing in his Diary: "This has been a day of gloom and doubt. Everybody seems filled with vague distrust and recklessness. The idea seemed to be reached by Lincoln when chatting with the volunteers this morning he said 'I don't believe there is any North! The Second Regiment is a myth. Rhode Island is not known in our geography any longer. You are the only Northern realities.' Seward's messengers sent out by the dozens do not return. The Seventh and Butler's are probably still at Annapolis."[1]

The panic spread widely in the days following the secession of Virginia. General Taliaferro with state troops had seized the Norfolk Navy-Yard, the ordnance headquarters of the navy. The action of Commodore Paulding in spiking the great guns there and towing out the frigates *Congress* and *Cumberland* just before Taliaferro's arrival prevented an attack on Washington by water. But the land ways were still open and Lee had ordered the planting of a battery on Arlington Heights. Things moved swiftly now, and those southern officers of the army and navy who had been hesitating resigned and left for home. Many who would have remained in the service left under domes-

[1] Unpublished Diary of John Hay, Library of Congress.

tic pressure. They laid the blue aside with broken hearts. Some, torn between two allegiances, took a more summary way of settling the problem. One distinguished officer met a friend from the North on the street, shook him warmly by the hand, and went home and shot himself. This tragedy was not the only one of the sort. All was confusion and distress in the Capital city and none knew what the morrow would bring forth. Rumors of the most alarming sorts followed one another. The high officers of the government could not conceal their alarm and they haunted General Scott's quarters till late at night. The panic spread to the people. In every sort of vehicle they fled. In carriages, when they had them, in wagons or drays they left, or when these failed they loaded the things they most wanted to save on lowly push-carts and departed from the city that they thought doomed.[2]

To understand the situation certain things must be remembered. Many of the officers of both the army and navy that Washington knew best had gone South. The wave of enthusiasm for war that was sweeping the South was also known. What the North would do was not so well known, as yet. The attitude of Maryland was still undefined, but the party in favor of following Virginia seemed to be powerful. Would the riots in Baltimore be repeated and the troops for which Lincoln called be unable to reach Washington? Worst of all was the uncertainty about Lincoln himself. We know him to-day as the greatest of all the great figures that that epic time brought forth. To Washington in '61 he was merely an accident of politics, a local politician who had risen from obscurity because of the situation rather than from inherent worth. What could his uncouth ignorance do in the impending

---

[2] *Records of Columbia Historical Society*, Vol. 21, p. 103.

struggle with that brilliant statesman at the head of the
Confederacy who had been the master of two Administra-
tions and who knew every trick of the game?

Lincoln's panic did not last long. On May seventh while
he was calmly looking out of the White House window
watching the movements of two strange steamers, "resting
the end of his telescope on his toes sublime," Hay spoke
to him of a proposition of an enterprising patriot to ex-
terminate the whites of the South and set up a black republic over which the North would establish a protec-
torate while the blacks raised the cotton. And Lincoln
answered him:

"Some of our Northerners seem bewildered and dazzled
by the excitement of the hour. . . . For my own part, I
consider the central idea pervading this struggle is the
necessity that is upon us of proving that popular government is not an absurdity. We must settle this question
now whether, in a free government, the minority have a
right to break up this government whenever they choose.
If we fail it will go far to prove the inability of the people
to govern themselves. There may be one consideration
used in the stay of such final judgment but that is not
for us to use in advance: that is, that there exists in our
case an instance of a vast and far-reaching disturbing element, which the history of no other free nation will
probably ever present. That, however, is not for us to
say at the present. Taking the government as we found
it, we shall see if the majority can preserve it."[3]

Meanwhile the problem of the passage of troops through
Maryland was solved and they began pouring into Washington to undergo the same process of intensive preparation that Lee was putting his regiments through at Rich-

―――――――
[3]Hay Diary.

mond. Under the leadership of General Irvin McDowell, a careful man as Lee knew, who would follow meticulously as Scott directed, they were being shaped. Both armies were to be fitted for the task if their commanding generals could have their way. But unfortunately there were the politicians to be placated, and they wanted a battle fought and the issue settled. For only a few dreamed that more than one battle would be necessary. And the people followed the politicians. Could anything be more ridiculous, they asked, than two hostile armies of almost equal strength facing each other for weeks and not firing a shot? The newspapers were screaming for action, Greeley's voice more strident than the rest: "If the men in Washington are ready to do their duty let them see to it that the Stars and Stripes float over Richmond before the twentieth of July. The nation's cry is 'Forward to Richmond! Forward to Richmond!' The Rebel Congress must not be allowed to meet there on the twentieth of July."[4] It was not the last time that Greeley's unwisdom was to mislead.

So on the sixteenth of July, yielding to popular clamor and political necessity the unprepared army of the North began its march to Bull Run.

The tale of that fateful day has been often told. They thought it would be a sort of a glorified picnic in Washington and Richmond and rode out in carriages to see it. They found out it was no picnic before nightfall. It is not necessary to tell that story here again. Lee had no part in it except that of preparation. The armies of victory were commanded by Beauregard and Johnston. Lee was in Richmond where the partizans of Johnston were beginning to call him "the dress parade and parlor

---

[4]*New York Tribune,* June 27, 1861.

GENERALS THOMAS J. (STONEWALL) JACKSON, JOSEPH E.
JOHNSTON AND ROBERT E. LEE

general."[5] He wrote to Mrs. Lee, six days after the battle, "I wished to partake in the former struggle and am mortified at my absence. But the President thought it was more important that I should be here."[6] It had not yet been decided, when the battle was fought, just what his position was. In consequence he was chary about issuing instructions, and Johnston before the battle resented orders, saying that he himself was the ranking general.[7] But in spite of Johnston's resentment Lee writes to him after the victory: "I almost wept for joy at the glorious victory achieved by our troops. The feelings in my heart could hardly be repressed on learning the brilliant share you had in its achievement."[8]

It was a paralyzing victory. The South was filled with joy. Lieutenant Paxton wrote to his young wife, whom he had left at Thorn Hill in the Valley of Virginia: "We spent Sunday last in the sacred work of achieving our nationality and independence. The work was nobly done, and it was the happiest day of my life, our wedding day not excepted. I think the struggle is over forever."[9] There were some of the Confederate leaders who thought all conditions favorable to a march through Maryland either to capture the Federal Capital or to occupy the strategic point at the junction of the Baltimore and Ohio Railroad at Relay House. Thousands of Marylanders, whose sympathies were with the South, they declared, would have increased the numbers of the Confederate army. Howard and Montgomery Counties in Maryland were teeming with food for men and horses. Half a mil-

---

[5] Dodd, *Davis*, p. 254.
[6] *R. and L.*, p. 37.
[7] Dodd, *Davis*, p. 252.
[8] Quoted by Bradford, p. 204.
[9] Paxton, p. 12.

lion rounds of ammunition for small arms had been captured, enough for the venture. The occupation of Relay House would produce the immediate evacuation of Washington by the Federals, the transfer of the seat of war to Pennsylvania, the accession of Maryland to the Confederacy, and fifty thousand more men as recruits as fast as they could be armed, for Baltimore would clothe and equip them.[10] After the second battle of Bull Run Lee at once invaded Maryland, and Johnston wanted to do so now. It is possible that the reason for the failure to do so was Lee's absence from Richmond. At this critical moment Lee was withdrawn from the President's councils and sent to western Virginia and the President refused to listen to those who wanted to move North.[11] So the South failed to gather the results of its victory. And while they hesitated in Richmond Washington moved swiftly to repair the loss. Congress authorized the enlistment of half a million men for three years. Their eyes were open at last to what the war meant. It was "the very fillip they needed" to waken their manhood to the task.

[10] Fitzhugh Lee, p. 110.
[11] Maurice, *Lee*, p. 71.

CHAPTER XIV

The West Virginia Campaign

THE approaches by land from the Northern States to the Confederacy fall largely into four groups. The first led directly to Richmond through Maryland and Washington. The second ran through the broken country that lay west of the mountains of Virginia and opened a way to the Shenandoah and thence to Richmond. The third crossed Tennessee by way of Nashville and Chattanooga, and after passing the mountains went to Atlanta, the back door of the Confederacy. The fourth took the river-way down the Mississippi through Corinth and Vicksburg. This last was the scene of Grant's brilliant movements which cut the Confederacy in two with the fall of Vicksburg. The third Sherman took on his way to the sea, smashing in the back door. The first covered the country of Lee's great victories, the scene of his enduring fame. Here he was invincible, until starvation and attrition left him only the shadow of an army. But in the field covered by the second group, to which he was now going, he was to suffer a defeat almost as far-reaching in its effects as that of Gettysburg, a defeat further, that, if it had not been for Davis's absolute confidence in him, might have ended his career.

The differences between western Virginia and the Tidewater were wider and higher than the mountain ridges that stretched between them. They reached back over long years. While the wealth of the east was great the broken valleys of the west had produced little more than a competence for the rugged and simple folk that dwelt among them, "the rude peasantry of the mountains," as the proud dwellers in the great houses in the Tidewater thought of them.[1] When the movement for secession began it found steadfast opposition in this section. On November 12, 1860, the citizens of Preston County in a great mass meeting denounced secession as treason. Two weeks later a similar meeting at Morgantown declared that the success of the Republican ticket did not constitute a justification for any state to leave the Union.[2] In a speech made April sixteenth in the Richmond Convention by Alexander H. H. Stuart, who had been secretary of the interior under President Fillmore, he pointed out as among the consequences of secession that "it may result not only in a dissolution of the Union, but in another dissolution which, to me, would be more painful than the overthrow of the Union itself. It may result in the dissolution of the bonds which bind together the different great slopes of the State."[3]

This is exactly what happened and very quickly. A mass-meeting held at Grafton on April nineteenth, two days after the Convention had resolved on secession, declared that "if Eastern Virginia should secede from the Union the western part of the State would secede from Virginia."[4] A convention of representatives from thirty-five counties began its sessions in Wheeling on May thirteenth, led by the men who had fought unavailingly at

---

[1] I am not altogether sure that Lee did not feel this way. I have in my possession a letter written by a West Virginian, who was afterward to become well known in his native state and who was a boy when Lee's army camped for a while at his mountain town, in which he says: "I cannot get over Lee's attitude in regard to West Virginians. You know that his first campaign was in the mountains. He spent over two months in Pocahontas County in 1861. He was like the great god Budh!"

[2] Smith, p. 81.

[3] Robertson, p. 197.

[4] Smith, p. 186.

Richmond against leaving the Union.   The result was the formation of the loyalist government of Virginia with its capital in Wheeling, which Lincoln promptly recognized. While these events were transpiring Ohio troops commanded by General McClellan entered the state at Wheeling and Parkersburg.   These two bodies came together at Grafton, pressed on to Philippi, and surprised and routed a Confederate detachment there.   Thereupon ensued an active little campaign which ended in the death of the brilliant Garrett, in almost clearing the western country of Confederate troops, and in winning for McClellan the recognition which resulted in his being placed at the head of the Army of the Potomac.   It was then that Davis ordered Lee to western Virginia.

The object of all this fighting on the part of the Union forces had not been merely to secure for the loyalist people of the western section the new government they had set up but also to secure for the North the control of the Baltimore and Ohio Railroad, the shortest line between Washington and the Mississippi River.   Lee had seen the strategic value of this railroad and in his headquarters at Richmond had planned the expedition, which was to operate against important bridges and tunnels about Cheat River, and which ended in Garrett's defeat and death.[5] He was now sent to attempt himself the thing which the others operating there had failed to do.

He writes to Mrs. Lee a few days after his departure: "I enjoyed the mountains as I rode along.   The views are magnificent—the valleys so beautiful, the scenery so peaceful.   What a glorious world Almighty God has given us! How thankless and ungrateful we are and how we labor

---

[5] Nicolay and Hay, Vol. IV, p. 333.

to mar his gifts!"[6] But he was to have other things than scenery to absorb his mind in the weeks immediately ahead. He was to find that the people he had come to rescue from the "invaders" did not want to be rescued. He writes again to Mrs. Lee: "Our citizens beyond this are all on their side. Our movements seem to be rapidly communicated to them while theirs come to us slowly and indistinctly."[7] The "rude peasantry" were not siding with the Tidewater, in spite of those persuasively eloquent speeches that Davis thought Governor Wise would make when he sent him to this region. Wise had been more successful in getting Virginia into the Confederacy than he ever proved to be in defending it as a part of the Confederacy.

And Davis was learning that the North had no monopoly of political generals. He was to suffer from them as did Lincoln. Two of these in western Virginia, Wise, and Floyd, also an ex-governor and Buchanan's secretary of war, were engaged in a petty quarrel between themselves when Lee arrived. (Floyd was afterward to display his incompetence at Fort Donelson and to slip out of that doomed stronghold at night leaving to another the un-pleasant task of surrender.) Incompetence had done its worst with the men. Taylor, who was one of Lee's aides, wrote: "Never did I experience the same heart-sinking emotions as when contemplating the wan faces and the emaciated forms of those hungry shivering men of the army at Valley Mountain."[8]

Nor did the men with whom Lee was expected to win battles know much about the meaning of war or the ways of a soldier. A non-commissioned officer in charge

---

[6] R. and L., p. 39.

[7] Ibid., p. 41.

[8] Taylor, p. 17.

of a group who were throwing up intrenchments seated himself on a log beside General Loring, who had passed on his rounds to observe the work. The corporal observed, "General, we officers have a good time, don't we?" General Loring looked at him and asked his rank. He replied, "Corporal." The General was noted for his ability with profanity and he proceeded to display it, and when he had withered the corporal he ordered him to take a spade and make the dirt fly.[9] Not only corporals but privates had to learn much of what such a thing as discipline meant. For weeks it rained daily and in torrents, making the roads almost impassable to wagons, so that adequate provisions could not be brought up. It was cold, so cold that Lee writes on August twenty-ninth: "I have on all my winter clothes and am writing in my overcoat."[10] The men accustomed to the heat of southern summers could not stand the cold. They were sorely afflicted with measles and a malignant type of fever which prostrated hundreds of each command.[11]

With such conditions to face what could any man do? Nevertheless on September eleventh Lee had his plans ready for an attack on the northern forces under Reynolds who were holding Cheat Mountain. The several columns of his army reached their assigned positions in safety and everything seemed ready for a surprise attack. The signal for the combined attack was to be the opening of fire by a designated detachment. But the commander of that detachment found the position he was to attack stronger than he expected and he did not give the signal. They were compelled to withdraw and the enterprise failed. There-

---

[9] Worsham, p. 87.

[10] R. and L., p. 42.

[11] Taylor, p. 16.

after the northern commander was on his guard and no further opportunity to destroy his force presented itself. All that Lee could do was to keep the Union forces away from the passes to the Shenandoah until winter stopped the possibility of operations in the mountains. Then his troops were withdrawn and western Virginia was lost to the Confederacy.

Perhaps no event in Lee's military career has brought forth so many explanations and none is so difficult to understand in spite of all the explanations. Bishop Peterkin, who served as a young officer in this campaign and who was afterward one of Lee's volunteer aides, declared thirty years later that "to him the reasons for General Lee's retreat were far from clear."[12] And his afterward adoring cavalry leader, Jeb Stuart, wrote to his wife after the reports of the campaign were published: "With profound personal regard for General Lee he has disappointed me as a general."[13] Davis in a Memorial address made in Richmond in 1870 said: "He came back, carrying the heavy weight of defeat, and unappreciated by the people he had served, for they could not know, as I knew, that if his plans and orders had been carried out, the result would have been victory rather than retreat. You did not know it; for I should not have known it had he not breathed it into my ear only at my earnest request, and begging that nothing be said about it."[14]

Lee's own explanation was given after the war was over to his friend General Starke, as they sat talking over the events in which they had shared. He declared that if he had fought a battle at Sewell Mountain when his forces

[12] *Church News*, October, 1894.

[13] Thomason, p. 131.

[14] *R. and L.*, p. 52.

were drawn up before those of Rosecrans that it would have been without substantial results.   He was seventy miles from the railroad and his base of supplies, the roads were heavy with mud and if he had fought and won the battle, and Rosecrans had retreated, he would never have been able to follow him.   "But," said General Starke, "your reputation was suffering, the press was denouncing you, your own State was losing confidence in you and the Army needed a victory to add to its enthusiasm."   And Lee answered, "I could not afford to sacrifice the lives of five or six hundred of my people to satisfy public clamor."[15]

But what Lee might have said was that no general in the circumstances could remedy the stupid blindness of the incompetent politicians masquerading as soldiers who had got the army into the state in which he found it.   Floyd and Wise had forced Virginia into the Confederacy.   They now were largely responsible for losing the western portion of it for the Confederacy.   But Davis had his share in the responsibility.   He had been unwilling to see, early enough for proper action, that the Ohio line was among the most important portions of the Confederacy's frontier, that he could better watch the enemy standing upon the banks of the Ohio than on the high mountain ridges.   His armies were scattered in ineffectual places along the coast, while he expected Lee with a few thousand to hold this strategically valuable territory.   He was to be guilty of this fatal mistake at other times, notably at Gettysburg.   It was not only measles and mud that caused Lee's failure.   Yet when all that has been said, Lee can not wholly escape the blame of failure.   Many will find with Peterkin that the reasons for his retreat are "far from clear."

---

[15] Long, p. 494.

With his withdrawal the South lost western Virginia and the North gained enormous advantages. The adherence of this section to the Union cut down the available military strength of Virginia by forty thousand men and reduced its territory by about two-fifths. It carried over into Kentucky and Tennessee, and gave new courage to the loyalists in those states. It deprived the Confederates of the advantage of defending the line of the Ohio River, and made impossible raids toward Pittsburgh, and the Great Lakes, and the lines of communication between the East and the West. The great industrial centers were safe from surprise attacks. Western Virginia formed a mountainous buffer protecting Ohio and western Pennsylvania and released many regiments that might have been required for their guarding. Above all, it insured to the North the control of the Baltimore and Ohio Railroad, the only line directly connecting Washington with Cincinnati and St. Louis, thus making possible the quick transfer of troops from the Potomac to the Mississippi. If one will take a map and follow the narrow strip of territory, belonging now to West Virginia and reaching east to Harper's Ferry, known as the Eastern Panhandle, one will see how the astute Lincoln shaped his new state to protect this invaluable railroad. Its position had a large part too in molding the strategy of the Union armies, for their leaders were enabled thus to attack both flanks of the Confederacy. Its possession was easily worth an army.

So it will be seen that the loss of the campaign did much to lessen the results of Virginia's secession. For the victories Lee gained before Richmond in the years that followed meant only the temporary setback of the northern forces. They came again and again and finally they stayed. But never again did the gray soldiers control western Virginia with all that meant to the Confederacy. Its loss was the first serious blow that the South was to suffer in that long campaign of cutting off this bit and that, as a savage hacks the limbs from the living body, until only the bleeding torso is left.

Lee was ordered back to Richmond, where the *Examiner* hailed him as "Evacuating Lee." Davis sent him to Charleston to command the Department of South Carolina, Georgia and Florida where his engineering skill was to be employed in the erection of defenses. The *Examiner* noted his departure for his new command "where it is to be hoped that he will be more successful with the spade than with the sword." But the clamor that rose about him might have ended his career had not Davis stood firmly behind him. It became necessary for the President to write to the Governor of South Carolina telling him what manner of man he was. Yet through all those difficult months, as Davis afterward declared, "with a magnanimity unequalled, he stood in silence, without defending himself or allowing others to defend him, for he was unwilling to offend anyone who was wearing a sword and striking blows for the Confederacy."[16] Davis would never give him enough soldiers, but he never could let Lee go.

---

[16] *R. and L.*, p. 52.

CHAPTER XV

Adviser to the President

SHORTLY after Lee's departure for Charleston Jones wrote in his Diary in Richmond: "General Lee has now been ordered South for the defense of Charleston and Savannah and those cities all safe!"[1] Lee himself did not agree with this verdict, for he writes to his daughter on November fifteenth, "Another forlorn hope expedition. Worse than West Virginia."[2]

There were elements about the assignment which were sufficient to make him feel that it was "another forlorn hope expedition." The North had command of the sea and the efficiency of its navy was increasing rapidly. The coast-line of the Confederacy, reaching from the entrance of the Chesapeake to the mouth of the Rio Grande, was indented with numerous bays, inlets and harbors which afforded not only means of protection to the blockading forces, but also opened a way of attack to the coast country. The defenses devised by the sometimes amateur engineers had been often injudiciously located and hastily erected, and so offered little resistance to the enemy when attacked. Already several points of exceeding importance to the Confederate defense had fallen to northern troops. It was a serious situation which confronted Lee on his arrival.

The engineering ability which had made for him a reputation in the old army was soon brought to bear on the

---

[1] Jones, Vol. I, p. 96.
[2] *R. and L.*, p. 55.

situation. Defenses began to rise rapidly. The troops engaged in these operations became enfused with some of his energy. Before the winter was over he had made Savannah and Charleston impregnable. Attack after attack upon them failed and it was not until the war was nearly over that they were finally taken by Sherman after his march to the sea. So a wide section of country was saved to feed the armies of the Confederacy, and the principal rail lines from the Potomac to the Mississippi through the Confederacy were covered. He had lost western Virginia but he had saved this coast country. But this is not the kind of service that wins mention in dispatches, nor was it the service in which he wanted to be engaged. It was the defense of Richmond and Virginia that ever held his thoughts.

The winter, as may be imagined, was a very busy one with all this construction at widely separated points to be supervised. He had a great deal of territory to cover and it kept him continually on the move. But the letters written during this period are full of interesting bits for the wife on whom the horrors of war were hard and whose invalidism was increasing. He tells her at length of a visit to the old Greene mansion where his father had died: "The garden was beautiful, enclosed by the finest hedge I have ever seen. It is of wild olive. . . . A magnificent grove of live-oaks envelops the road from the landing to the house."[3] And again from Savannah in February when Virginia was deep in mud and winter: "Here the yellow jasmine, red-bud, orange tree, etc., perfume the whole woods and the japonicas and azaleas cover the garden."[4] On Christmas Day he sends his daughter "some sweet

---

[3] *Ibid.*, p. 61.
[4] *Ibid.*, p. 65.

violets which I gathered for you this morning while covered with the dense white frost, whose crystals glittered in the bright sun like diamonds and formed a brooch of rare beauty and sweetness which could not be fabricated by the expenditure of a world of money."[5] In another letter he tries to encourage his wife in her anxiety—how often is this note to be found in his letters to her!—"The news from Kentucky and Tennessee is not favorable, but we must make up our minds to meet with reverses and overcome them. I hope God will at last crown our efforts with success. But the contest must be long and severe, and the whole country must go through suffering. It is necessary we should be humble and taught to be less boastful, less selfish, and more devoted to right and justice to all the world."

It was not only the news from Kentucky and Tennessee which was "not favorable." It was a gloomy winter for the Confederacy. The hope of European recognition, on which they pinned their early confidence, was beginning to dim. Lincoln had been shrewd enough to surrender Commissioners Slidell and Mason, who had been seized while passengers on the British steamer *Trent* by the indiscreet Captain Wilkes, and while the surrender was a bitter pill for the North to swallow it ended the chance of a war with England. The North was being ably served by its agents in Europe, far more ably than the South. It might have been better for the South had Mason never reached the other side.

Gold was selling in Richmond at a premium of fifty per cent. The price of the ordinary necessities had risen a hundred per cent. Men were wearing their last year's clothes, and women were ransacking the attics for dis-

---

[5] Jones, *Reminiscences*, p. 385.

carded finery with which to keep up a brave appearance. The railroads were beginning to break down for lack of iron for repairs. This was interfering sadly with the schedule of troop movements. Beauregard was calling on the churches to take down the bells from their steeples and turn them into cannon, and cherished copper kettles were being given up in many a kitchen. The blockade was growing tighter, and it was difficult to ship cotton and tobacco, the two crops for which Europe would pay gold. The gold in circulation at the beginning of the war had vanished and the Treasury was offering notes to be paid when the war should end in victory.

The military situation was serious. There were many who, like Lieutenant Paxton, thought that Bull Run had ended the whole matter of fighting. That battle sent the South to sleep. But as the winter wore on they woke with alarm to find themselves menaced on all sides. Paxton, now a major, writes to his wife on December fifteenth: "I sometimes look to the future with much despondency. I think most of our volunteers will quit the service when the year expires and the news I get from Rockbridge gives me but little reason to hope that many more will volunteer to fill their places thus made vacant in our army. If they come at all I fear it will be by compulsion."[6]

In February, 1862, an unknown Ulysses S. Grant captured Forts Henry and Donelson, commanding the roads into the Confederacy by the valleys of the Tennessee and Cumberland Rivers, thereby turning over the control of Tennessee to the North. A large army under the command of General McClellan was being prepared about Washington to remedy the disaster of Bull Run. And the enlistments of the greater part of the southern army, par-

---

[6] Paxton, p. 36.

ticularly the veterans who had driven McDowell from Bull
Run, were about to expire. Davis had sought to arouse
new hatred of the North and new enthusiasm for the war
in the biting words of his message to Congress in November:

"Our people now look with contemptuous astonishment
on those with whom they had been so recently associated.
They shrink with aversion from the bare idea of renewing
such a connection. When they see a President making war
with the assent of Congress; when they behold judges
threatened because they maintain the writ of habeas corpus,
so sacred to freedom; when they see justice trampled under
the armed heel of military authority, and upright men and
innocent women dragged to distant dungeons upon the
mere edict of a despot; when they find all this tolerated
and applauded by a people who had been in the full enjoyment of freedom but a few months ago—they believe that
there must be some radical incompatibility between such
a people and themselves. With such a people we may be
content to live at peace, but the separation is final, and for
the independence we have asserted we will accept no alter-
native."[7]

Davis himself, before long, was to follow the course of
Lincoln in these things which he now denounced. His
speech had little result in arousing enthusiasm. The Richmond correspondent of the *Charleston Mercury* wrote his
paper on the occasion of Davis's inauguration (he had been
provisional president up to this time) that the gathering
of people from all points of the Confederacy demonstrated
a great amount of dissatisfaction with the Administration
and its handling of affairs.

"At present they have no one to look to, no leader. I

[7]Dodd, *Davis*, p. 257.

find no man who knows what to do. Mr. Boyce proposes
Toombs and Beauregard as Generalissimos, to whom the
whole conduct of the war can be entrusted. But how to
effect this? Who can control the President? Will he agree?
Both of these gentlemen have already experienced the im-
practicable temper of the President. Were they to accept
the post they would not be able to retain it. . . . The President has proposed to hand his name down to history as one
who combined in his own person all the best qualities of
Napoleon and Washington. He will not resign. Therefore we are compelled to look about for other aid."[8]

It was indeed a perilous situation which confronted the
Confederacy. No one in authority seemed able to envisage
the war, or to plan the measures necessary. Then Davis did
the one thing that gave Lee his opportunity and made possible a rapid change in the situation. He called him back
to Richmond to be his military adviser. It was a position
rather anomalous in character, involving an immense
amount of work which did not appear on the surface, and
consequently was not generally appreciated. He was
directed to exercise a constant supervision over the condition of affairs at each important point, to keep thoroughly
informed as to the resources and necessities of the commanders of the various armies, as well as of the dangers
they had to meet, and so to be ready to advise the President,
who was the constitutional commander-in-chief, as to the
action to be taken. As the official orders put it he was
charged "with the conduct, under the President, of all the
military operations in the Confederacy."[9] Even with that
limiting clause, "under the President," his chance had
come. It can not be said that the appointment was greeted

---

[8]*Charleston Mercury*, February 23, 1862.
[9]*O. R.*, Vol. IV, p. 223.

with enthusiasm in Richmond. They had not forgotten the previous fall. But the same correspondent who had hammered Davis a fortnight before saw things a little differently: "Could the President refuse himself the pleasure of interfering with Lee and not get jealous of him, our destiny would be safe in his hands."[10] But that Lee sensed the difficulties of that "under the President" will be seen from this letter to Mrs. Lee who was at the White House, their other estate, on the day after his return from Richmond:

"My dear Mary: I have been trying all the week to write to you, but have not been able. I have been placed on duty here to conduct operations under the direction of the President. It will give me great pleasure to do anything I can to relieve him and serve the country but I do not see either advantage or pleasure in my duties. But I will not complain, but do my best. I do not see at present that it will enable me to see much more of you. In the present condition of affairs no one can foresee what may happen, nor in my judgment is it advisable for anyone to make arrangements with a view to permanency or pleasure. We must all do what promises the most usefulness. The presence of someone at the White House is necessary as long as practicable. How long it will be practicable for you and Charlotte to remain there I cannot say. The enemy is pushing us back in all directions, and how far he will be successful depends much upon our efforts and the mercy of Providence. I shall, in all human probability, soon have to take the field, so for the present I think things had better remain as they are. Write me your views. If you think it best for you to come to Richmond I can soon make arrangements for your comfort and shall be very glad of your company and presence. We have experienced a great affliction both in our private and public relations. Our

[10]*Charleston Mercury,* March 6, 1862.

good and noble Bishop Meade died last night. He was very anxious to see you, sent you his love and kindliest remembrances, and had I known in time yesterday I should have sent expressly for you to come up. But I did not know of his wish or condition until after the departure of the cars yesterday. Between 6 and 7 P.M. yesterday he sent for me, said he wished to bid me goodbye, and to give me his blessing, which he did in the most affecting manner. Called me Robert and reverted to the time I used to say the catechism to him. He invoked the blessing of God upon me and the country. He spoke with difficulty and pain, but was perfectly calm and clear. His hand was then cold and pulseless, yet he shook mine warmly. 'I ne'er shall look upon his like again.' He died during the night. I presume the papers of to-morrow will tell you all. . . ."[11]

Bishop Meade was the clergyman who had married them years before at Arlington. Was the troubled soldier, who had to meet the enemy "pushing us back in all directions," thinking of that wedding-night as he trudged home to his quarters in threatened Richmond?

---

[11] R. and L., pp. 66-67.

Chapter XVI

The Defense of Richmond

THE stage was now set for the scene in which Lee was to emerge as one of the great commanders of history. It was a serious situation that confronted him as he assumed his place as the military adviser of the President. The Confederate forces for the defense of Richmond were disposed in this way. Magruder with less than thirteen thousand men held the Yorktown line, defending the Capital from an attack by way of Fortress Monroe, on the southeast. To the westward there were two armies, a small force beyond Staunton holding the passes into the Valley from western Virginia, and Jackson's at Woodstock, half-way between Staunton and Winchester, totaling less than five thousand. The main army of about fifty thousand under J. E. Johnston lay north of Richmond, with the Rappahannock before it, barring the direct road from Washington.[1] To overcome these combined forces of less than seventy-five thousand McClellan had assembled about Washington a well-equipped host of about one hundred and eighty thousand men. By the middle of April an army under McDowell of thirty thousand was preparing to advance by the direct land route to Richmond, which crosses the Rappahannock at Fredericksburg. Banks was in the northern end of the Shenandoah with nearly twenty thousand and Frémont with fifteen thousand was advancing through western Virginia toward the southern end of that great

---

[1]Maurice, *Lee*, p. 92.

Valley, while McClellan had landed with his main army at Fortress Monroe and was headed up the Peninsula.[2] Thus Richmond was threatened on all sides by a vastly superior host, splendidly equipped. It was a situation beside which all that had gone before was child's play.

The way up the Peninsula before McClellan, after landing his army at Fortress Monroe, was through the oldest settled territory in the land, but it had never been fully settled, and wholly cleared. It was a land of slow winding rivers. There was the James on the south. Richmond lay on its north bank about seventy miles away. North, and about fifteen to twenty miles away, ran the York. There were many marshes and lily-beds along its slow winding reaches. The Peninsula is divided, in its upper portion, by the Chickahominy, which runs about four miles north of Richmond and goes to swell the James. It is a swifter stream but there are marshes along its banks, wooded marshes, masked by underbrush and creepers. Here and there throughout this land of rivers you come on level plateaus that rise swiftly from the water. No roads are good, but the best of them run along the plateaus. These alone are possible for wheeled transport. None of them was marked as McClellan's great host began its blundering way through this difficult land, this mosquito-ridden watery wilderness, that yet had little water in it that was fit for man to drink. That army was to find those swamps as great a barrier as Johnston's entrenchments. But they were not thinking in Richmond of these difficulties their foe had to meet in that spring of '62 as McClellan's ponderous machine began its slow and steady progress up the Peninsula. At least not many of them were. They had other things to think about.

[2]*Ibid.*, p. 94.

By mid-May he was established within sight of the spires of Richmond, and the citizens lay awake at night listening to the sound of his great guns. The news that came from other portions of the Confederacy did not lend much courage to its defenders. Grant had swept their comrades from the most of Tennessee. New Orleans had fallen to the fleet of Farragut. Even Davis began to despair and ordered the archives of the Confederacy to be packed for quick shipment. Johnston demanded the concentration of all the troops in eastern Virginia and North Carolina in order to hazard all on a great battle with McClellan. Then Lee put in motion the plans which were to save Richmond.

He knew that the reason that determined Davis to hold on to Richmond was that which was operating in the mind of Lincoln with regard to Washington—namely, the effect of the loss of the Capital on public opinion both at home and abroad. The chances of European intervention seemed to be growing dim, but once let the Confederate flag wave over the white dome in Washington and recognition would come swiftly. And the heart of the North—already realizing that war was a long matter—would fail. So Washington had to be preserved at any price. This was the main idea behind the plans now put into effect. Richmond was to be saved by threatening or appearing to threaten the Capital of the enemy. The first move was Jackson's. His little army had been increased to about seventeen thousand. They were not many but they moved swiftly and they were willing to follow their astounding leader wherever he wanted to go. The things that happened in the Valley campaign are almost unbelievable, the distances they marched, the armies they defeated, the fear they aroused through all the North. First Jackson moved south, and beyond Staunton checked Frémont's advance. Then just as swiftly, he turned and moved northward and met Banks at Winchester and completely routed him. Lee ordered him to press on toward Harper's Ferry and threaten an attack on Washington. This led Lincoln to recall McDowell, who was pressing on to join McClellan. McClellan had made his dispositions with the idea that McDowell would join him; having thrown his right across the Chickahominy. With his army thus divided Johnston fell upon him in the battle of Seven Pines. It was a drawn combat, but in it Johnston was wounded. He had ridden out to the front of the battle in order to avoid seeing Davis, whose daily visits were more than Johnston could bear, and thus received his wound.[3]

Davis immediately appointed Lee to the command of the Army of Northern Virginia in his place. It was an appointment that aroused no popular enthusiasm in Richmond. The *Examiner* announced that "Evacuating Lee, who had never risked a single battle with the invader, is commanding general." Not many weeks were to pass before that verdict was violently reversed. Meanwhile Lee went on with his plans. And they were as daring as they were successful.

Jackson was ordered to prepare to join Lee before Richmond. But in order to use him as Lee planned it was necessary to keep McDowell near Washington or McDowell would have followed and thus neutralized the effects of Jackson's movements. So a portion of Lee's army was entrained openly as though they were going to join Jackson, in the presence of northern prisoners, who were not any too securely guarded after that. Soon McClellan and Lincoln both heard that a considerable force

---

[3] Maurice, *Statesmen and Soldiers,* p. 36.

had joined Jackson and that with these Jackson was planning a new offensive in the Valley. He completely deceived Lincoln, who telegraphed McClellan he could send no more troops because Jackson was being heavily reenforced. With this deception successful he got away to Lee and joined him, leaving seventy thousand northern troops prepared for his attack in various parts of Virginia or its borders.

In the meantime Lee had received other reenforcements so that he had with Jackson about eighty-seven thousand men with which to oppose McClellan and his one hundred and nine thousand. With these he began the Seven Days' Battles which ended in McClellan's withdrawal to his new base at Harrison's Landing on the James River, and ended the northern hope of the early capture of Richmond.

The maneuver by which Lee achieved this astonishing result had been briefly outlined in a letter to Jackson on June eleventh:

"Leave your enfeebled troops to watch the country and guard the passes covered by your cavalry and artillery, and with your main body . . . move rapidly to Ashland by rail or otherwise, as you may find most advantageous, and sweep down between the Chickahominy and Pamunkey, cutting up the enemy's communications, etc., while this army attacks General McClellan in the front. He will thus, I think, be forced to come out of his entrenchments, where he is strongly posted on the Chickahominy, and apparently preparing to move by gradual approaches on Richmond. Keep me advised of your movements, and if practicable, precede your troops, that we may confer and arrange for simultaneous attack."[4]

On June twenty-third Jackson had everything ready

[4] O. R., Vol. XII, part III, p. 910.

and rode ahead, sixty miles by country roads without pause, for the conference that Lee had desired. They met at Lee's headquarters two miles out of Richmond on the Nine Mile Road. With them were the division commanders, Longstreet and the two Hills. Jackson told them that his troops were fifty miles away but that they would be on hand and ready by the twenty-sixth. So on the twenty-sixth the battles began at Mechanicsville, although Jackson had not come up. In fact his movements through that day have never been explained. But the pounding began despite his absence and by evening Fitz-John Porter, commanding McClellan's right wing, found that the Confederates were beyond his flank and that he must withdraw. The next day at Gaines' Mill, with Jackson up, the attack was renewed and by night Lee was in undisputed possession of the north bank of the Chickahominy.

There remained for McClellan the choice of retreating down the York River to his old base at Fortress Monroe or of attempting to establish a new base on the James. He chose the latter and to do it had to carry out a difficult flank movement, with the chance of being overwhelmed while the movement was in process. This Lee attempted, but his combination failed because again Jackson was late, and he suffered heavy losses. A further attack on McClellan at Malvern Hill found him ready in a way unexpected of a retreating army and still further losses resulted. So that McClellan was able to reach his new base at Harrison's Landing on the James. But Richmond was saved, and the great expedition from which Lincoln expected so much ended in complete failure.

That McClellan was not entirely destroyed was due not merely to the skill with which he conducted the retreat but as well to the poor staff work and the inability of the

Confederate leaders to carry out the plans that Lee devised and to effect the combinations that he desired. It was, of course, the first time he had commanded a large army in battle and there is little doubt that he had not taken into consideration the difficulties that had to be faced in making the combinations necessary with leaders who were working together for the first time in actual battle. Perhaps he risked too much, but the necessity was great. And he won his great object, the relief of Richmond.

And Richmond was ecstatic. They were gallant folk, they who wore the gray, and they did not yield easily to despair, no matter how hard the day. And gallantly had they stood to the testing in those days when McClellan's guns grew louder by day and the light of his camp-fires more brilliant by night. The women nursed by day in the hospitals, which grew more crowded all the time, and at night they looked more beautiful than ever to the men who danced with them under the gleaming chandeliers, and then, kissing white hands farewell, galloped off to the lines on the Chickahominy. There were many weddings that spring and early summer, and for some the days of wedded bliss were brief. For after Malvern Hill the sound of the Dead March was heard all day long through the streets. "The empty saddle and the led war-horse—we saw and heard it all. Now it seems we are never out of the sound of the Dead March in Saul. It comes and it comes, until I feel inclined to close my ears and scream."[5] So runs an old Diary.

But Richmond never did scream. And now its faith had won. Lee had driven the invader back, and it had new tales of gallantry to tell. Of "Prince" John Magruder "who played his ten thousand before McClellan like fire-

---

[5] Chesnut, p. 88.

flies and utterly deluded him."[6]   Of Jeb Stuart who rode at the head of his cavalry clear around McClellan's army. Of Ambrose Hill's young soldiers who went back time after time to the charge holding the line for Jackson who was late. Of the color-bearer, James Taylor, who was shot three times before he gave in. Then he said as he handed the colors to the man next to him, "You see I can't stand it any longer," and fell dead.[7]

But the losses had been terrible. The number of gray men killed and wounded and missing amounted to about twenty thousand and McClellan's loss was sixteen thousand. Of course his losses could be and were replaced, while the Confederate losses were growing harder to make up every day. His losses in materiel were also enormous. He left behind or burned great quantities of stores. The Confederate ordnance officers picked up and reconditioned during the Seven Days thirty-one thousand stand of small arms, and they took besides fifty-two pieces of artillery. But the greatest loss to the North was in morale. It was another of those heavy blows which deepened the lines in Lincoln's face. McClellan, the young Napoleon in whom the North had trusted, had accomplished nothing after a year's effort and the expenditure of vast treasure.

With the South it was the reverse. May had opened with no promise of hope for the Confederacy. The coming of July brought a new rush of joy. Richmond was saved. Lee had done it, Lee and that amazing Jackson. They who only a few weeks before had doubted were "now throwing up their caps for Robert E. Lee."[8] But there was no elation in Lee's heart at this swift turn of the tide.

---

[6] *Ibid.*, p. 196.

[7] *Ibid.*, p. 199.

[8] *Ibid.*, p. 196.

He writes to Mrs. Lee on July ninth:

"I have returned to my old quarters and am filled with gratitude to our Heavenly Father for all the mercies He has extended to us. Our success has not been so great or complete as we could have desired, but God knows what is best for us. Our enemy met with some heavy loss, from which it must take him some time to recover, before he can recommence his operations."[9]

There have been some who thought that this swift reversal of conditions was due more to the constitutional limitations of McClellan than to Lee's brilliant generalship, but that is unfair to both men. McClellan was no weakling. Lee's own opinion of him was high. He was asked afterward which in his opinion was the ablest of the Union generals; and bringing his hand down on the table he replied with emphatic energy, "McClellan, by all odds!"[10] And Grant long after the war declared, "If McClellan had gone into the war as Sherman, Thomas, or Meade, had fought his way along and up, I have no reason to suppose he would not have won as high distinction as any of us."[11] But he had been suddenly thrust into high position with heavy responsibilities after his initial success in West Virginia. He was charged with the enormous task of reconstructing an army out of the shattered remnants of Bull Run, of taking the raw levies that came from all over the land, arming them, drilling them, giving to them the mind of a soldier. He had behind him a people anxiously demanding results. Greeley was still clamoring, "On to Richmond." And the very Administration which had ap-

[9] *R. and L.*, p. 75.

[10] Long, p. 233.

[11] Maurice, *Statesmen and Soldiers*, p. 66.

pointed him was not sure of him because he had been a supporter of Douglas.   Not that this affected Lincoln, but it did undoubtedly create mistrust on the part of some of Lincoln's advisers.   And it profoundly affected McClellan himself, for he did not trust Lincoln.   He was to write later of Lincoln in his narrative of these days that "he is honest and means well."[12]

It is little wonder that under the circumstances McClellan was a bit overly cautious, refusing to move until he saw every mile ahead.   And his lack of trust in Lincoln created a situation which fitted splendidly into Lee's plans. He left Washington without imparting to Lincoln his scheme for the protection of the Capital, and in consequence when Jackson defeated Banks at Winchester and opened the road to Harper's Ferry Lincoln grew alarmed and refused him the reenforcements he needed.   Yet in spite of all this he was a great general, the greatest the North had produced up to this time.   The difficulty in the way of his success was that he was confronted, through the wounding of Johnston, with one of the supreme soldiers of all time.   General Scott was right, Lee was worth an army.

The shell which wounded General Johnston at Seven Pines was the hardest blow to northern hopes that the war produced.   It changed the whole Confederate army and its method.

Before Lee took command the troops were sickly, half-fed and had little heart for their task.   The camps were at once removed to healthier locations, supplies of fresh beef and bread were secured, and a new spirit spread through the ranks.   The troops improved in appearance, the discipline became better, they went into battle with

---

[12] *McClellan's Own Story*, p. 91.

shouts and when in it they fought like tigers. "A more marked change for the better was never made in any body of men than that wrought in his army by General Lee."[13]

The ride to fame had begun!

---

[13] Snow, p. 58.

CHAPTER XVII

Some Portraits

THERE were other names to be remembered as the result
of that campaign for the defense of Richmond and those
that followed, the names of the men who stood around Lee
and aided him to victory. They were an extraordinary
group. Before going further in the story of the campaigns
it is necessary to glance at their portraits. The men whom
they led have left much material for their re-creation.
And it is impossible to understand that war without knowing something about this extraordinary group that surrounded the great captain and carried out his plans. He
could not have done the things he did without them. And
when the third of the four had fallen the end was not far
off. A British student of the war has this to say about
them: "It was the personality of the American generals,
more so than their knowledge which stood them in such
good stead, and in the end it is this indefinable quality, always prolific in a forming nation, and generally deficient
in a formed one, which is one of the greatest assets of
generalship. . . . Thus we see that to appreciate the history
of great battles above all we must appreciate the person-
alities of the generals who waged them, those men who
wielded armies as their men wield weapons and who imbued
these living instruments with their determination to conquer."[1]

That they did imbue their men with determination to

[1] Fuller, pp. 7-8.

conquer is unquestioned, and had the Confederacy been as ably led politically as it was in the field the outcome of the war might have been different.

The man who next to Lee among the armies of the gray has touched the heart of the world is Thomas Jonathan Jackson, born in the mountains of western Virginia, of good Scotch-Irish stock and known and loved by the name of "Stonewall." They said he was a stern soldier, who drove his men hard. Yet there are still a few bent old gray-haired men, who followed him as boys, whose eyes light up at the mention of his name as they do at none other. The study of his campaigns is required in every military school in the Western World, but it is the man we want now. He was one inch above six feet in height, a gaunt and awkward-looking man. His beard and mustache were of reddish-brown and he wore them tolerably full, but they did not hide the cold firmness of his mouth. His nostrils were thin, his eyes dark and piercing and with a peculiar glitter in them. His uniforms were rusty and ill-fitting and without the decorations of rank—except when in the fall of '62 Jeb Stuart gave him a splendid new coat, glittering with gold braid. He wore a queer black cadet cap pulled low over his eyes, great horseman's boots and a leather stock which propped up his chin and sawed his ears. One who followed him to the end at Chancellorsville left this record of his first sight of him:

"A sort of Don Quixote, gaunt, bony and angular, riding an old stiff Rosinante, which he pushed into a trot with great difficulty. . . . He rode leaning forward with his knees drawn up, owing to the shortness of his stirrups; raised his chin up in the air in order to look beneath his cap brim, and from time to time moved his head from side to side, above his stiff leather collar, with an air of profound abstraction. Add to this a curious fashion of slapping his right hand against his thigh, and the curt, abrupt 'Good—very good!' which was jerked from his lips when any report was made to him: and there is Colonel T. J. Jackson of the Virginia forces."[2]

He was reticence itself, without any of the small talk of good comradeship, and seemed to those about him to be most of the time lost in his own thoughts. He had the strange habit of stopping and throwing up his hands as though he were supplicating the Invisible. And indeed he lived as ever in that Presence. In religion he was like most of his race, a Presbyterian of the sternest creed. He not only believed in predestination, but he had the very definite belief that he would never fall by the hands of the enemy—which indeed he never did, his own men firing the fatal volley in the gathering dusk of the evening of the day of his greatest victory. Over and over he has been compared with Cromwell. And there was much of that stern captain in him, as when he came through the woods by the Chancellorsville House and found the hosts of the enemy in bivouac, totally unaware that he had brought his whole force through the forest by an old lumber road and was ready to fall upon them. And those who rode beside him said he rubbed his hands together and smiled as Samuel may have done before he hewed Agag to pieces before the Lord. Or on that other day when an officer rushed up to him with the question:

" 'Did you order me to advance over the field, sir?' 'Yes,' said Jackson. 'Impossible, sir! My men will be annihilated! Nothing can live there! They will be annihilated!' 'General——,' said Jackson, 'I always en-

[2]Cooke, *Surry*, p. 80.

deavor to take care of my wounded, and bury my dead. You have heard my order—obey it!' "[3]

It is little wonder they called him hard. But he won battles. And that of course is the purpose of war. And there is one other thing which was said about him by one of the men who marched to his orders in that demanding Valley campaign: "There was something about General Jackson that always attracted his men. It must have been his faith."[4]

When Jackson fell at Chancellorsville, Lee called young Jeb Stuart to take his place and finish the battle. He is another of the immortals of that tragic epic, a gallant combination of Puritan and Cavalier. He came of the same stock as Jackson and the Valley gave him to the world. He never failed Lee but once, and that was on the field where so many failed him—Gettysburg. But that is another story. He was not thirty when the war began, and only a year and a few months more than that when he fell at Yellow Tavern. He was one inch less than six feet high, strong and sturdy, large-boned, with long arms and legs and a short body, and he looked best on a horse. He had the blue eyes of his race, but when the battle drew on they grew dark and piercing. When he rode at the head of his squadrons in the war he wore a great brown beard and spreading mustaches, which showed red lights in the sun, but there is a West Point portrait taken when he was graduated which shows him clean-shaven, with a long jaw and too short a chin. They called him "Beauty Stuart" in the Academy days, and the irony that youth knows best was in that name.

There was no mistaking his arm of the service. He was

---

[3] Cooke, *Stonewall Jackson*, p. 248.

[4] Worsham, p. 164.

General Thomas J. (Stonewall) Jackson   General J. E. B. Stuart

General James Longstreet   General A. P. Hill

General Richard S. Ewell   General Joseph E. Johnston

a cavalry man all over, looking as though he were born to the saddle. His boot-tops covered his knees, his spurs of gold were bright and shining. His sword was a light French saber, and he wore it belted over a sash of yellow silk with tasseled ends. He wore a red rose in his jacket in the months when roses bloomed and when the roses faded a love-knot of red. And from his wide-brimmed hat a gorgeous plume floated in the wind. Oh, there were days when after a hard ride he came in coated with Virginia mud or sheathed with Virginia dust, but when he could he was the resplendent soldier, all gold and glitter.

He rode big horses, hunters, sorrels or bays, and he decked them with a brilliant yellow breast cap with a blazing heart in the center. And he wore out his mounts as he wore out his men in those long rides around the enemy. He demanded as much of his men as did Stonewall. In the Gettysburg campaign he kept them fifty hours in the saddle, until they fell asleep and the horses stumbled and rolled against one another in the ranks. Only then did he grant them an hour's rest.[5] But other than this he was wholly unlike Stonewall. He was in love with life, with people, and people were drawn to him. "He drank deep of life and had a gusto for it all—fine horses and the beauty of women and the gallantry of men, the rich splendor of the seasons in Virginia, the crash and excitement of battle and the bright face of danger."[6]

He had in his train a banjo player as kings of old their minstrels. That banjo player is almost as immortal as himself. As they rode through those Virginia roads he would call Sweeney up beside him and bid him strike up. And above the clank of sabers and the tread of horses the

---

[5]Thomason, p. 3.

[6]*Ibid.*, p. 5.

Virginia forests would ring with gay ballads, "O Lord Ladies, don't you mind Stephen" or "The Old Gray Mare," while Stuart would lie back in his saddle with laughter or join in the chorus like an uproarious boy. And when he went dashing at the head of his troopers on that day of Chancellorsville he was singing: "Old Joe Hooker, won't you come out of the Wilderness," with Sweeney riding beside.

Yet it was not merely laughter. A letter to his brother written early in the war gives the key to his method: "We must make up in quality what we lack in numbers. . . . Therefore I strive to inculcate in my men the spirit of the chase."[7]

But if his spirit was not as dolorous as Stonewall's his religion was just as real. He had become a Christian early in life and he was always a Christian. On the frontier when the only service he could attend was that of the Episcopal Church, he was confirmed in that. And he writes to his brother in '63: "Pray for me in the coming struggle. With me no moment of the battle has ever been too momentous for prayer."[8] And he lived as though he meant it.

With all his love of life no scandal was ever breathed about his name.

How strangely different these from Lee, "so cold, quiet and grand," "the best representative of the aristocratic principle in all American history." Yet the three were bound together by a mutual trust. Jackson had said of Lee in those dark days early in '62, when the failure of the West Virginia campaign was causing others to doubt him, "Lee is a phenomenon. He is the only man I would follow

---

[7]*Ibid.*, p. 9.
[8]*Ibid.*, p. 10.

blind-fold."[9]   When Jackson was wounded Lee sent this
message: "When a suitable occasion offers, give him my
love, and tell him that I wrestled in prayer for him last
night, as I have never prayed, I believe, for myself."[10]
And Stuart, who once had doubted him, came to look "up
to the commander with childlike love and admiration."[11]
When Stuart fell at the Yellow Tavern there is this record:
"When one of his staff entered and spoke of Stuart, General
Lee said, in a low voice, 'I can scarcely think of him without weeping.' "[12]   And afterward in Lexington he told
Wade Hampton "General Stuart is my ideal of a soldier."[13]

The war took both Jackson and Stuart, Jackson when
the tide of the Confederacy was at its flood, Stuart in the
days when the tide was fast ebbing never to flood again.
Gallant figures! They ride for ever down the years, Jackson on his old stiff Rosinante, Stuart like a knight with his
white plume flying.

There are two others who must not be forgotten, one
who also fell and one who survived, Ambrose Hill and
James Longstreet. Hill came from Culpeper, where they
all did not think of him as much as Davis did when he gave
him his commission as colonel, for an old aunt of his
laughed when she heard it. "The Confederacy must be
pretty hard up," she thought, " if they made Ambrose Hill
a colonel." He had his day in Mexico, in that training
school for the larger struggle and served with George H.
Thomas in Bragg's battery. He was tall and slender, a
handsome man, with bristling red hair and a beard like all
the rest. His eyes had a twinkle in them, but the twinkle

---

[9] Cooke, *Lee*, p. 265.
[10] *Ibid.*, p. 403.
[11] *Ibid.*, p. 267.
[12] *Ibid.*, p. 403.
[13] Thomason, p. 3.

could turn to a blaze when gusts of anger shook him. He
was withal a modest man, always ready, a hard fighter, one
of the finest soldiers in the army, "he had the best division
when he had a division, and one of the best corps when he
had a corps."[14]   And when Jackson lay dying he called
in his delirium, "Order A. P. Hill to prepare for action,
pass the infantry to the front."   And as the shadows
gathered on that last evening for Lee the last words that
those who watched over him heard—with a ring of the old
command about them—were: "Tell Hill that he must
come up."   But Hill had gone before his old commander.
He fell before Sheridan's attack at Five Forks in the last
battle of Lee's army.

And last there is James Longstreet. "Old Pete" his
soldiers called him, and Lee "his Old War Horse." He was
the only one of the group who was not a Virginian. South
Carolina had mothered him. He had been a major in the
old army and had served also in Mexico, winning his brevet
for gallantry. He had been one of Grant's groomsmen,
when that young lieutenant married Julia Dent. He was a
big man and burly, and a long beard covered his face and
fell down over his faded coat. They loved beards in that
army! He was slow and deliberate, and somewhat obstinate, holding fast to his own opinions. This dogged determination was to serve him often in good stead, but it
served him ill at Gettysburg when he could not agree with
Lee. Lee, he thought, took too many risks. So he did, but
Lee was his superior and his was the responsibility. Yet
Lee loved him and stood by him.

All four are among the immortals of America's military
history. Without them to help Lee might never have done
the things he did in Virginia.

---

[14] Long, p. 43.

CHAPTER XVIII

The Tattered Army

BUT leaders are not all. They must have men who will follow where they lead, the human pawns in the great game. Lee had them. Daring and brave as were his lieutenants, his men ranked up with them. And the resulting combination was amazing. The Army of Northern Virginia in the summer of '62 and on until those July days when its heart was broken at Gettysburg was the most unusual fighting machine that this American land has ever seen. And even after Gettysburg it fought for two long years with desperate valor. It was always outnumbered, it was usually half-starved, it was in rags most of the time, it was often poorly armed, but it won victory after victory. Before any one can know the story of Lee he must also know something of the instrument with which he achieved so greatly.

The men who made up that host came from high places and from low, from great plantation houses and from little mountain cabins. There were some who were horsemen almost before they could walk. They followed Stuart in his wild forays, as he played havoc with Yankee wagon-trains, and compelled surprised telegraph operators within the northern lines to send impudent messages to the northern Quartermaster-General complaining about the quality of the mules they had captured. And there were some to whom the rifle was more familiar than any other tool, marksmen and sharpshooters who had won their skill on squirrels' heads. There were men who carried Greek Testaments in their knapsacks and there were those who could not read. But high-born or lowly they learned to take what came, and they were ever ready for a song or a battle.

An English officer, who was with Lee as an observer, left this impression of them: "The Confederate has no ambition to imitate the regular at all; he looks the genuine rebel; but in spite of his bare feet, his ragged clothes, his old rug, and tooth-brush stuck like a rose in his button hole, he has a sort of a devil-may-care, reckless, self-confident look which is decidedly taking."[1] "The veriest tatterdemalions who ever with their rags affronted the sun"[2] was the verdict of one of them. To an old regular only their muskets would have given them the right to the name of soldiers, but their method of using them removed all doubt. Often they were faint, half-starved, weary unto death with marching and fighting, but their bayonets were bright.

And they were half-starved more often than they were fully fed. When the day's march was done Johnny Reb would open his haversack, an uninviting bag of a store-room greasy with bacon fat and grimy with dirt, and extract his chunk of bacon, usually wrapped in an old rag; he would draw his ramrod from his musket and running it through the slices of meat hold them in the flames. When they caught fire he would hold them over the toasted crackers and let the hot grease fall drop by drop upon them. Then he would fill his old battered tincup with water and, propping it upon the coals, pour in the handful of roasted rye which passed for coffee, and when this boiled

---

[1] *Blackwood's Magazine*, September, 1863.
[2] Cooke, *Hammer and Rapier*, p. 98.

his meal was ready.[3] So it was breakfast, dinner, supper.
The menu seldom varied, except when some chicken indis-
creetly interfered with his march, or some charitable soul
shared its plenty with him.

Even in the early months of the war this was the usual
ration. If the Confederacy had had ample supplies to
feed them its means of transportation were wholly inade-
quate. It had begun the war with crippled transport and
it ended it with its transport ruined. To Johnny the capture of a northern supply train was an event. It meant a
full meal at last, as on the night that Jackson raided Pope's
storehouses and the supplies of the sutlers who followed
his army at Bull Run. " 'Twas a curious sight to see our
ragged and famished men helping themselves to every
imaginable article of luxury or necessity, whether of clothing, food, or what not. For my part, I got a tooth-brush,
a box of candles, a quantity of lobster salad, a barrel of
coffee and other things which I forget. Our men had been
living on roasted corn since crossing the Rappahannock
and we had brought no wagons, so we could carry away
little of the riches before us. But the men could eat one
meal at least. So they were marched up and as much of
everything eatable served out as they could carry. To see
a starving man eating lobster salad and drinking Rhine
wine, bare-footed and in tatters, was curious; the whole
thing was indescribable."[4]

But supply trains were not captured every day. There
were times, as in the late fall of '64, when the men were
more than half-starved. Supplies were so low that many
could stand it no longer and desertion grew. "For the first
time the morale was shattered, their spirits broken. I have

---

[3]Hunter, p. 146.

[4]Cooke, *Hammer and Rapier,* p. 100.

seen stalwart men sit and brood for hours. No more the light jest went around; no more was heard the cheerful merriment; the men who laughed in the smoke of battle and never flinched at any hardship, had become complaining and mutinous."[5] That they stayed at all was because of Marse Robert. They knew that he was telling the truth when in a general order issued in November, '64, he reminded them: "The welfare and comfort of the army is the object of his most anxious solicitude and no efforts have been spared to provide for its wants." They knew further that he was not faring much better than they, that there were distinguished guests who came to visit him who, being asked to dine, had to content themselves with the simple luxury of boiled cabbage. He lived habitually in a tent. Even when he was ill his staff had almost to compel him to take shelter under a roof. When friends sent him delicacies they went to the men in the hospital tents. Nor did he end with sharing these. One winter night in January, '64, when a cold rain was falling a courier soaked to the skin rode up to his headquarters. He had come a long way from another detachment with dispatches. Lee pulled a chair to the fire and bade the man warm himself while he read the messages he had brought. When he had warmed himself he rose to go and the General asked him if he had no rubber coat. On receiving a negative reply he walked to the wall and taking down his own gave it to the man in spite of his protests.[6] There were times, and these times were many, when his men had to suffer, but he shared, as far as a commander could, their hardships.

Not that he took these sufferings quietly. His correspondence with Richmond is full of earnest appeals for

---

[5] Hunter, p. 663.

[6] *Ibid.*, p. 664.

supplies, and vivid accounts of what the army was going through. He sets forth plainly the fact that the state of the army often made impossible the movements he had planned, but always the complaint is not against the men, but against the conditions which caused it. He writes, October, 1863, after his movement around General Meade's right, to Manassas: "The want of supplies of shoes, clothing and blankets is very great. Nothing but my unwillingness to expose the men to the hardships that would have resulted from moving them into Loudon in their present condition induced me to return to Rappahannock. But I was averse to marching them over the rough roads of that region, at a season, too, when frosts were certain, and snows probable, unless they were better provided to encounter them without suffering."[7] Another letter written at the same time to the Secretary of War setting forth the same facts, concludes: "I think the sublimest sight of war was the cheerfulness and alacrity exhibited by this army in pursuit of the enemy under all the trials and privations to which it was exposed."[8] And still another written to Mrs. Lee, which under no circumstances can be thought of as an official excuse for failure, tells the same tale of care for that army: "I should certainly have endeavored to throw them north of the Potomac; but thousands were barefooted, thousands with fragments of shoes, and all without overcoats, blankets, or warm clothing. I could not bear to expose them to certain suffering."[9]

There is plenty of evidence that the men were willing to suffer what they did because they trusted him and knew that he was doing all he could. A private once wrote to

[7] *R. and L.*, p. 103.

[8] *Ibid.*, p. 104.

[9] *Ibid.*, p. 111.

him saying that he could not carry on with the rations provided, asking the General if he knew what they were, and stating that if they could not be bettered the men would still do the best they could. Lee answered by publishing a general order explaining the situation. The man was answered, not condemned.

There was considerable criticism of his methods of discipline, yet his was a disciplined army if by discipline is meant the means by which its purposes are accomplished. These men accomplished the things he wanted done, in spite of the difficulties under which they suffered and that is the primary purpose of discipline. So that his method worked, worked so satisfactorily that one who had to meet his blows, General Hooker, testifying before the Committee on the Conduct of the War, said: "With a rank and file vastly inferior to our own, intellectually and physically, that army has, by discipline alone, acquired a character for steadiness and efficiency, unsurpassed in my judgment, in ancient and modern times. We have not been able to rival it nor has there been any other near approximation to it in other rebel armies."[10] Henderson, who does not agree with Hooker that southern soldiers were intellectually and physically inferior to their northern opponents,[11] offers an explanation for their obedience to discipline: "The Confederate States were free from the aggressive independence of the North. Obedience was a quality which they had previously experienced. Throughout their history their people had unreservedly committed their political destinies to the members of their great houses, and they followed them now as loyally in the field."[12] Be

[10] Jones, *Reminiscences*, p. 28.

[11] Henderson, *Science of War*, p. 198.

[12] *Ibid.*, p. 200.

that as it may there was certainly no such willingness to follow through in any of the other Confederate armies as was found in that of northern Virginia.

They performed impossible maneuvers and they won astounding victories. And the secret of it all was their trust in their leader. "Uncle Robert will get us into Washington yet, you bet he will" was what they said after Gettysburg.[13] And that trust deepened into devotion. Men say that Lee is the idol of the South. That is true if by that is meant that which calls forth reverence. And that reverence was spread by the men who had followed him the long years to Appomattox. Such things have always a reason, a reason too deep for the understanding of that pleasant group of little souls that made up the present popular cult of idol-breakers.

---

[13] Bradford, p. 121.

Chapter XIX

The Routing of Pope

LEE had saved Richmond, but he had not destroyed his opponent. Had his plans been fully carried out this might have been accomplished, but Jackson, for once in his brilliant career, had not acted with his usual vigor and McClellan had slipped through the swamps of the Peninsula. It was the one failure in a remarkable campaign. It raises a point which will be frequently met in the study of the campaigns which follow, the failure of Lee to interfere with his subordinates when he saw that his plans were not being carried out. It was but seldom that Jackson failed to carry them out, but Longstreet was guilty often of failure to do exactly as he was ordered. He was an obstinate man and he had not the vision of Lee, and this lack was to work havoc many times, and especially at Gettysburg.

Of course it is a hard thing for a commander to draw the line correctly between undue interference and excess of liberty. Lee himself described the principles which guided his conduct in battle: "My interference in battle would do more harm than good. I have to rely on my brigade and division commanders. I think and work with all my power to bring the troops to the right place at the right time; then I have done my duty. As soon as I order them forward into battle, I leave my duty in the hands of God." While as a system of command the principle is sound yet in armies of the size which Lee directed some more direct intervention when battle is joined is necessary. "Lee was disposed to err on the battlefield in not asserting his authority enough. He suffered, as the French say, from the defects of his qualities, for it is probable that, if his character had allowed him to be more assertive, he would not have inspired in those he led the devotion which made them endure as men have rarely endured."[1]

McClellan was safe in his lines at Harrison's Landing on the James River and he was still in a position to make a serious threat against Richmond. He was only twenty miles away, in a secure position, in possession of the best possible lines of communication both for supplies and re-enforcements, which the navy could keep constantly open, and rightly located to move on the city from the rear. McClellan proposed to cross the James River and attack Petersburg and cut off the railroad which connected Richmond with the South. This is exactly the plan which Grant two years later was to follow through to success. And this was what Lee expected him to do. He said, to those in his confidence, that Richmond could be assailed to greater advantage in this way.[2] But Fate intervened to save Richmond again, this time in the guise of northern politicians.

The old mistrust of McClellan on the part of certain of Lincoln's advisers asserted itself immediately on the news of his defeat, and a clamor arose for his removal. Chase, Secretary of the Treasury, led the demand.[3] Of all of the men who surrounded Lincoln, Chase is the least worthy of honor. Every move he made looked toward his choice as Lincoln's successor. It was the popular thing now to demand McClellan's removal. So Chase led the demand.

[1] Maurice, *Lee,* p. 144.
[2] Cooke, *Lee,* p. 100.
[3] Nicolay and Hay, Vol. VI, p. 3.

The President himself was averse to it. In the meantime
Halleck, who had served with some distinction in the West,
had been appointed general-in-chief and had arrived in
Washington. After apparently agreeing with McClellan's
plan he suddenly reversed his position and joined with those
seeking his removal, and recommended that McClellan and
his army be withdrawn from the Peninsula. On the third
of August, McClellan was ordered to bring back his troops
and turn over his command to Major-General John W.
Pope. Nothing could have happened to suit Lee better.

A word about this Halleck, as he was to have a serious
effect on Lee's fortunes. Nicolay and Hay damn him with
faint praise: "His integrity and his ability were alike
undoubted. His deficiencies were rather those of temper-
ament. In great crises he lacked determination and self-
confidence, and was always more ready to avoid than to
assume embarrassing responsibility."[4] Those farther removed from the conflict do not deal with him so kindly.
He was throughout the war a thorn in Grant's side, as he
would have been in that of any bold captain. He was a
pedant who, having studied the theories of war, imagined
that the following of certain strategical rules and tactical
maxims constituted all that was required of a general.
Had he been in command of Braddock's forces on the
Monongahela he would have done exactly as Braddock did.
If Scott thought Lee would have been worth an army corps
to Lincoln it is not too much to say that Halleck was always worth a corps to the Confederates. This time he
was worth more than that to them, for his refusal to endorse McClellan's plan and his lifting the threat to Richmond from the rear released Lee for cooperation with
Jackson in a brilliant operation which ended in the flight

---

[4]*Ibid.,* Vol. VI, p. 2.

of Pope's army to the fortifications around Washington.

Lincoln made many mistakes before he found Grant, but Pope was among the worst. He had won distinction by his capture of Island Number 10 in the Mississippi just before McClellan's defeat, and when Lincoln felt it unwise longer to resist the demand for the latter's removal, he called Pope to Washington, where he made a favorable impression on the members of the Cabinet and was offered the command.

When Lee learned of Pope's appointment, he sent for Longstreet, who had been in the same class with Pope at West Point, to learn what sort of man they had to deal with. This was his usual method. His military secretary bears testimony as to his care in this particular: "He studied his adversary, knew his peculiarities and adapted himself to them. His own methods no one could foresee; he varied them with every change in the commanders opposed to him. He had one method with McClellan, another with Pope, another with Hooker and yet another with Grant."[5] What Longstreet told him we do not know, but he must have appraised him of the facts about Pope, for Lee proceeded now to take risks such as he took with no other commander who opposed him throughout the war. Perhaps he was aided in this by the address which Pope issued to his army on taking command:

"I have come to you from the West, where we have always seen the backs of our enemies; from an army whose business it had been to seek the adversary and to beat him when he is found; whose policy has been attack and not defense. . . . I presume I have been called here to pursue the same system and to lead you against the enemy. . . . I desire you to dismiss from your minds certain phrases

[5] Long, p. 430.

which I am sorry to find so much in vogue amongst you. I hear constantly of 'taking strong positions and holding them,' of 'lines of retreat' and 'bases of supply.' Let us discard such ideas. The strongest position a soldier should desire to occupy is one from which he can most easily advance against the enemy. Let us study the probable lines of retreat of our opponents, and leave our own to take care of themselves. Let us look before us and not behind. Success and glory are in the advance, disaster and shame lurk in the rear."[6]

Lee surely had his measure after reading that proclamation, and action speedily followed. He sent Jackson to harass Pope and check his advance before McClellan moved from Harrison's Landing. Ambrose Hill was sent with his division to reenforce Jackson, and Lee in his letter to Jackson announcing Hill's departure gave the laconic command: "I want Pope suppressed."[7] He had probably just read Pope's proclamation! As soon as Lee learned that McClellan's forces were leaving the James for the Potomac he put into operation the plans already formulated and entrained the first of his troops that evening. He had decided to use his central position to overwhelm Pope before the Army of the Potomac had completed its circuitous voyage. On his joining Jackson there followed a movement as bold and original as is to be found in the history of war. The problem was to defeat Pope before McClellan's army joined him. To attack in front would be a slow and costly process.

Lee determined to divide his army (he had fifty-five thousand effectives to Pope's seventy thousand) and to send one portion of them under Jackson along the Blue

---

[6] Nicolay and Hay, Vol. VI, p. 5.
[7] Maurice, *An Aide-de-Camp of Lee*, p. 121.

Ridge to come in a great circle upon Pope's communication with Washington. It was an enormous risk for he could spare Jackson only twenty-four thousand men. There are many who have thought of the maneuver as contrary to all rules of war. Perhaps it was, but there was a Jackson to perform it and a Lee behind it. Much depended on speed, and Jackson knew it. For the time he seemed to have forgotten the existence of roads. The column moved apparently on the theory that where two men can place their feet an army can pass. When they came to fences, they threw them down; when they met with streams they waded. Jackson thus advanced across open fields, by strange country roads, and comfortable homesteads, on and on, as if he would never cease. It was the "beeline" he was taking. When the Confederates were marching over nearly the same ground in June, 1863, a soldier asked an old negro where they were going. "You are taking the same road as Mas' Jackson took last year, only he took the nigh-cuts."[8] In consequence of this almost impossible maneuver Pope awoke to find Jackson in his rear and Lee moving rapidly to join him. Possibly there were some in his army who felt like reminding him of what he had to say about "lines of retreat"!

Pope had great storehouses in his rear at Bull Run where were gathered the supplies for the campaign. Jackson moved to destroy these. His men carried off as much as they could transport and burned the rest. The black smoke clouds rising into the sky carried the word to Pope that his army was faced with starvation. He issued orders to move at dawn on Bull Run "to bag Jackson and his whole crowd." But Jackson had moved off into the night as swiftly as he had come, and concealed his army in the

---

[8] Cooke, *Hammer and Rapier*, p. 97.

woods, so that Pope kept marching and countermarching sixty thousand of his troops all day within gunshot of his position without discovering him. The next day in order to prevent Pope's further movement eastward and his junction with the Army of the Potomac, Jackson attacked with his small force. While he lost heavily he succeeded in his plan of further bewildering his already bewildered foe and opened a way for Lee to join him. Longstreet did not move as rapidly as Lee desired, in spite of Lee's orders given three times that fateful morning of August twenty-ninth. Thus Pope was probably saved from annihilation.

On the thirtieth the attack by the combined Confederate forces was made, and Pope was decisively defeated on the same field of Bull Run from which McDowell had been driven the year before. The battle on that bleak plain dotted with pine-trees was one of the most desperate and one of the bloodiest of the whole war, yet one who was near Lee on that day was "vividly impressed by the air of unmoved calmness which marked his countenance and demeanor. Nothing in the expression of his face and no hurried movement indicated excitement or anxiety."[9] And when the day ended Pope with the thoroughly demoralized remnants of his army was flying to the safety of the fortifications at Washington, having lost, in addition to the stores burned by Jackson, thirty guns, twenty thousand rifles, seven thousand prisoners and thirteen thousand five hundred killed and wounded. He had learned some things not mentioned in his proclamation!

Lincoln promptly relieved Pope of his command and again called McClellan to his old post, explaining to a member of his household: "We must use the tools we have. If he [McClellan] cannot fight himself he excels in mak-

[9] Cooke, Lee, p. 119.

ing others ready to fight."[10]   And some one like that was desperately needed in that shattered army.   McClellan wrote from his headquarters at Alexandria on September first: "This week is the crisis of our fate."   Never were there truer words.   Day after day Washington looked to see the red battle flags of Lee's host gleaming on the Arlington hills.   Never had the overthrow of the Confederacy seemed more hopeless.   In two brief campaigns Lee had entirely altered the whole situation, so that the British Minister in Washington wrote to his government: "All hope of the reconstruction of the Union appears to be fading away, even from the minds of those who most desire it."[11]

---

[10] Nicolay and Hay, Vol. VI, p. 23.

[11] *Ibid.*, Vol. VI, p. 88.

CHAPTER XX

The First Invasion of the North

BUT in spite of Washington's fears Lee's battle flags were not to wave on Arlington hills. He had no intention of attempting a direct attack on Washington's formidable defenses. But he did deem the time ready for the invasion of the North. His objects in the movement were perfectly clear. He wanted to keep the northern armies out of Virginia until the rains of winter made impossible further movements and thus save its harvests for the Confederacy. Also he wanted the North to know something of the devastation of battle. He desired as well to attach Maryland to the Confederate cause and secure from it many recruits for his army. Most of all he hoped to break the war spirit of the North by his threat at northern cities, and a victory near the borders of Pennsylvania. Then Davis was to join him and offer peace to the North on the single condition of southern independence. This would come at a time when the Congressional elections were being decided. If Lincoln should refuse this offer, with Lee's victorious army in a secure position in northern territory, the North, he thought, in its fright would be likely to return the opposition party to power in such numbers as to force Lincoln's hand.[1] It was a bold and ambitious plan. Lee wrote to Davis after the movement of his army began:

"The present position of affairs places it in the power

[1]Dodd, *Davis*, p. 278.

of the Government of the Confederate States to propose with propriety to that of the United States the recognition of our independence. For more than a year both sections of the country have been devastated by hostilities which have brought sorrow and suffering upon thousands of homes, without advancing the objects which our enemies proposed to themselves in the beginning of the contest. Such a proposition coming from us at this time could in no way be regarded as suing for peace, but being made when it is in our power to inflict injury upon our adversary would show conclusively to the world that our sole object is the establishment of our independence and the attainment of an honorable peace."[2]

And of course he hoped, as did Davis, that success in this campaign would hasten the thing on which the hopes of the Confederacy had rested from the beginning, European recognition. The blockade was beginning to pinch badly. If England and France could have a favorable opportunity to interfere, Richmond felt confident they would. Lee's two previous campaigns had given great encouragement to the friends of the Confederacy in London and Paris. A victory won in the North might settle the question. Although he did not know it the British government was seriously considering intervention at the time he began his march northward.

On the fourth of September the first of his troops crossed the Potomac above Leesburg singing "Maryland, My Maryland." Lee himself was suffering from a painful injury received a day or two after the last battle. He had been standing by his horse with his arm through the bridle, when a squadron of northern cavalry suddenly appeared on the brow of the neighboring hill. In the excitement which followed his horse gave a quick start and he

[2] O. R., Vol. XIX, part II, p. 600.

was thrown violently to the ground breaking some of the bones in his right hand. He was consequently unable to handle a horse during the campaign and spent most of it in an ambulance, or on horseback with a courier leading his mount. By the seventh he had occupied Frederick and was well-placed to threaten either Washington, Baltimore or Philadelphia and to cut the communications of the Capital with the remainder of the country.

There is no question that the movement had a frightening effect on the North. Valuables were buried in the little Pennsylvania towns and women and children were sent away to safety. The folk in the eastern cities trembled as they picked up their morning papers fearing to read that Lee had again outwitted McClellan and was moving down the broad valleys toward Harrisburg and the Susquehanna. The Governor of Pennsylvania summoned all the able-bodied men within the state to be ready for marching orders. The next day he telegraphed the Mayor of Philadelphia that Lee had moved his army from Frederick to the Cumberland Valley and was preparing to march on Philadelphia. "Every available man is needed at once. Stir up your population tonight. Form them in companies and send us twenty thousand men tomorrow."[3] The North was getting its first taste of invasion. But events were shaping to ease the fear.

Harper's Ferry was held by northern troops and the way to the Valley was barred, threatening Lee's line of communication. He decided to divide his army again and send Jackson to take Harper's Ferry. When this was captured Jackson could rejoin him in one day's march. Meantime McClellan began to move on the fifth from Washington. "Lincoln's stern and repeated injunction

---

[3] McMaster, *Lincoln's Administration*, p. 242.

'You must find and hurt this enemy now' had to be obeyed."[4]

Then two things happened which interfered with Lee's plans. Jackson was delayed in the taking of Harper's Ferry. And on the thirteenth a northern soldier found a copy of Lee's order disclosing his entire plan and the disposition of his forces, which was promptly placed in McClellan's hands. It was his tremendous opportunity. Jackson was many miles away, and Longstreet was near Hagerstown. Had McClellan moved speedily he might have destroyed Lee's army piecemeal, but McClellan was not Jackson. He did not reach Lee's position until the seventeenth, four days after the information as to his opponent's plans had reached him. A citizen of Maryland, who was a southern sympathizer, was present in McClellan's headquarters when Lee's order was delivered to him and he speedily acquainted Lee with the fact that his opponent had knowledge of his plans. His delay gave Lee all he could have asked for, an opportunity for forty-eight hours to study his ground and reshape his plans. Also to get Longstreet and Jackson back with the main forces. Jackson had no fear of night marches. On the seventeenth the battle began.

The field of Antietam is a quiet field to-day. The Potomac rolls along in peaceful manner on the west, and beyond it rise the Virginia hills. To the east lies the Antietam creek. Gently rolling fields, where the harvests are sown and reaped, stretch away to the waters. The sleepy little Maryland town of Sharpsburg lies on its edge, and one can see the church spires of Shepherdstown over beyond the river. There on that September day was waged one of the most desperately fought struggles of the war,

---

[4] Nicolay and Hay, Vol. VI, p. 132.

and the most unnecessary that Lee ever waged. For the best he could have hoped for was to beat off McClellan. The ground he chose for the battle was admirable for defense but left him little opportunity for a counter-stroke such as he gave Pope after Manassas. It gave him a chance for a display of splendid valor, but little more than that. Perhaps no battle that he fought has drawn upon him such criticism.

His army was in poor condition. It had gone through two long campaigns and it was greatly weakened in numbers. Henderson estimates that twenty thousand stragglers and deserters were absent from the ranks.[5] The long marches, the hard fighting, and the excessive hardships they had passed through had told on them and "never had the army been so ragged, dirty and ill-provided for as on this march."[6] Longstreet declared: "Sickness and weakness that creep into an army from irregular food collected in the stress of the march, were no trifling impediments to the maintenance of our ranks in vigorous form."[7] The wonder is not that they did not win the battle but that they were able to fight at all.

Lee's own report was that he fought with less than forty thousand, but it is generally supposed that this is an under-estimate.[8] He had written Davis before starting that "we cannot afford to be idle and though weaker than our opponents in men and military equipments, must endeavor to harass them if we cannot destroy them."[9] But Davis did not move to send the necessary reenforcements.

McClellan, on the other hand, reported that he had

---

[5] Henderson, *Science of War*, p. 203.
[6] Long, p. 206.
[7] Longstreet, p. 288.
[8] Maurice, *Lee*, p. 153.
[9] O. R., Vol. XIX, p. 590.

eighty-seven thousand men.[10] Lee's flanks were protected by the Potomac, and across his front ran the Antietam creek. McClellan was forced to make frontal attacks under difficult conditions. His troops charged with supreme gallantry, but the attacks were disjointed. There had been no opportunity for entrenching and the southern men had simply to stand up under withering artillery fire and hold off the infantry attacks, while on the northern side the utmost of valor was shown in the steadiness with which the charging lines faced the sheeted flame of the Confederate defense. They perished by regiments.

All day long the battle went on, with little success for either side. Lee's handling of his little army was superb. The next day he planned to hit back, but he was hindered by the lay of the ground from making the attack on the northern right that he desired. So on the next night he withdrew across the Potomac, while McClellan remained with the bulk of his army watching the passage. Lee had lost in killed and wounded nearly ten thousand of the very flower of his army.

A drawn battle, the military historians call it. But the campaign was a failure.[11] It ended the first threat against the North, and it stopped the progress of the Army of Northern Virginia which began with the Seven Days. It put an end for ever to the idea that Maryland would leave the Union and throw in its lot with the Confederacy. It ended the hope of a dictated peace, at least for this year. The North rallied quickly from its fears and gave loyal support to the Administration in the November elections. But most of all it made possible a stroke that Lincoln had been planning for some time, of which only he saw the

---

[10] Nicolay and Hay, Vol. VI, p. 131.

[11] Fitzhugh Lee, p. 215.

far-reaching effect, but which in the end proved to be a
heavier blow to the Confederacy than the loss of many
battles. Longstreet's comments on this are to the point.

"The full significance of Sharpsburg (Antietam) to the
Federal authorities lay in the fact that they needed a
victory on which to issue the Emancipation Proclamation,
which President Lincoln had prepared two months before
and had held in abeyance under the advice of members of
his Cabinet until the Union should win a success. Although this battle was by no means so complete a victory
as the President wished, and he was sorely vexed with
General McClellan for not pushing it to completion it was
made the most of as a victory, and his Emancipation Proclamation was issued on the 22nd of September, five days
after the battle. This was one of the decisive political
events of the war and it at once put the great struggle
outwardly and openly upon the basis where it had before
only rested by tacit and covert understanding. If the
Southern army had been carefully held in hand, refreshed
by easy marches and comfortable supplies, the Proclamation would not have found its place in history. On the
other hand, the Southern President would have been in
Maryland at the head of his army with his manifesto for
peace and independence."[12]

Possibly! But however that may have been it was Lincoln's opportunity, and he took it.

---

[12]Longstreet, pp. 288-89.

CHAPTER XXI

Lincoln's Counter-Stroke

THE North had not yet produced a soldier who was able to master Lee. But in the political part of the struggle Lincoln was outwitting Davis. An English officer who had been an observer with the Confederate forces, could write in the foremost English review of the day that the United States was "now merely a military despotism of a portion of states striving under the dictatorship of an insignificant lawyer to crush out the freedom of the rest."[1] But that "insignificant lawyer" was proving himself the superior of the master of Cabinets. For wars are not finally won on the battle-field. Battles, maneuvers, are not the end but the means to the end. The end in all wars is to break the will to war of the opposing people. And greater in its final effect on the conflict than all victories that Lee had won in that fateful summer of '62 was Lincoln's Emancipation Proclamation. No one had expressed that result better than Longstreet in the words already quoted: "It at once put the great struggle outwardly and openly upon the basis where it had before only rested by tacit and covert understanding."

The mind of the North was by no means clear on the question of slavery when the war began, and Woodrow Wilson is probably right in his contention that "had the war been short and immediately decisive for the Union the Federal power would not have touched slavery in the

---

[1] *Blackwood's Magazine,* January, 1863.

States."[2] It must always be remembered that Lincoln was not elected as an Abolitionist nor was the Republican party an abolitionist party, but an anti-slavery-extension party. Its opponents in the election of '60 charged it with being an abolitionist party, but the platform on which Lincoln ran is clear, and his own position is definitely set forth in the First Inaugural.

The war in the beginning, from the northern view-point, was a war to preserve the Union, and that only. But the struggle dragged on, and Lincoln saw that in the end it would arouse the forces of the North as they had not been aroused if the war were made a war against slavery, and the question finally settled that had plunged the nation into this terrific conflict. The North needed a motto to be inscribed upon its battle flags, and that motto "freedom." It would at once lift the struggle to a moral plane such as it had not occupied before. He knew the North was not yet ready for the move he was prepared to make, not any more ready than his Cabinet had shown itself to be when he first proposed it, but he believed it would be when it saw as he saw. Nevertheless it was a daring stroke and he risked his own political downfall when he made it. He himself declared to his Cabinet that in those troubled days after the second battle of Bull Run, when he was weighing the whole matter in his mind, he placed on God the responsibility of the decision, resolving that he would take as a sign for action any military success by which Lee would be driven back across the Potomac.[3] Then came the news of Antietam. An English historian, in a recent study of the war, makes this comment:

"For those who have any belief in the purposive guidance

---

[2] Wilson, p. 226.
[3] Nicolay and Hay, Vol. VI, p. 160.

of the world, who realize the magnitude of Lincoln's decision, who see him as the leader of a great people asking for a sign from the Lord of Hosts, and who then read the remarkable story of the campaign of Sharpsburg, it is hard to dismiss the conviction that a hand mightier than Lee's was shaping the march of events and watching over the carnage of those fateful September days."[4]

The Emancipation Proclamation was of course without constitutional warrant. It carried no other authority than that of Lincoln as commander-in-chief of the armed forces of the nation. He could, as a military measure, free the slaves within territory occupied by those forces, but he could not abolish an institution which legally existed. Nevertheless it accomplished the purpose he had in mind as an announcement of policy.

Its results were wide-spread. It was not long until the North awoke to its meaning, and found it had a cause to fight for with enthusiasm. It rallied behind him that far from insignificant body of citizens who had been doubtful whether it was right or expedient to maintain the Union by force of arms. But its immediate result was to give a new weapon to the political opposition to Lincoln, a weapon that was used with some effect in the November elections. It also had a far-reaching effect on the South. The leaders received it with violent expressions of anger, but there were, as we remember, many in the South who questioned the validity of its "peculiar institution," and there can be little question that it had the result of undermining their will to war, a result not immediately seen. The Union men in the border slave states were dismayed. They had been definitely declaring that the war was solely for the preservation of the Union, and that slavery would

<hr>

[4]Knowles, p. 111.

not be touched. The Proclamation put them in an embarrassing position, but they held loyally.

Its widest and most far-reaching effect was abroad, and this probably more than any other was what Lincoln was striving for in determining to issue the Proclamation. For years there had been in Europe a growing demand for the abolition of human slavery. This demand was particularly strong in Great Britain. Yet the attitude of Europe was favorable to the South and the danger was great that this might extend to the point of intervention. Louis Napoleon was on the throne of France and he, in defiance of the Monroe Doctrine, was engaged in an attempt to set up an empire in Mexico for his protégé, Maximilian, a project which the agents of the Confederacy assured him they would not oppose if successful. Great Britain's major industry of cotton-spinning had suffered seriously from the cutting off of its normal supply through the blockade, and, as we have seen, the government was on the point of intervention when Lee moved northward. The grim men in the Chancelleries were not of the sort who viewed republics with favor, and this seemed their chance.

Lee's victories of the summer had given impetus to the movement for the recognition of the independence of the Confederacy and intervention. Mr. Gladstone, the British Chancellor of the Exchequer, had declared in a speech at Newcastle in September, amid the applause of his audience, that the people of the Southern United States were now to be regarded as a nation: "There is no doubt that Jefferson Davis and the other leaders of the South have made an army; they are making, it appears, a navy; and they have made what is more than either—they have made a nation."[5]

And the same issue of the important *Review* which

---

[5] *Blackwood's Magazine*, November, 1862.

contained the account of the speech, contained also a demand for intervention:

"Not only does international law justify our recognition of the Southern Confederacy, but humanity demands that we should take measures to put an end to such horrible war. . . . And if the great powers of Europe—or at least England, Russia and France—would solve the difficulty which each power separately feels, by agreeing to undertake a joint mediation, and, if necessary, intervention, they would render an important service to civilization, humanity and mankind at large, and would show a better example of a 'Holy Alliance' than any which yet stands recorded in the pages of history."[6]

Louis Napoleon had presented the proposal for such intervention to Great Britain and Russia in October before these words appeared in print. Such intervention would probably have· meant the ending of the war, as France's intervention had in the revolutionary struggle. It was the thing for which all the resources of the Confederacy were being utilized. Davis kept dangling before the men of the Chancelleries Lee's victories of the summer. The news of the Proclamation was received by the newspapers of Great Britain with bitter anger, for their editors saw the effect it was sure to have in arousing the sentiment of those opposed to slavery to any further move on the part of the government looking toward intervention. That is exactly what happened. The strength of popular sympathy with the North became so clear that even during the excitement and friction aroused by the activities of the *Alabama* there was never any likelihood that the government would depart from its attitude of neutrality. Lord John Russell even went so far as to admonish Gladstone

[6] *Ibid.*

to be a little more careful in his speeches.[7] Louis Napoleon did not dare act singly. Lincoln, by his bold action, put the South in the wrong before the opinion of the world, and prevented that foreign recognition of the Confederacy which he dreaded.[8] Thus the statesman outwitted the soldier and robbed Lee's victories of that summer of what would have been their widest reaching effect. The moral victory was thus won by the North, and in strategical effect it compensated for all the victories that Lee had won.

Nor were they slow in realizing this in Richmond. The *Examiner,* commenting on the Proclamation which it called a mere "brutum fulmen," sought to cheer its readers with the assurance that it was "the most egregious folly which Lincoln's government has committed since the beginning of the War." Yet it revealed its fear of the consequences of that "folly" for in calling on Davis to do something it declared:

"The efforts and victories of the Southern Confederacy up to this time have been only blundering blows of a blind giant. When the enemy rubs up against the military power, the army hits, sometimes with striking effect. But the success is all barren, isolated and without ulterior consequences. . . . But the most victorious general, and the bravest army cannot bring a continental war one jot nearer a conclusion if they are but atoms in a discordant mass governed by changing chances, if unsupported, if left destitute of supplies at the moment when advance is possible, if crippled by the jealousy, or tethered by the timidity of an incompetent government."[9]

Not all of Lee's obstacles were in the field.

[7]Dodd, *Davis,* p. 289.
[8]Wilson, p. 226.
[9]*Richmond Examiner,* October 2, 1862.

CHAPTER XXII

Fredericksburg

AFTER crossing the Potomac Lee proceeded by easy
marches to the lower Valley of Virginia, where he spent
the next weeks recruiting his army, and seeking to refit it
for the winter. An English officer who spent several
months with him at this time, has left his account of the
way things were managed at his headquarters:

"In visiting the headquarters of the Confederate Generals, but particularly those of General Lee, any one accustomed to see European armies in the field cannot fail to
be struck with the great absence of all the pomp and circumstance of war in and around their encampments. Lee's
headquarters consisted of about seven or eight pole tents,
pitched with their backs to a stake fence, upon a piece of
ground so rocky that it was unpleasant to ride over it—
its only recommendation being a little stream of water
which flowed close by the General's tent. In front of the
tents were some three or four wagons, drawn up without
any regularity, and a number of horses roamed loose about
the field. The servants, who were of course slaves, and
the mounted soldiers called couriers, who always accom-
pany each general of a division in the field, were un-
provided with tents and slept under the wagons. Wagons,
tents, and some of the horses were marked U.S., showing
that part of that huge debt in the North had gone to
furnishing even the Confederate generals with camp equipment. No guard or sentries were to be seen in the vicinity,
no crowd of aide-de-camps, loitering about, making themselves agreeable to visitors, and endeavoring to save their

generals from receiving those who have no particular business. A large farmhouse stands close by, which, in any
other army would have been the general's residence pro
tem, but as no liberties are allowed to be taken with personal property in Lee's army, he is particular in setting a
good example himself. His staff are crowded together two
and three in a tent; none are allowed to carry any more
baggage than a small bag each and his own kit is but very
little larger. Everyone who approaches him does so with
marked respect, although there is none of that bowing and
scraping of forage caps which occurs in the presence of
European generals."[1]

The next weeks brought to Lee one of the great sorrows
of his life. His daughter, Annie, to whom he was especially
devoted, died at the Warren White Sulphur Springs in
North Carolina. Word had reached him shortly after
Antietam of her serious illness. But he could not leave
to go to her. Then came the news that she was worse.
One morning the mail came and the letters were distrib-
uted, but no one knew whether he had received any
further word. At the usual hour he summoned his military secretary to know if there were any matters of routine
that required his attention. He looked over the papers
presented to him and gave the necessary orders. His
secretary left but returned in a few minutes to report
another matter and found the General bowed in grief, an
open letter in his hand containing the word of his daughter's death. His army and its needs required his first
thought, then his private grief.[2] But to his other daughter
he wrote: "In the quiet hours of the night when there is
nothing to lighten the full weight of my grief, I feel as if
I should be overwhelmed."[3]

---

[1] *Blackwood's Magazine*, January, 1863.
[2] Taylor, p. 76.
[3] *R. and L.*, p. 80.

He had made duty the stern guide of his days. He must follow unflinchingly now. And if he must go on there were others also who must do the same, come what may. There is another letter written from the camp by Elisha Paxton, now a brigadier-general, to his wife which shows the thoughts that were coming to some of them. He had written her in October when it had seemed as though McClellan would advance across the Potomac: "I think we will have another battle near this place and I feel sure it will be a splendid victory for us. Our victories, though, seem to settle nothing; to bring us no nearer to the end of the war. It is only so many killed and wounded, leaving the work of blood to go on with renewed vigor."[4] On November 2, 1862, he wrote to her the things which were in his heart, and he seems to be writing for that whole army when he says:

"We then hoped a few months would end the war, and we would all be at home again. Sadly we were disappointed. Many of our comrades have gone to their long home and many more disabled for life. And now when we look to the future, we seem, if anything, farther from the end of our troubles than when we began. Many of us are destined to share the fate of our dead and wounded comrades, a few may perhaps, survive the war, enjoy its glorious fruits, and spend what remains of life with those we love. We all hope to be thus blessed, but for my part I feel that my place must be filled and my duty done, if it cost me my life and bring sorrow to the dear wife and little ones who now watch my path with so much anxiety and pray so fervently for my safe deliverance. The sentiment which I try to hold and cherish is God's will and my duty to be done, whatever the future may have in store for me. I am glad to feel, Darling, that although I have been writ-

---

[4] Paxton, p. 66.

ing to you for almost eighteen months, and this has been the substitute for our once fond intercourse, I feel that when I write now that I miss you none the less than I did when this cruel war first placed the barrier of separation between us. I hope as fondly as ever that the day may come when we will live in peace and quiet together. Eight years ago today, Love, we began our married life, very happy and full of hope for the future. Thus far it has been made of sunshine and shadow, joy and sorrow, strangely intermingled. The darker side of life has for a long time predominated; may we not hope for a change of fortune ere long?"[5]

It was not alone in the Commander's tent that there was to be found a weary heart. But they fought on!

There were troubles also in Richmond. Davis was having difficulties with his Congress, and with the governors of some of the states who could not see eye to eye with the President. There were many changes in his Cabinet. Jones, who from his post in the war office was seeing many things, records his impression of the leaders in his Diary on November 14, 1862: "Never before did such little men rule such a great people. Our rulers are like children or drunken men riding docile horses, that absolutely keep the riders from falling off by swaying to the right and the left and preserving an equilibrium. There is no rule for anything, and no stability in any policy."[6] And again on December second he tells of the results of speculation in the Confederate Capital:

"God speed the day of our peace! Our patriotism is mainly in the army and among the ladies of the South. The avarice and cupidity of the men at home, could only

---

[5] *Ibid.*, pp. 68-69.

[6] Jones, Vol. I, p. 189.

be excelled by ravenous wolves; and most of our sufferings are fully deserved. Where a people will not have mercy on one another how can they expect mercy? They depreciate the Confederate notes by charging from $20 to $40 per bbl. for flour; $3.50 per bushel for meal, $2 per lb. for butter, $20 per cord for wood, etc. When we shall have peace let the extortionists be remembered! Let an indelible stigma be branded upon them! A portion of the people look like vagabonds. We see men and women and children in the streets in dingy and dilapidated clothes; and some seem gaunt and pale with hunger—the speculators, and thieving quartermasters and commissaries only, looking sleek and comfortable. If this state of things continues a year or so longer, they will have their reward. There will be governmental bankruptcy, and all their gains will turn to dust and ashes!"[7]

These conditions in Richmond were not without effect upon the army. Among Paxton's letters is this:

"The President's patriotic appeal, I see, is answered by the committee of one county 'Hay, twenty cents per pound' by that of another 'Wheat, $6.50 a bushel.' I do not believe there is such a scarcity as to justify such figures, but the famine is of Christian charity and public spirit. Men wish to grow rich upon the miseries of their country, and there is no limit to their extortions. All seem holding back what they have in the hope that a starving army will raise the price of bread and meat still higher. God will give us the blessing of independence and peace as soon as we deserve it; and our prayer should not be so much for victory to our arms as for patriotism and charity to our people, wisdom and integrity to our rulers."[8]

But in spite of personal sorrows and all the other troubles

[7] *Ibid.*, p. 200.
[8] Paxton, p. 100.

of the time Lee went ahead with the preparations for the battle that he saw had to be fought before winter set in. He wrote to the Secretary of War on December third that several thousand of his men were barefoot and suggested "that shoes be taken from the extortioners at fair price."[9]   The problem of stragglers and deserters which bothered him before Antietam and which was to become acute after Gettysburg now began to loom large in his correspondence with Davis.   He writes: "In connection with the subject of straggling . . . the destruction of private property by the army has occupied much of my attention.   A great deal of damage to citizens is done by stragglers, who consume all they can get from the charitable and all they can take from the defenseless, in many cases destroying stock and other property."[10]   He again issued strict instructions to his army against this evil, and one of the few recorded instances of his loss of temper was caused by violation of this order.. He was riding along in the rear of his lines when he came across a soldier who had stolen and killed a pig which he was conveying to his quarters.   This flagrant disregard of his command threw the General into a hot passion.   Though usually disinclined to capital punishment, he determined to make an example of this pilferer and ordered the man to be arrested and taken back to Jackson with the directions to have him shot.[11]   But Jackson was just going into action, and knowing that Lee would probably feel differently after thinking it over, he gave the man a chance to save his life by showing his courage in the front line of battle.

Lincoln was by this time wearied anew by McClellan's

[9] Jones, Vol. I, p. 202.
[10] Maurice, *Lee*, p. 160.
[11] Long, p. 222.

inaction and replaced him by General A. E. Burnside. Burnside's plan was to move rapidly on Richmond by way of Fredericksburg, basing himself on Acquia Creek, thus removing his communications from the danger of an attack from the Valley. But again slowness interfered with his plans. His advance reached the heights opposite Fredericksburg on November seventeenth, but the pontoons necessary for the crossing of the Rappahannock had not arrived. So nothing was done although the number of Confederate troops in Fredericksburg was very small. While Burnside waited for his pontoons Lee hurried a portion of Longstreet's corps to Fredericksburg and promptly followed with the rest of his army, so that when Burnside was ready to cross he was ready for him.

It had not been Lee's intention to fight on the Rappahannock. He had planned to let Burnside cross that river, falling back before him as he advanced until he reached the North Anna. He had written Jackson on November nineteenth: "As to the place where it may be necessary or best to fight I cannot now say. . . . I do not now anticipate making a determined stand north of the North Anna."[12] What he desired was to lengthen Burnside's lines of communication so that he might strike at them with the daring Stuart. And if he could draw his enemy in to the woods and swamps of eastern Virginia with the rains and mud of early winter coming on he might play havoc with him. Nor was such a possibility unlikely when one considers the commander with whom he had to deal. Burnside was Lincoln's worst mistake. But again the political situation interfered. Davis feared to take the risk of permitting the enemy to come within twenty miles of the Capital, particularly as since Bragg's failure in the

[12] *O. R.*, Vol. XXI, p. 1021.

West the affairs of the Confederacy in that section were in a serious condition, and he feared that Burnside's advance would work havoc in Tennessee and on the Mississippi. So Lee was compelled to fight at Fredericksburg.

The Rappahannock, where Burnside had to cross it, is a stream about four hundred yards wide. The Stafford Heights, a steep line of hills, reach down to the water on the side where the northern forces lay. On the opposite side is Fredericksburg, lying on a level plateau which stretches out to another line of hills behind the town. On these Lee's army was disposed. Thus a river and a plain lay between the two armies and the northern troops had to cross both to reach Lee's position, which was well covered with woods. These woods were Burnside's undoing, for he thought he was attacking only a portion of Lee's army with Jackson still far away. As it was he had not even a remote chance of success. His men had to advance across the open plain under the direct fire of the Confederate batteries on the heights and though Fitzhugh Lee, who was in the battle, gives high praise to "the dauntless courage displayed by the Federal officers and men,"[13] not even courage could win against such odds.

As the fog lifted on that morning they who watched behind the guns on Marye's Heights beheld the whole northern host in battle array, one hundred thousand strong. As the long line of blue moved steadily forward, its bayonets gleaming in the sun, with the artillery behind them roaring out its throaty defiance, men held their breath and those who stood beside Lee heard him say: "It is well that war is so terrible or we might grow fond of it."[14] But their task was beyond human endeavor, and division

[13] Fitzhugh Lee, p. 230.
[14] Jones, *Life,* p. 208.

after division recoiled from the shock, leaving their dead upon the field. The two armies waited on their arms the next day to see which would move. That night Burnside withdrew across the river under cover of a violent storm, having lost nearly thirteen thousand in killed and prisoners. As McClellan had been unable to pursue across the Potomac after Antietam so Lee was now unable to follow Burnside across the Rappahannock, for the northern guns on Stafford Heights would have done to him what he had done to Burnside. The battle was thus, as Paxton feared it would be, "one of those victories which seem to settle nothing; to bring us no nearer to the end of the war." It was only "so many killed and wounded." The whole battle is impossible to comprehend, either from the point of the attackers or the attacked. Again there was immense slaughter with no apparent result. It was another instance, of which there were many before this war was done, of Lee's yielding to Davis when he should have held firm. Jackson told D. H. Hill, "I am opposed to fighting here. We will whip the enemy but gain no fruits of victory. I have advised the line of the North Anna but I have been overruled."[15]   And Jackson was right.

---

[15] Dabney, *Stonewall Jackson*, p. 595.

Chapter XXIII

The Loss of His "Right Arm"

After the battle of Fredericksburg the two armies lay looking at each other from their respective positions for four months. The bottomless mud of Virginia roads did not conduce to speedy operations or in fact to any sort of operation on the part of infantry. The daring Stuart kept up his raids on the supply depots behind the northern lines to the advantage of his needy army, and on December twenty-sixth during one of these raids he cut the telegraph lines and sent a message to General Meigs, the northern Quartermaster-General, complaining of the quality of mules supplied to the Army of the Potomac! It was another hard winter for Lee's men and they needed all that Stuart could gather. The meat ration was but a quarter of a pound and the number of men without boots and blankets ran to thousands. The *Richmond Examiner* for December thirteenth describes the march through the city of a portion of Lee's army on its way to another part of the state "many of the men walking barefoot through the melting snow."

Lee's letters through this period are full of longing for his family. He writes to his daughter Mildred on Christmas Day:

"I cannot tell you how I long to see you when a little quiet occurs. My thoughts revert to you, your sisters and mother; my heart aches for our reunion. Your brothers I see occasionally. . . . I have no news, confined constantly to camp and my thoughts occupied with its necessities and duties. I am however happy in the thought that General Burnside and his army will not eat their promised Christmas dinner in Richmond."[1]

Again on February 23, 1863, to his daughter Agnes:

"I read yesterday, my precious daughter, your letter and grieved very much when last in Richmond at not seeing you. My movements are so uncertain that I cannot be relied on for anything. The only place I am to be found is in camp, and I am so cross now that I am not worth seeing anywhere. Here you will have to take me with the three stools—the snow, the rain and the mud. The storm of the last twenty-four hours has added to our stock of all and we are now in a floating condition. But the sun and the wind will carry off all in time and then we shall appreciate our relief. Our horses and mules suffer most. They have to bear the cold and rain, tug through the mud, and suffer all the time with hunger. The roads are wretched, almost impassable."[2]

Another change in commanders in the northern forces brought a new opponent to be studied, "Fighting Joe" Hooker. Many reenforcements had come to the northern camp across the river, while Lee had found it necessary to detach large numbers of his men for service in other hard-pressed places, relying on the Virginia mud to keep Hooker inactive. But even so he was not sure of Hooker. The same letter continues: "General Hooker is obliged to do something. He is playing the Chinese game, trying to frighten us. He runs out his guns, starts his wagons and troops down the river and creates an excitement gen-

---

[1] Long, pp. 242-43.
[2] *Ibid.*, pp. 243-44.

erally." But that Lee was not so frightened as to have lost his sense of humor is to be seen in this letter to his wife:

"The cars have arrived from Richmond and brought me a young French officer, full of vivacity and ardor for service with me. I think the appearance of things will cool him. If not the night will, for he brought no blankets."[3]

The dreary winter dragged on. Paxton wrote to his wife in March that "it has been so long since I have heard a musket or a cannon that I have almost forgotten how it sounds."[4] He tells her how at least a portion of that army spent their evenings. "Today I went to our chapel to hear Dr. Hoge, who preached a very fine sermon, General Jackson being one of the audience. We have preaching in the chapel twice on Sunday and, I think, pretty much every night. It looks odd to see a church full of people and all of them men. It would be really refreshing to see a woman among them, to give the audience the appearance of civilization."[5]

With the coming of spring Lee began to plan for the summer's campaign. He told Davis that he thought it important that they should assume the offensive by the first of May. He wanted to send Jackson sweeping through the Valley again with a new threat on Washington and thus compel Hooker to withdraw north of the Potomac. Then this was to be followed by another invasion of the North. But before Longstreet, who had spent the winter south of the James, could rejoin him, Hooker began his movement which ended in the battle of Chancellorsville,

---

[3] *R. and L.*, p. 93.
[4] Paxton, p. 91.
[5] *Ibid.*, p. 90.

the greatest of Lee's victories. It more than any other
battle displays Lee's ability for calculated daring.

Hooker's plan called for Stoneman with his cavalry to
make a wide circle around Lee's left and cut his communications with Richmond, while Sedgwick was to make a
demonstration against Lee's front at Fredericksburg.
While this was going on Hooker was to march up the
Rappahannock and cross it and come down behind Lee's
lines through the Wilderness to Chancellorsville. Chancellorsville is not a village, but a farmhouse about ten miles
from Fredericksburg, situated with its outbuildings on the
edge of that forest which was to become so famous the
next summer as the Wilderness. The maneuver failed,
because Stoneman was delayed by bad roads and swollen
rivers, and Hooker had no cavalry when the battle was
fought, and also because Lee discerned the plan from the
very outset and took measures to meet it. He left Early
with his division to watch Sedgwick and concentrated the
rest of his forces to meet Hooker as he came through the
Wilderness. Then he made the move which calls forth
Maurice's estimate that this was the greatest battle. He
had strongly entrenched his position on the edge of the
Wilderness and he decided to hold it with fifteen thousand
men, while Jackson made one of his famous circling movements. He marched off at dawn by a road through the
woods that had been discovered during the night, to fall
on Hooker's right flank. On his arrival at a point near
where he expected to run into the northern forces he made
a careful reconnaissance, and discovered Hooker's men in
groups, chatting, smoking and playing cards, while in the
rear they were butchering beeves.

"Stonewall's face bore an expression of intense interest

during the five minutes he was on that hill. His eyes had a brilliant glow. The paint of approaching battle was coloring his cheeks, and he was radiant to find no preparation had been made to guard against a flank attack. He made no reply to the officer with him; his lips were, however, moving, for, sitting on the horse in sight of and close to Howard's troops, he was engaged in an appeal to the God of Battles."[6]

So writes one who was with him in that conflict. When he heard Jackson open his attack Lee himself attacked in front so as to prevent Hooker diverting troops to meet the flanking movement. These bold tactics won the victory. As Hooker retired behind the Rappahannock, Lee made a swift march and fell on Sedgwick, who also was forced back. One only appreciates the tremendous nature of this victory when one remembers that Hooker had one hundred and thirty-three thousand men at the beginning of the campaign while Lee had only fifty-six thousand.

But the victory cost him dearly. At the end of the day, as his men were crushing the northern right, and victory was assured, Jackson fell mortally wounded by his own men. He had ridden out to reconnoiter the lines in his front, and on his return was mistaken for the enemy and he fell with three bullets in him. As he was being carried to the ambulance he gave his last order to General Pender, who had expressed doubts as to whether he could hold his position, "You must hold your ground, General Pender, you must hold your ground, sir."[7] At first it was thought his wound was not mortal. His left arm was amputated and it was thought all was well. To Lee, who had sent him a message congratulating him on his victory, he

[6] Fitzhugh Lee, pp. 247-48.

[7] Long, p. 257.

made the reply: "General Lee is very kind but he should give the glory to God." After the amputation Lee sent him the word "that if he had lost his left arm I have lost my right." Pneumonia set in. He became delirious: "Order A. P. Hill to prepare for action," he cried. "Pass the infantry to the front rapidly. Tell Major Hawkes——" He stopped and added quietly, "Let us cross the river and rest under the shade of the trees."[8]

That chance volley in the woods was the heaviest blow that Lee and the Confederacy suffered. One wonders what would have happened had Jackson been at Gettysburg! Lee wrote to his wife: "In addition to the deaths of officers and friends consequent upon the late battles you will see that we have to mourn the loss of the great and good Jackson. Any victory would be dear, at such a price."[9] And to one of his officers he said, "I had such implicit confidence in Jackson's skill and energy that I never troubled myself to give him detailed instructions. The most general suggestions were all that he needed." Jackson died in the hour of victory. It was reserved for Lee to continue the struggle through its last and most tragic stages.

But never again did Lee venture to divide his army in the face of the enemy. No more in the story of these battles is there to be found those brilliant daring movements which made numbers of no account and won victory in the very moment of defeat. The Confederate chaplain who prayed: "When in Thine inscrutable decree it was ordained that the Confederacy should fail it became necessary for Thee to remove Thy servant Jackson" came very near reaching the heart of the matter.

---

[8] Fitzhugh Lee, p. 251.

[9] R. and L., p. 94.

Two days after the battle on May seventh, before Jackson's condition became serious, Lee issued his General Order 59. More than anything else it shows the spirit of the man in the hour of his greatest triumph.

"With heartfelt gratification, the General Commanding expresses to the army his sense of the heroic conduct displayed by officers and men, during the arduous operations in which they have just been engaged.

"Under trying vicissitudes of heat and storm, you attacked the enemy, strongly intrenched in the depths of a tangled wilderness, and again on the hills of Fredericksburg, fifteen miles distant, and by the valor that has triumphed in so many fields, forced him once more to seek safety beyond the Rappahannock. While this glorious victory entitled you to the praise and gratitude of the nation, we are especially called upon to return our grateful thanks to the only Giver of victory for the signal deliverance He has wrought.

"It is, therefore, earnestly recommended that the troops unite on Sunday next in ascribing to the Lord of Hosts the glory due unto His name.

"Let us not forget in our rejoicing the brave soldiers who have fallen in defense of their country; and while we mourn their loss, let us resolve to emulate their noble example.

"The army and the country alike lament the absence for a time of one to whose bravery, energy, and skill they are so much indebted for success.

"The following letter from the President of the Confederate States is communicated to the army as an expression of his appreciation of its success:

" 'I have received your dispatch, and reverently unite with you in giving praise to God for the success with which He has crowned our arms.

" 'In the name of the people, I offer my cordial thanks to yourself and the troops under your command for this addition to the unprecedented series of great victories which your army has achieved.

" 'The universal rejoicing produced by this happy result will be mingled with the general regret for the good and the brave who are numbered among the killed and wounded.'

"R. E. LEE, General."

Chapter XXIV

The Second Invasion of the North

VICTORY brought to Lee new and heavy responsibilities. His immediate problem was as to the next move. It was not an easy problem. He had defeated, in one battle after another, the best that the North could send against him. McClellan, Pope, Burnside, Hooker, each at the head of an army larger and immensely better equipped, had in turn gone down before that Army of Northern Virginia. But each time the North had come back with larger armies and new equipment. The one man that Lee apparently could not beat was that despised country lawyer, Lincoln. Every time an army was scattered he gathered another, for every leader that failed he found a new one to take his place. How long could this keep up? Lee knew that time was on the side of the North. He had won victories, but they were costly victories, costly most in men. He could capture materiel from the North but he could not fill the gaps in his ranks with northern prisoners. There were no signs of that thing in which Davis trusted, European intervention. In fact the signs were the other way since that master-stroke of Lincoln in the issuing of his Proclamation. Something had to be done and done quickly. It was the crisis of the war and of Lee's career as a leader of the armies.

There were ominous things happening in the West. The North had a leader there who was forming the habit of victory, a man whom Lee faintly remembered as a rather untidy lieutenant whom he had sent back to his quarters one day to clean up during the Mexican affair, and who had dropped out of the army shortly after that. He was not able to estimate him as he had the other officers whom he had been called on to meet in Virginia. Now this man Grant was driving Pemberton into Vicksburg to shut him up with an army of thirty-five thousand men. That army was important to the Confederacy, with its man power growing less with every battle fought. And Vicksburg was important, tremendously important, for it was the last stronghold left to the South on the Mississippi. Grant was determined to take it and thus cut the last means of communication between the states east of that great artery and those that lay to the west, Louisiana, Arkansas and Texas, states that had furnished some of the best regiments and quantities of much needed supplies.

The inefficient Bragg, kept in command by one of Davis's queer aberrations, was at Tullahoma, unable to cope with the northern forces under Rosecrans at Murfreesboro. If Rosecrans should move upon him the slight hold the Confederacy had on Tennessee might be broken. Johnston was in Mississippi trying to come to Pemberton's aid at Vicksburg, and not succeeding. The same hesitancy he had shown in the Peninsula was again in evidence. The western armies badly needed a leader who was willing to take chances. In the eastern theater of war Hooker was entrenched on the heights across from Fredericksburg, in an almost impregnable position, rebuilding that army that Lee had shattered at Chancellorsville. He was evidently preparing, in spite of the severe blow the morale of his men had suffered, to advance in some other way on Richmond.

Truly the problem that Lee had to meet was not an easy

one. And Jackson was gone. Whatever move Lee would make, he had to make without his "right arm." True, Stuart remained, that gay and daring Stuart whom he had put in Jackson's place after that fatal wounding. And Stuart had charged Hooker's lines with exceeding gallantry at the head of his troops, his plume flying like Navarre's at Ivry, and singing as he rode, "Old Joe Hooker come out of the Wilderness." And that charge had contributed greatly to the victory at Chancellorsville. Still he was not Jackson.

There were divided counsels in the Confederacy. Longstreet had urged on Secretary of War Seddon, and he in turn urged Lee, that his own division be sent to the West to join Johnston and the combined forces move at once to reenforce Bragg, who should be directed to attack Rosecrans and destroy him and then march on the Ohio River and Cincinnati. Longstreet argued that Grant's was the only army that could be drawn on to meet this move and that thus Vicksburg would be relieved and the peril of the Confederacy being cut in two would be removed.[1] Johnston agreed with him that this was the best possible plan.

Lee, on the contrary, held that if he sent Longstreet to the West his forces would be so weakened that he would not be able to bar Hooker's threatened move on Richmond. The proof that he was wrong in this is to be seen in the fact that in September he did send Longstreet's corps west with no peril to Richmond. The solution of the problem that he urged on Davis was that he should again invade the North, this time moving into Pennsylvania through the Cumberland Valley and make a new threat to isolate Washington. He argued that a victory in the northern

---

[1] Longstreet, p. 331.

territory near to the great cities of the East would bring
new terror to the North, and that Lincoln would be sure
to call on Grant for aid. Thus Pemberton at Vicksburg
would be relieved and his army set free to unite with
Johnston. In addition, after his victory, he would con-
solidate his position in northern territory and then offer
Lincoln peace on terms that would recognize the
Confederacy. He was still thinking as he had before
Antietam.

His biggest difficulty was with Davis, who was still holding to his theory of a defensive war, believing that thus
he could wear out the North and induce European intervention. Davis as well was having his difficulties with
local fears throughout the Confederacy, which called for
the detachment of many small bodies of troops to defend
places which were, in the last, of no great importance to
the big issue. One of the strongest criticisms of Davis's
theory of the conduct of the war is to be made right here.
By not taking the state governments fully into his confidence as to his plans he allowed many troops to be idle
in small garrisons who were badly needed in the big operations. It is worthy of note that in the early summer of
'63 there were one hundred and ninety-three thousand
Confederate troops scattered between the Mississippi and
the Rappahannock while Lee marched into Pennsylvania
with only seventy-three thousand.[2]

And while Davis finally gave his consent to Lee's plan
it is perfectly evident that he never grasped the meaning
of that plan in its entirety, but saw it only as a defensive
stroke, a move to free Virginia from the Army of the
Potomac and release his Capital, Richmond, from its threatening danger. This can be seen in the reasons he sets forth

---

[2]Maurice, Lee, p. 193.

for giving his approval to Lee's project in his own narrative of the war:

"It was decided by a bold movement to attempt to transfer hostilities to the north side of the Potomac, by crossing the river and marching into Maryland and Pennsylvania, driving the foe out of the Shenandoah Valley. Thus it was hoped that General Hooker's army would be called from Virginia to meet our advance towards the heart of the enemy's country. In the event, the vast preparations which had been made for an advance on Richmond would be foiled, the plan of the summer campaign deranged, and much of the season for active operations be consumed in the new combinations and dispositions that would be required. If beyond the Potomac some opportunity should be offered so as to enable us to defeat the army on which our foe most relied, the measure of our success would be full, but if the movements only resulted in freeing Virginia from the hostile army it was more than could fairly be expected from awaiting the attack which was clearly indicated."[3]

It is always easy to be wise after the event. Looking back there is one thing that is fairly evident and that is that Lee did not see in that summer of '63 far beyond the borders of his own Virginia. Yet the Confederacy was greater than Virginia and to keep it from being cut in two by the fall of Vicksburg he should have taken the same desperate chances that he took when he divided his army before Pope at the second Manassas or again before Hooker at Chancellorsville. But the fact seems to be that he did not sense the problem except in the phase for which he was immediately responsible. Grant's position before Vicksburg could have been made perilous. He was at a

[3]Davis, Vol. II, p. 438.

great distance from his base of supplies and wholly dependent on the Mississippi River for his communications. Batteries properly planted on the river-banks could have
stopped his transports and he would have then been in a
difficult position. Had Lee gone west with Longstreet's
corps and taken over the command of Bragg's army, and
put new spirit into it as he did when he took over Johnston's
command in the Peninsula, he could have driven Rosecrans
back and cut Grant's communications. He could then
have moved on Vicksburg and Grant would have been between the relieving army and the garrison under Pemberton. It would have been a serious situation for him,
with his surrender not unlikely. This would have left the
whole West open for Lee's movements. The divisions left
on the Rappahannock could have held Hooker for a month,
and in that time Lee could have threatened so many
vital points that instead of Lincoln's allowing Hooker to
press on to Richmond he would probably have called on
him for aid in the West.

Apparently Lee could not see this. It would appear
that at least in this early summer "he was unable to focus
the war as a whole, as one picture. He could see bits of it
clearly enough, but the whole was beyond his vision."[4]
In direct contrast with this is Lincoln's attitude. From
the very opening of the conflict he saw the importance of
gaining and keeping control of the Mississippi, because of
the substantial results therefrom for the North through
the keeping in line of those sections of the Middle West and
Northwest to which the open navigation of the great river
was vital, and as well the effect it would have in crippling
the South. Constantly Lincoln maintained a vigilance
over the Union garrisons at river points, and a recent

---

[4] Fuller, p. 376.

student of Grant's campaigns goes so far as to claim that the reason Lincoln did not call Grant east to succeed Mc-Clellan was that he "wanted him kept in the West to work out the Union's destiny on the Mississippi."[5]

Davis had been at first opposed to the plan for the invasion of the North. Being from Mississippi himself he saw the importance of holding Vicksburg. But Lee was insistent. For once Wolseley's telling phrase did not apply; he was not "subservient to the civil authorities." Finally, when it was evident that Grant had Pemberton tightly shut up in Vicksburg, Davis decided to place the whole military situation before the Cabinet for decision. All of May twenty-sixth was spent in discussion, with all the members of the Cabinet present, although Lee does not seem to have been there. Davis laid before them Lee's plan and the Cabinet agreed to it, although the tall bearded Postmaster-General, John Reagan, opposed it with great intensity. He was from Texas and he felt that the movement into Pennsylvania meant the abandonment of the West. But he was overruled and Lee's plans approved. Davis's confidence in Lee led him to give it his support against his own judgment. But he never grasped the fact that if the invasion was to be made at all it should be made with every man, horse and gun that could be gathered from the whole of the Confederacy. It was "the Confederates' last throw for victory"[6] and every resource should have been thrown into the scale. That it was not can be seen from the fact that Lee crossed the Potomac with only seventy-three thousand men, only a little more than a third of the troops Davis had east of the Mississippi.

There has been much controversy over this decision, but

---

[5] Conger, p. 45.
[6] Maurice, *Statesmen and Soldiers*, p. 54.

it does seem as though the final responsibility was Lee's. And since he had persuaded the Confederate authorities to approve the plan, he, knowing the stakes at issue, should have compelled Davis to furnish him all that was necessary to push the campaign through to a successful conclusion. A few more regiments would have turned the scale at Gettysburg. Henderson, in his lecture on the battle delivered to British officers at Aldershot, gave it as his opinion that "at Gettysburg General Lee's whole army suffered from over-confidence. Face to face with an army they had beaten so often with inferior numbers they relaxed precautions."[7] And Colonel Freemantle of the Coldstream Guards, who was present with Lee throughout the entire campaign, records in his Diary on the evening of that fateful July fourth: "It is impossible to avoid seeing that the cause of this check to the Confederates lies in the bitter contempt felt for the enemy by all ranks."[8] Is this the explanation of Lee's failure to make Davis see he needed every available man? Had he begun himself to be over-confident?

This is certain. Lee's plan failed. Not only did he not win the battle on the northern soil of which he had dreamed, but on the very day that word went out to the nation that his defeated host was turning back to the Potomac the further message told that Pemberton had surrendered Vicksburg with thirty-two thousand men and seventy-two cannon. No further commentary on Lee's plan as a means of relief need be made. Had he won at Gettysburg Vicksburg would have fallen just the same. This compelled the further surrender of Port Hudson with seven thousand men, and the last Confederate stronghold

---

[7]Henderson, *Science of War*, p. 305.

[8]*Blackwood's Magazine*, September, 1863, p. 324.

on the Mississippi was gone, and that great river ran in Lincoln's compelling phrase "unvexed to the sea." The Confederacy was cut in two and the portion west of the river was virtually denied any further participation in the conflict. It was the most crushing blow the Confederacy had received and one from which it never recovered. It would seem, at least in this campaign, that the British soldier Fuller, is right in his judgment that "in Lee with all his greatness, there is something parochial."[9] Perhaps to him Virginia loomed too large! The movement was disastrous from every view-point. It should never have been attempted without definite assurance that all the power available was behind it. As a move to aid Vicksburg it came too late. And with the fall of that stronghold the way was now open for Grant's grand strategy, that was to take Atlanta and then sweep on through the Confederacy to the sea, while Lee was held at Petersburg in the brilliant but impotent defense of the Capital whose country was being slowly cut away.

It was high tragedy for the South. Men may contend that Gettysburg was a drawn battle. Be that as it may, there is no question about the result on the South. "This disastrous movement into Pennsylvania," wrote a member of the Confederate Congress to the Secretary of War, "and the fall of Vicksburg, the latter especially, will end in the ruin of the South without foreign aid in some shape. The failure of the Government to reinforce Vicksburg, but allowing the strength and flower of our army to go North, when there could be but one fate attending them, has so broken down the hopes of our people that even the little strength yet remaining can only be exerted in despair."[10]

[9] Fuller, p. 380.
[10] Quoted by Fuller, p. 376.

That it was a desperate stroke is the admission of Lee's military secretary, Long, too loyal to his cause to place the blame where it rests, on Davis, who would not see how desperate it was, and on his chief who should have made him see:

"Lee fought, and knew that he fought for a great stake. That he did not succeed and that the moment came too late, even if it had been successful, to affect the result at Vicksburg, detracts nothing from the brilliancy of the conception.   The one pertinent thing is that the Confederate general saw that by a single bold and successful stroke it might be possible virtually to end the war and secure the independence of the Southern Confederacy. That success was possible is shown by the narrow chance by which it failed.   It had been well said that when the Confederate charge at Cemetery Ridge for a while seemed successful, the Muse of History took up her pen to record the birth of a new nation."[11]

But that very Muse is impatient of blindness!

---

[11] Long, pp. 429-30.

CHAPTER XXV

The March on Gettysburg

By June fifth the Army of Northern Virginia was gathered at Culpeper. Its morale had never been better. On June seventh Lee reviewed the entire cavalry corps on the plain near Brandy Station. They had been preparing for days for the event, mending, cleaning, polishing, until the brasses shone as they seldom did in that army that cared more for its rifles than for its looks. Stuart had put on his West Point manners and worried the life out of his home-spun colonels, who thought more of battles than of reviews. But it was a sight to remember when the day came, eight thousand bronzed troopers riding before their beloved General-in-Chief, first at a walk and then at a gallop.

The distinguished folk that came from Richmond were more than ever satisfied with their army and surer than ever of what they would do when they got to Pennsylvania. Lee himself was quite cheered by the sight. He writes to Mrs. Lee the next day: "I reviewed the cavalry in this section yesterday. It was a splendid sight. The men and horses looked well. They have recuperated since last fall. Stuart was in his glory. Your sons and nephews are well and flourishing."[1]

The British observer, Colonel Freemantle, records in his Diary his impressions of the infantry just after the march into Pennsylvania began:

---

[1] *R. and L.*, p. 96.

"The soldiers of this division are a remarkably fine body of men, and look quite seasoned and ready for work. Their clothing is serviceable, so also are their boots; but there is the usual utter absence of uniformity as to color and shape of their garments and hats; gray of all shades and brown clothing with felt hats predominate. The Confederates are now entirely armed with excellent rifles, mostly Enfields. When they first turned out they were in the habit of wearing numerous revolvers and bowie-knives. General Lee is said to have mildly remarked, 'Gentlemen, I think you will find an Enfield rifle, a bayonet, and sixty rounds of ammunition as much as you can conveniently carry in the way of arms.' They laughed and thought they knew better, but the six-shooters and bowie-knives disappeared, and now none are to be seen among the infantry.... At no period of the war, they say, have the men been so well-equipped, so well clothed, so eager for a fight, or so confident of success—a very different state of affairs from that which characterized the Maryland invasion of last year, when half the army were barefooted stragglers, and many of the remainder unwilling and reluctant to cross the Potomac."[2]

But Lee had more than reviews to think of before the northern movement began. General Pleasonton, who had been at West Point with Stuart, also knew something about cavalry fighting. So Hooker sent him across the Rappahannock with orders to find Stuart and whip him. He did not succeed in doing this when he came to Brandy Station, but he gave Stuart one of the hardest fights he ever had before he withdrew.

The battle was the beginning of a train of circumstances which brought much anxiety to Lee. His second son, Rooney, one of Stuart's brigadiers, was dangerously wounded toward the end of the day's fighting. As soon

---

[2] *Blackwood's Magazine*, September, 1863, p. 367.

as he was well enough to be moved he was taken to Colonel Wickham's place, Hickory Hill, where his wife could nurse him. He had married the Colonel's daughter, Charlotte Wickham, and there were few to whom Lee gave the outspoken affection that he did to this gay gentle lady. His "darling Chass" he called her, and he had paused on those strenuous days when he was driving McClellan down the Peninsula to write her a long letter in which he tells her, among many things, that "Summer returns when I see you."[3]

Just before the battle in which Rooney was wounded there had been some threats on the part of the northern authorities to hang some captured Confederate navy officers, whose status was a bit dubious in the practise of the seas, as pirates. Davis had promptly retaliated by setting aside an equal number of northern captives whom he said would hang if the threat were carried out. Word came to Washington of the situation of Rooney, and a raiding party was sent to capture him, and when Stanton had him safe in Fortress Monroe he announced, with an air of triumph, that if the officers were hanged Rooney Lee would follow. The whole tale is a nasty one, showing a side of Stanton we do not like to think about. Rooney was held captive until the spring of 1864, although Davis offered to give any in exchange that the North desired.

And while Rooney lay in prison his wife died. Lee had written to her on his return from Gettysburg, while his thoughts were filled with the care of his broken army: "Nothing would do more harm than for him to know you were sick and sad. How could he get well? So cheer up and prove your fortitude and patriotism. What, too, should I do? I cannot bear to think of you except as I

---

[3] Jones, *Reminiscences*, p. 391.

have always known you, bright, joyous and happy."[4] And after she was gone he wrote his boy as he waited Grant's attack in the Wilderness: "God knows how I loved your dear, dear wife, how sweet her memory is to me, and how I mourn her loss."[5] Shadows were growing thicker for him every year. But there was no loss of courage!

As the march northward began Lee gave strict orders against the maltreatment of the non-combatant population in the country through which they hoped to pass and directed that payment should be made for whatever supplies should be taken for the troops. He had no desire to alienate the peace party of the North by any ruthless conduct by his army. This peace party was much in his mind in all the planning for the campaign. Davis had said again and again that reunion with the North was unthinkable. Lee wrote him a letter at this time which is as near a rebuke as he ever gave the Executive. He tells him that such assertions, which out of respect for Davis he attributed to the press, were short-sighted in the extreme. The southern leaders should encourage the idea that peace might bring a restoration of the Union in order to hearten those in the North who were looking for that end. "If we once receive overtures for a cessation of hostilities," he argues, "we can fight as staunchly for entire and final separation as we have been doing with arms in our hands."[6] The letter is a bit puzzling from Lee, quite at variance with his usual straightforward way of dealing with things. There is no record of any reply from Davis.

But in spite of his policy of conciliation, the rich country through which they passed was compelled to yield them

---

[4]*Ibid.*, p. 400.
[5]*Ibid.*, p. 401.
[6]Dodd, *Davis*, p. 308.

immense booty for which they paid in Confederate notes, which the stolid Pennsylvania farmers did not receive with great eagerness. In the British Diary is this entry:

"Major Moses tells me that his orders are to open the stores in Chambersburg by force, and seize all that is wanted for the army in regular and official manner, giving in return its value in Confederate money on receipt. The storekeepers have doubtless sent away their most valuable goods on the approach of the Confederate Army. Much also has been already seized by Ewell, who passed through nearly a week ago. But Moses was much elated at having discovered a large supply of excellent felt hats, hidden away in a cellar, which he annexed at once. Ewell, after the capture of Winchester, advanced rapidly into Pennsylvania, and has already sent great quantities of horses, mules, wagons, beeves, and other necessaries back; he is now at or beyond Carlisle, laying the country under contribution and making Pennsylvania support the war, instead of poor, used-up and worn-out Virginia."[7]

On June twenty-third the passage of the Potomac began. On this day Lee made a mistake which was to have far-reaching consequences. Stuart asked permission to ride around the rear of the northern army, which was then at Leesburg, then to cross the river cutting communications and getting what information he could. After this he was to join the advance guard of Lee's army near the Susquehanna. Stuart had made a number of such raids with invariable success, and he counted on being able to carry this one through successfully. But it was a fatal thing at this critical time. Owing to Hooker's crossing the river earlier than they expected the whole northern army was interposed between Stuart and Lee, and he was unable to

[7] *Blackwood's Magazine*, September, 1863, p. 372.

THE VIRGINIA MEMORIAL AT GETTYSBURG

The bronze Lee on his great horse watching the ground where his hopes died.

join the advance guard until the battle was nearly over. A commander without cavalry in a strange and hostile country is like a blind man. Lee lost Jackson, his "right arm," at Chancellorsville. He was without his "eyes" at Gettysburg. Perhaps if he had had them many things would have been different. One thing surely would have happened: had Stuart been present to scour the country and keep his commander informed of the enemy's position, Lee would have secured the heights at Gettysburg on the first day which he was afterward to attempt to take at such cost. For on the morning before the battle began Hill's corps was at Cashtown and Ewell's at Heidlersburg, both less than ten miles from Gettysburg. They could have easily anticipated the northern advance guard had Lee known.[8] In fact it is not likely that a battle would ever have been fought at Gettysburg had Lee known of Meade's approach. His chances of success would have been greater, had he been able to wait, as at Fredericksburg, in a carefully prepared position for Meade's attack. But he was groping about like a blind man in a country he did not know and stumbled into battle.

As Lee marched north toward the Susquehanna, things had been happening with the Army of the Potomac of which he knew nothing. It had a new commander totally unlike Hooker, Meade, a tall thin Pennsylvanian, with a long thin nose and a cool mind that carefully considered every move. His troops called him "the damned old goggle-eyed snapping turtle." He moved about as rapidly as a turtle, but we remember the fabled race with the hare! Meade had a way of getting there too, though he tried Lincoln's patience after Gettysburg. Lee thought the Army of the Potomac was still in Virginia, but by June

[8]Henderson, *Science of War*, p. 287.

twenty-eighth it had been concentrated at Frederick. Lee learned of this on the twenty-ninth and hastened word to his scattered units to come together. On the thirtieth the armies were groping toward one another, and a division of northern cavalry under General Buford occupied the town of Gettysburg. It was only a small force, but Buford handled it so skilfully that he gave the impression that he had a very much larger body with him to Heth who came from Cashtown to get shoes for his division in Gettysburg and found Buford there. Had Stuart been where he ought to have been the chances are that this small force would have been driven out and the heights seized, and Meade forced to fight an offensive battle instead of a defensive. As it was Heth retired, leaving Hancock, who had hurried up on hearing the firing, in possession.

When morning came Heth told Hill, his corps commander, that if he had no objection he would take his whole division back to Gettysburg and get those shoes, to which Hill replied, "None in the world."[9] But when he reached McPherson's Heights two miles west of Gettysburg, he ran into Hancock's skirmishers. A few scattering shots and the battle was on which was to decide the fate of the American nation, one of the decisive battles of the world. And it was not begun as Lee desired it, nor Meade, but by the action of a minor officer who wanted shoes for his men to replace those worn out on Pennsylvania's metaled roads.

[9] Fitzhugh Lee, p. 290.

CHAPTER XXVI

The Battle

How can any one tell the story of those three epic days when one hundred and seventy thousand men toiled and struggled and sweated and died about and in and through that little Pennsylvania town. It stands sheltered in the curve of a broken line of hills, that in the shape of a giant fish-hook lie there in the valley, as though the great Master-Builder had cast them aside when He was making His mountains. Culp's Hill is the point of the fish-hook, Cemetery Ridge the center, and the salient of the Peach Orchard the shaft, running on into the Round Tops. Pilgrims from all the earth find their way to it and listen to the singsong tale that the guides tell of this charge and that struggle. It has given names to the world that will not soon be forgotten, the Peach Orchard and Little Round Top, the Wheat-field and Devil's Den. Names like that are to be found over all the English-speaking world, but when one utters them, one thinks of Gettysburg. And looking over the ground where his bravest fell, sits, on his great bronze charger, the man whose name we repeat with reverence and with sadness, whether our fathers wore the blue or the gray—Lee! Lee and Gettysburg, they are inseparable! There

> "He cast his stone
> Clanging at fortune, and set his fate on the odds!"[1]

---

[1] Benet, *John Brown's Body*, p. 283.

And that fate was failure. For that stone returning wounded him, and wounded most the cause for which he fought.

On the first day the battle was with the South. Heth, seeking those shoes, drove eastward carefully, for he did not know what lay in front. The thin blue line gave way before him, its commander handling his men skilfully. Over Seminary Ridge they went, past the little college and into the town. Reynolds was killed, the gallant Reynolds, whom every one thought Lincoln would name in Hooker's place. Hancock had arrived with his Eleventh Corps and he held the Confederates at bay until Ewell came down from the north, and drove them through the town to the heights east of it. There Hancock made the momentous decision to hold and entrench. Lee arrived on the field about three o'clock. He saw the northern troops fleeing through the town and he sent his aide, Colonel Taylor, to Ewell, to say to him that he could see the enemy retreating and that "it was only necessary to press those people to secure possession of the heights, and that *if possible* (italics mine) he wished him to do so."[2] But Ewell was not Jackson and he did not think it "possible," and the day closed with Hancock entrenching. Lee missed Stuart. He would have known if it were "possible" had Stuart been there to see him.

During the night he gave orders to Longstreet to attack at dawn. But Longstreet had felt from the first that the battle here was a mistake and had urged a turning movement around Meade's left. Again he urged it on the morning of the second, but Lee was firm. Never had Lee missed Jackson more than here. He did not argue. He moved as directed. But the sun rose higher and higher, and Long-

---

[2] Taylor, p. 95.

street did not move. It was three o'clock in the afternoon before his battle flags were set forward. That saved the North from disaster. By the time he moved, fresh forces had arrived and the line was strongly held. The heights were saved for Meade. Well might Lee say after the war, "Had I had Stonewall Jackson at Gettysburg I should have won the battle."[3] Had Jackson been in Ewell's place the first day or in Longstreet's the second the result might have been different.

So the third day dawned. The men in blue had been entrenching during the night, bringing up cannon. The heights were bristling with them ready for the gray lines that were to attempt to cross the fields below. The ground before the Round Tops, Meade's left, was not favorable for an advance, so Lee decided to send Longstreet against the center on Cemetery Ridge with a massed infantry attack, and Ewell against the right on Culp's Hill. Again Longstreet was to move at dawn, but again he hesitated. A delay of several hours took place, during which Ewell launched his attack and was driven back at the point of the bayonet. Then at one o'clock the Confederate massed batteries on Seminary Ridge opened fire, and Meade's guns answered from Cemetery Ridge. For two hours the cannon roared—until the smoke hung like a great pall over the valley between the ridges. Then the northern fire began to slacken, and some of their guns were drawn back. The moment seemed favorable, the Confederate ammunition was beginning to run low, and Longstreet gave permission for the advance. They who watched from the heights saw long gray lines of infantry come through the smoke. It was the beginning of Pickett's charge.

While men live they will tell that story. It was as use-

---

[3] Jones, *Life*, p. 237.

less as Balaclava and as magnificent! The lines swiftly moved across the meadows. They crossed a fence. There was almost a mile to go before they made the contact. But on they came as though they were marching in review. The Confederate cannon ceased. The guns should have gone forward after Pickett's men, but they failed to do so. Now Pickett was climbing the slope of Cemetery Ridge. A fearful blaze of fire burst from the crest, and the batteries that had been withdrawn and were waiting for this moment rushed forward and began firing at point-blank range. Still Pickett went on. Lee saw his men enter the cloud of smoke on the Ridge. He caught glimpses of their battle flags waving on the crest as the smoke lifted. But Pickett had only fifteen thousand, and many of these he had left in the meadows and on the slope. The other divisions of the twenty-five thousand Lee had planned for the assault never moved. Pickett could not hold, and his line went reeling back. In that moment on the crest they had reached the high-water mark of the southern flood:

"Where the bronze, open book could still be read
By visitors and sparrows and the wind!
And the wind came, the wind moved in the grass,
Saying . . . while the long light . . . and all so calm . . .
   'Pickett came
   And the South came
   And the end came,
   And the grass comes
   And the wind blows
   On the bronze book
   On the bronze men
   On the grown grass,
   And the wind says
   "Long ago

Long
Ago!" ' "4

And across the meadow from the bronze book near the
clump of woods where he sat on Traveller that July day to
watch the charge sits the bronze Lee on his great horse,
guarding the ground where they died. And where his
hopes died!

On the fourth he began the retreat. The rain poured in
torrents and through the rain they marched. Every road
south was crowded, long miles of misery, of broken hopes.
And every road led now to Appomattox.

4 Benet, p. 295.

Chapter XXVII

Back to Virginia

As ONE stands by the great bronze book and looks out over the field on a summer day the battle seems to be one of the long-gone forgotten things with which the past is crowded. We speak of it in terms of movements as we would of some machine. But they who shared in it thought of it in terms of human agony. It was not the bronze men who stand so placidly on the lines who fought it, but men who hoped and dreamed and prayed, men who knew wounds and weariness, men who died in dreadful agony, men who knew the bitterness of failure, or the exaltation that follows triumph. The battle is meaningless unless we think of them.

The British officer to whose Diary we are indebted for much in the story of this campaign has left a picture of that dreadful third day which makes us forget the bronze men. It is just after Pickett's charge.

"I soon began to meet many wounded men returning from the front; many of them asked in piteous tones the way to a doctor or an ambulance. The further I got, the greater became the number of the wounded. At last I came to a perfect stream of them flocking through the woods in numbers as great as the crowd in Oxford street in the middle of the day. Some were walking alone on crutches composed of two rifles, others were carried on stretchers by the ambulance corps; but in no case did I see a sound man helping a wounded to the rear, unless he carried the red badge of the ambulance corps. They were still under a heavy fire, the shells were continually bringing down great limbs of trees, and carrying further destruction amongst this melancholy procession. I saw all this in much less time than it takes to write it, and although astonished to meet such vast numbers of wounded, I had not seen enough to give me any idea of the real extent of the mischief. When I got up close to General Longstreet, I saw one of his regiments advancing through the woods in good order; so thinking I was just in time to see the attack, I remarked to the General that 'I wouldn't have missed this for anything.' General Longstreet was seated on the top of a snake fence at the edge of the wood, and looking perfectly calm and unperturbed. He replied, laughingly, 'The devil you wouldn't. I would like to have missed it very much; we've attacked and been repulsed.'

"Soon afterwards I joined General Lee, who had in the meanwhile come to the front on becoming aware of the disaster. . . . He was engaged in rallying and encouraging the broken troops, and was riding about a little in front of the woods, quite alone—the whole of his staff being engaged in a similar manner further to the rear. His face, which is always placid and cheerful did not show signs of the slightest disappointment, care or annoyance; and he was addressing every soldier he met with a few words of encouragement, such as, 'All this will come right in the end; we'll talk it over afterwards; but in the meantime all good men must rally. We want good and true men just now, etc.' He spoke to all the wounded men that passed him, and the slightly wounded he exhorted 'to bind up their hurts and take up a musket' in this emergency. Very few failed to answer his appeal, and I saw badly wounded men take off their hats and cheer him. He said to me, 'This has been a sad day for us, Colonel—a sad day; but we can't expect always to gain victories.' He was also kind enough to advise me to get into some more sheltered position. Notwithstanding the misfortune that had so suddenly befallen him, General Lee seemed to observe everything, however trivial. When a mounted officer began licking his horse for shying at a bursting shell, he called out 'Don't whip him, Captain, don't whip him. I've got just such another foolish horse myself, and whipping does no good.' "[1]

General Imboden, for whom Lee sent that night after the retreat had been decided on, that he might guard the trains back to Virginia, left this description of Lee after the night had come:

"He threw his arm across his saddle to rest himself and fixing his eyes upon the ground, leaned in silence upon his equally weary horse. . . . 'General,' I remarked, 'this has been a sad day for you.' . . . He looked up and replied mournfully: 'Yes, it has been a sad day, a sad day for us,' and immediately relapsed into his thoughtful mood and attitude. Being unwilling again to intrude upon his reflections I said no more. After a minute or two he suddenly straightened up to his full height, and turning to me with more animation, energy, and excitement of manner than I had ever seen before, he addressed me in a voice tremulous with emotion, and said: 'General, I never saw troops behave more magnificently than Pickett's division of Virginians did today in their grand charge upon the enemy, and if they had been supported as they were to have been, but for some reason not yet explained to me they were not, we would have held the position they so gloriously won at such a fearful loss of noble lives, and the day would have been ours.' After a moment he added in a tone almost of agony: 'Too bad! Too bad! Oh too bad!' "[2]

The bronze men there on the field are so calm. They show many things, but they do not show what these old pictures show of that human agony.

---

[1] *Blackwood's Magazine*, September, 1863, p. 301.
[2] Old Scrap-Book: Clipping from *The Galaxy*.

CHAPTER XXVIII

The Retreat and Its Consequences

LEE sent off his heavy trains, with Imboden guarding them, on the fourth. All day long he waited for Meade to attack but no attack was made. That night the army began to march toward Virginia. All night long it rained, it rained in torrents, on the men plodding along in the mud, on the wounded in the wagons—springless wagons, seventeen miles of them and all agony! The little streams were rising. Was the Potomac rising? Would they be able to cross?

That was the question Lincoln was asking himself in Washington. Vicksburg had fallen on the same day as Lee's repulse. Washington again was safe. He was a happy man after all these months of anxiety. If Meade would only follow and smash Lee, with his back to the swollen river, the war would be over. He sent message after message urging Meade to push forward and fight. But Meade was a cautious man. All of Lincoln's commanders were cautious men it seemed, except Grant. Meade wired that he was scouting for the weak point in Lee's army. That weak point was not easy to find. Also, that he had called a council of war. Halleck telegraphed him at Lincoln's direction, "Call no council of war. It is proverbial that councils of war never fight. Don't let the enemy escape."[1] But while Meade was preparing to attack, Lee got over the river on the night of the thir-

---

[1] Fitzhugh Lee, p. 305.

teenth, his men singing—or some of them—as they splashed through the fords in the dark: "Carry me back to Old Virginny." Even in spite of all they had seen of plenty in Pennsylvania Virginia looked pretty good to them. They always won there.

On the fourteenth Meade sent Lincoln another telegram saying that he "had driven the invader from our soil." Lincoln cried in his despair: "We had them in our grasp, and he let them go! When will our generals get over the idea that an army south of the Potomac has been driven from our soil. The whole country is our soil."[2] A few days later he said to John Hay, "We had gone through all the labor of toiling and planting an enormous crop and when it was ripe we did not harvest it." Still he added: "I am very grateful to Meade for the service he did at Gettysburg."[3] But even Lincoln, who saw farther than any man of his time, did not see the thing that was to follow from that defeat. No one saw it. It was one of those things that develop slowly. It began in the night, as Lee's weary army took its way back to Virginia over those mountain roads in the beating rain. His men had time to think and they realized that something had happened, something that had never happened before. They had been beaten! Lincoln had said that they had been at Antietam, but they did not believe him. Other than that the names that fluttered on their battle flags were the names of victories. But this they knew was no victory.

That this defeat was in a measure due to their own overconfidence did not add to their comfort. They knew now they had been over-confident, now and afterward. A line officer of one of the Virginia regiments in an address on

---

[2] Barton, *Lincoln at Gettysburg*, p. 34.
[3] Hay, Unpublished Diary, July 19, 1863.

Lee's birthday in 1876 spoke of the Pennsylvania campaign as a "campaign whose only fault was the generous fault of over-confidence in an army whose great deeds might, if anything, excuse it—an over-confidence, as we ourselves know, felt by every man he led, and which made us reckless of all difficulties, ready to think that to us nothing was impossible." It is always a hard blow to men's spirits to realize that their failure was their own fault, a blow to morale of the severest sort. The bitterness that was in their hearts they did not then tell to the world. Those men in gray did not wear their hearts on their sleeves. But a young Virginian wrote this in his Diary that night when they crossed back to their battle-torn land:

"Monday 13th. We started back across the river. I reached the pontoon bridge about 6:30 o'clock. And it came to pass as I sat upon the river bank and watched the trains crossing from Maryland to Virginia, our army giving up the offensive and assuming the defensive, that I thought upon the vanity of human expectations and so a long train of thought engaged my mind, and I pondered of the future and the past in their relations to the present. I thought of expectations and promises unfulfilled in this brief but not inglorious campaign, and as my mind recalled the farewell greetings e'er I left Virginia's shore, I could not forget how I had trusted to bring you a little memento, which would, alas, be but too appropriate in memory of the fallen brave."[4]

"The vanity of human expectations!" Yes, it was that thought that held them, as they "gave up the offensive and assumed the defensive"—for the rest of the war! Lee, whose brilliant attacks had excited the wonder of the world, passed now largely to the difficult task of defense.

---

[4] Peterkin Mss. Diary.

That army of his had many things to ponder over as it marched along in the rain. How different things were in Pennsylvania from what the home letters told them they were in Georgia, in the Carolinas, in the Valley of Virginia. Things might be going all right, or nearly all right, on the big plantations where they still had slaves, but on the little farms the women were having hard times, sowing their own crops, spinning their own wool and cotton, weaving their own cloth, searching the woods for dyes, for medicines, searching the attics for bits of discarded finery with which to keep up a brave appearance.[5] For the blockade was growing tighter and the things which once were looked on as necessities were now decided luxuries. Then the paper money with which they were paid was falling all the while. A private's pay for a month would scarcely buy one meal for his family or a year's pay buy him a pair of boots.[6] Even this was not paid for months, so that the whole task of supporting the family fell on the women.

There had been growing also a conviction in that army that this was a "rich man's war but a poor man's fight," for the wealthy planter's son was able to get a job in some government office or in some comfortable post far removed from the land of the long marches and the damp bivouacs and the battle's wounds and death. Jones, in the war office in Richmond, was writing in his Diary the thing that was in the minds of many of them: "Some 40,000 landowners and the owners of slaves are at their comfortable homes or in comfortable offices, while the poor and ignorant are relied upon to achieve independence."

It was hard to keep always marching and fighting when

---

[5] Hague, *A Blockaded Family*, p. 51.

[6] Lonn, p. 10.

they thought of these things. But they had fought, one battle after another. They had marched, long weary distances, often shoeless over flinty roads. Washington's was not the only army that left a blood-marked trail. They had lain, when sick or wounded, in wretched makeshift hospitals, wrapped in thin blankets, rarely with straw pillows under their heads. They could have stood all this if their families at home had been properly cared for. But with this burden falling on the women it was different. And especially was it different when they got letters like this that Edward Cooper got from his wife down in North Carolina:

"My dear Edward: I have always been proud of you, and since your connection with the Confederate Army, I have been prouder of you than ever before. I would not have you do anything wrong in the world, but before God, Edward, unless you come home, we must die. Last night I was aroused by little Eddie's crying. I called and said, 'What is the matter, Eddie?' and he said, 'O mamma! I am so hungry.' And Lucy, Edward, your darling Lucy; she never complains, but she is growing thinner and thinner every day. And before God, Edward, unless you come home, we must die.

"Your MARY."[7]

Yet month after month they had endured things which seemed impossible. There had been a few desertions, very few on the whole when everything is considered. Nothing beyond the number that most armies have.

This march into Pennsylvania had opened their eyes to the fact that things were not like that in the North. The wheat stood thick and heavy on the fertile limestone fields.

---

[7] *Ibid.*, p. 13.

There were fat cattle in the meadows, and the vegetable gardens and the berry patches and the orchards seemed like paradise to those who had lived long on scanty rations of bacon and flour or parched corn. There were men working in the fields, and loafing in the evening about the village streets, plenty of men, young men too, who would long ago have been conscripted had they lived in Dixie. And when they were asked why they were not in the army they told them that they were not needed. And they told them further that it was like that all over the North. Wealth, power, inexhaustible—how could they ever win against such foes? They had beaten them time and again and every time they had come back with fresh forces. Now at last the North had beaten them, and the North had all this that they had never realized before, this store of untouched resources, for future battles, for battle after battle, until they were crushed. Oh! they were brave, those men of the Army of Northern Virginia, as brave as ever followed a leader; but what is bravery when it is overwhelmed with facts! And those facts kept following them as they wound through the mountain passes with the wounded ahead in wagons, and their guns rumbling after, and across the Potomac, never to cross it again.

That Gettysburg was a moral defeat of the first order for the Confederacy is to be seen in the immediate increase in desertions. This began to be reflected in the record of deserters slipping over to the northern lines at once and continuing all through August and September, 1863. A Virginian writes in July, 1863: "A good many deserters are passing the roads daily and greatly increase the demoralization. These deserters almost invariably have their guns and accoutrements with them when halted, and asked for their furlough or their authority to be absent from their commands, they just pat their guns and defiantly say, 'This is my furlough!' and even enrolling officers turn away as peaceably as possible, evidently intimidated by their defiant manner."[8] So serious did this become that on August 3, 1863, Davis issued a proclamation calling on all absentees to return to the camps.[9]

From this time onward desertion continued to be a factor that caused Lee increasing trouble. The marvel is, when one considers the conditions under which they fought, that it was not worse. It speaks volumes for the devotion of the men of his armies to him their beloved leader that they stuck as they did. Whatever men may think of the political leaders of the Confederacy it must always be a cause of pride to an American that these private soldiers of Lee's army endured what they did and endured it for so long.

But from Gettysburg on the tide of desertion steadily rose until in the last year of the war the machinery set up to cope with it was absolutely unequal to the task. The agony that it caused Lee as he saw his army melting before his eyes can be seen in his dispatches. November 18, 1864: "Desertion is increasing in the army notwithstanding all my efforts to stop it." January 27, 1865: "I have the honor to call your attention to the alarming frequency of desertion from the army. You will perceive from the accompanying papers, that 56 deserted from Hill's corps in three days." February 25, 1865: "Hundreds of men are deserting nightly and I cannot keep the army together unless examples are made of such cases." February 28, 1865, in a report showing 1094 desertions in ten days: "This defection in troops that have acted so nobly and

---

[8] *Ibid.*, p. 46.

[9] Jones, Vol. II, p. 4.

borne so much is so distressing to me that I have thought proper to give you the particulars."[10]

The end was not far when these dispatches were written. From the second year of the war there had always been desertion. But from Gettysburg on it increased amazingly, sapping the strength of the Confederate armies faster than additions could be made by conscription. And in addition the deserters helped to break down the morale of the folks back home. They were often organized into outlaw bands who threatened the lives and property of those who dared give information to the authorities that would lead to the arrest of the marauders. The people lost faith in a government unable to enforce its own decrees and compel obedience to its laws. And how, they asked, could an army win independence for them when it would not hold together? It was not Grant's strategy alone that destroyed the Confederacy. The memories of the quiet homes in the Cumberland Valley, of plenty while they starved, of man power so great and inexhaustible, that even youth could idle in the evenings in the streets of little towns, these were the things that haunted Lee's veterans from Gettysburg on and helped to break the will to victory. Gettysburg was not merely a defeat. It was the beginning of the break in morale.

The old yellowing pages of the Diary of the boy officer who had watched the crossing of the Potomac tell further of the morning of the twenty-third when they crossed the Blue Ridge to eastern Virginia, the land of their victories: "Before we started down the mountains the bands played very sweetly Kathleen Mavourneen."[11] And the sadness of the music matched the sadness of their hearts!

---

[10] Lonn, p. 28.

[11] Peterkin Diary.

Chapter XXIX

The Summer of '63

BUT loss of morale in his army was not the only difficulty Lee had to face in that fateful summer of '63. Bitterness and recrimination were the order of the day in the Confederacy. Censure was heard on every hand. Beauregard had opposed the invasion of Pennsylvania, urging rather a movement into the West which would have strengthened Bragg's army and enabled him to relieve Vicksburg. Now, with a wisdom after the event, Bragg wrote to him on July twenty-first that he had held the same opinion, but had been overruled by those in control, and because of his insufficient force had been compelled to fall back. A wave of despair swept the Cotton States, and the struggle already begun between Davis and the state authorities was intensified. The confidence of the southern people, in the words of Davis was "impaired so far as to give the malcontents a power to represent the Government as neglecting for Virginia the safety of the more southern states."[1]

The newspapers were filled with the word of failure. "There is to be no peace," cried the *Richmond Enquirer*, almost before Lee's shattered regiments were back across the Potomac. "All hope of a speedy peace depended on a decisive victory of Lee's army, and that success has not been decisive." Editors, safe among their ink-pots, were demanding to know how the South could win the war in this fashion. Lee must have been asking himself the same

---

[1] Davis, Vol. II, p. 448.

question and when late in July Davis wrote him concerning the mutterings of discontent that were heard in all quarters, adding "there are others, who, faithful but dissatisfied, find an appropriate remedy in the removal of officers who have not succeeded," he sent to the President his resignation. This letter is a remarkable revelation of the man himself, seeking in no way to avoid responsibility, but anxious as always to permit nothing to interfere with the success of the cause. He sets forth his belief that it "is natural and in many instances proper" that the want of success of a military commander should end in his removal, for no matter how great may be his ability "if he loses the confidence of his troops disaster must sooner or later ensue." He notes the "expression of discontent in the public journals" at the Gettysburg results, and reasons that some of the same discontent must exist in the army, although his "brother officers have been too kind to report it and so far the troops have been too generous to exhibit it." He therefore urges that Davis "take measures to supply my place." He goes on:

"In addition, I sensibly feel the growing failure of my bodily strength. I have not yet recovered from the attack I experienced the past spring. I am becoming more and more incapable of exertion, and am thus prevented from making the personal examinations and giving the personal supervision to the operations in the field which I feel to be necessary. I am so dull that in making use of the eyes of others I am frequently misled. Everything, therefore, points to the advantages to be derived from a new commander, and I the more anxiously urge the matter upon Your Excellency from my belief that a younger and abler man than myself can readily be obtained. I know that he will have as gallant and brave an army as ever existed to second his efforts, and it would be the happiest day of my life to see at its head a worthy leader—one that could accomplish more than I could perform, and all that I have wished. I hope Your Excellency will attribute my request to the true reason, the desire to serve my country and to do all in my power to ensure the success of her righteous cause."[2]

He concludes with the remarkable statement, "I have no complaints to make of anyone but myself." Not of Stuart, whose rash impetuosity had left Lee without his "eyes" up in that strange country when he needed them most. Not of Longstreet, whose obstinacy had made it impossible to seize the hour when victory might have been won. No complaints! After all it is something to have been born at Stratford. It comes out in the hour of testing.

Davis was guilty of many mistakes of judgment, but not this time. The man never is finer than in his answer:

"I do not doubt the readiness with which you would give way to one who could accomplish all that you have wished, and you will do me the justice to believe that if Providence should kindly offer such a person for our use, I would not hesitate to avail [myself] of his services. My sight is not sufficiently penetrating to discover such hidden merit, if it exists, and I have but used to you the language of sober earnestness when I have impressed upon you the propriety of avoiding all unnecessary exposure to danger, because I felt our country could not bear to lose you. To ask me to substitute you by some one in my judgment more fit to command, or who would possess more of the confidence of the army or of the reflecting men of the country, is to demand an impossibility."[3]

For some weeks Lee's army lay on the Rapidan, removing

_____
[2] Long, p. 497.
[3] Long, p. 499.

the marks of that bitter struggle among the Pennsylvania hills. The camp was a busy place, a vast repair shop. There was little likelihood of attack by the enemy for Meade had had to detach some of his regiments to put down the draft riots in New York. Lincoln had put the Draft Act of March third into effect when the struggle was going on at Gettysburg, and on July thirteenth the storm burst in the great city filled with foreign born to whom the Union meant nothing. The offices of the Draft were sacked, buildings were burned, and negroes were hung from lamp-posts. The casualties of the three days of rioting were over a thousand. The outburst against the draft spread to other cities. It was little wonder that Meade did not stir from his lines on the Rappahannock while this dreadful uncertainty was behind him.

Lee took advantage of this quiet to go to Richmond for a period of conference with Davis. Night after night they met on the second floor of the Confederate White House with the leaders of Congress and the members of the Cabinet. There were certain results of those conferences. Among them was the detachment of Longstreet's corps to aid in the critical operations in the West. But of greater importance was the decision to attempt no more to wrest a southern victory by an invasion of the North. Lee of course had never dreamed that he could achieve a conquest of the North, but he had thought that he could establish himself in northern territory and with a victory create the will to peace among those who opposed him. But Gettysburg ended that. From this time on he trusted to wearing out the patience of his enemy. By delay, by retreat, by swift maneuver, by compelling him to set up a wearing and a wearying siege, he hoped to hold the foe in check until the nation behind the army would cease to pour out blood and treasure and would demand peace. Defense is the key to every movement after Gettysburg, and in the months of war that remained he won the reputation which is his of one of the great defensive captains of all time.

It was not only the newspapers that poured out criticism hard to bear. He wrote his wife, "My heart sinks every-time the mail train comes," for he knew how the letters from home telling of the hardship there helped to damage further the morale of his men. Those that came to him were carefully answered. One of his secretaries complained in Mrs. Chesnut's drawing-room that "General Lee requires us to answer every letter, and to do our best to console the poor creatures whose husbands and sons are fighting the battles of the country."[4]

The battles of the West had taken their toll of men whom he trusted, and there is a bitter cry, such as we seldom hear from him, in a letter to Davis on September twenty-third, after the false report of Hood's death reached him:

"I am grieved to learn of the death of General Hood. I fear also from the accounts that General Wofford is dead. He was one of Georgia's best men. I am gradually losing my best men—Jackson, Pender, Hood. There was no braver soldier in the Confederate army than Deshler. I see he is numbered among the dead."[5]

On the ninth of October he crossed the Rapidan, and then ensued an uneventful campaign, of maneuver rather than of fighting. Both Lee and Meade sought time after time to take the other at a disadvantage, and each failed because of the alertness of his opponent. It was a conflict

---

[4] Chesnut, p. 259.
[5] *Gulf States' Historical Magazine*, Vol. III, p. 293.

of wits rather than bullets, and during the two months before winter came they marched back and forth over Virginia roads and in the end found themselves about where they began, without either winning any particular advantage. Then winter quarters until spring came bringing a new leader to the armies in blue, a different leader who was to write a different ending to the tale.

CHAPTER XXX

The New Opponent

ON MARCH 9, 1864, Lincoln took the most important step he had as yet taken toward the winning of the war. He appointed Ulysses S. Grant as lieutenant-general of the armies and placed the entire direction of military operations in his hands, with the solemn assurance that he should have everything he needed of arms and of men. Grant was thirty-nine years old when he came east to establish his headquarters with the Army of the Potomac, bringing with him the reputation of victory. He had the qualities Lincoln needed. He was not afraid of responsibility. He talked little, avoided show: a private's blouse with shoulder straps was his usual field uniform. Meade had a headquarters flag with a golden eagle emblazoned upon it. When Grant saw it first as they began the Wilderness campaign he is reported to have said: "What's this? Is Imperial Cæsar anywhere about here?"[1]

It has been the fashion latterly to sneer at Grant and to proclaim him as very much overrated. Such a fashion does nothing but set forth the colossal ignorance of those who further it. This man defeated in succession Floyd, Pillow, Buckner, Van Dorn, Pemberton and Bragg. And finally he achieved the task which had broken McDowell, McClellan, Pope, Burnside and Hooker, and in which Meade had been unable to succeed. He conquered Lee! Second-rate men do not do things like that.

[1]Fitzhugh Lee, p. 327.

Until Grant was placed in charge the North had no strategy. For years, in campaign after campaign, northern generals had sought to capture Richmond, as though that would have meant anything. Richmond was of so little value to Grant that after he took it he did not take the trouble to go and look at it. Scott had had a plan in the beginning of the war for a concerted attack from the north and west upon the Confederacy, which was very like that which Grant put into practise, but McClellan had contemptuously cast it aside.

But Grant from the first had his plan in mind and fought with one purpose, to cut the Confederacy in two on the Mississippi, and then, marching east through Georgia, destroy its sources of supply and take Virginia in the rear. This was behind his movement in Tennessee, carried out against the opposition of his superior, Halleck. This was the object of that brilliant Vicksburg campaign. And this is what he proceeded to carry through to consummation when he was made generalissimo. While he held Lee in "a bulldog grip" (as Lincoln put it) he sent Sherman on his great movement through Georgia, smashing in the back door of Richmond. Colonel Fuller of the British Army describes this movement as "a right flank wheel of over a thousand miles extending over three years in time, a strategical movement compared to which the German right flank wheel in 1914, however powerful, was child's play."[2] And he declares "that wheel is one of the most amazing manœuvres in military history." Second-rate men do not plan things like that, and further they do not carry them out.

If his present-day critics do not understand him they knew in the Confederacy what he was. Mrs. Chesnut

---

[2]Fuller, p. 47.

writes in her Diary on New Year's Day, 1864, what General Edward Johnston said of him:

"He is their right man, a bull-headed Suwarrow. He don't care a snap if men fall like the leaves fall; he fights to win, that chap does. He is not distracted by a thousand side issues; he does not see them. He is narrow and sure, sees only in a straight line. . . . He has the disagreeable habit of not retreating before irresistible veterans."[3]

And six months later Major Tyler of Lee's staff wrote to General Price of what others than he at headquarters must have seen:

"From first to last Grant has shown great skill and prudence, combined with remorseless persistency and brutality. He is a scientific Goth resembling Alaric, destroying the country as he goes and delivering the people over to starvation. . . . The game going on upon the military chessboard between Lee and Grant has been striking and grand, surpassing anything I have heretofore witnessed, and conducted on both sides with consummate mastery of the art of war. It is admitted that Lee has at last met a foe who matches his steel, although he may not be worthy of it. Each guards himself perfectly, and gives his blow with a precise eye and cool sanguinary nerve."[4]

Then there is the word of Lincoln written at the moment when the North was raging at Grant for the bloody failure at Cold Harbor:

"I have just read your dispatch. I begin to see it. You will succeed. God bless you all."

And finally it must always be remembered of him that

---

[3] Chesnut, p. 270.
[4] Quoted by Fuller, p. 375.

he is the one man who did the thing in which every one else failed—he defeated Lee! That is the surety of fame.

When he came east in the spring of '64 Lee had been carrying on his policy of delay for nine months. It was having its effect. The North was beginning to be war-weary. The national election was coming in the fall, and it seemed highly improbable in the temper of the nation that Lincoln could be reelected. With Lincoln out of the way the peace party would have the ascendent. The platform of the Democratic party was practically a surrender platform. Lincoln had to be reelected if the war was to be won, and to reelect him required that the will to war of the North be maintained and deepened. To this end victories had to be won before November came around. To shape the way for these, to make useless Lee's tactics of delay, was Grant's problem. He answered it—with blood—but he answered it. This is a fact his critics have overlooked. And in so doing they slur not only him, but the great soldier who led the forces opposed to him. It was a battle of giants, there on the Rapidan and on the Petersburg line, through that long dreadful summer and fall of '64. When it was over the end was in sight.

Yet not even the officers who fought under him were sure of Grant when he came east in '64. "It was not," he naïvely records in his *Memoirs*, "an uncommon thing for my staff-officers to hear from Eastern officers 'Well, Grant has never met Bobby Lee.' "[5]

---

[5] Grant, Vol. II, p. 292.

Chapter XXXI

Preparing for the Storm

THAT Lee was aware that unusual things were in the offing is to be seen from a letter written to Davis on March thirtieth: "I think we can assume that if General Grant is to direct operations on this frontier he will concentrate a large force on one or more lines, and prudence dictates that we should make such preparations as are in our power."[1] On April thirtieth he had reached the conclusion from the reports his scouts brought him that everything indicated that the Rapidan position was to be the object of a concentrated attack.

He has not been idle while the spring dragged on. His army was wretchedly clothed but they had begun to be used to that. One of the men who fought under him describes their appearance: "some with the bottoms of their pants in long frazzles, others with their knees out, others out at the elbows, and their hair sticking through holes in their hats."[2] Some of the men patched their clothing with any material they could get. A piece of red blanket supplied a seat for this man's trousers, while the next strode proudly along with his patched with black. But not all could get patches, and a girl by the side of the road watching the army pass told her mother, in answer to her question as to which were the officers, that "it was

---

[1] *O. R.*, Vol. XXXIII, p. 1245.

[2] Worsham, p. 175.

easy enough to tell because the officers' pants were patched
and the privates' pants were not."[3]

But if the men were ragged they were better armed than
they had ever been earlier. While the blockade was making it increasingly difficult to bring in munitions from
abroad great progress had been made in their manufacture
within the Confederacy. Those in charge of the munition
plants were growing more expert in turning out field-pieces
and heavier artillery, and small arms were being produced
in quantities. The supply of food that had been gathered in
the depots was also nearer the amount needed, although
forage for the horses, due to poor transportation facilities,
was by no means adequate. There is a vast meaning in a
phrase Lee uses in one of his letters immediately before the
opening of the campaign. "Now that the grass is spring-
ing" he hopes to be able to use his cavalry more effectively!
His letters to Davis must at times have proved wearisome
to that hard-pressed executive, so constantly does he keep
before him the needs of his soldiers. In his aide's phrase
"never had care for the comfort of any army given rise to
greater devotion."[4] He writes constantly to his wife urging the women of Richmond to knit socks and provide
other comforts for the men. He is a bit severe on those
whose chief interest lay in social festivities. He sends
through his son a message to the officers who had given a
ball at Charlottesville in April: "This is a bad time for
such things. We have too grave subjects on hand to engage
in such trivial amusements. I would rather the officers
should entertain themselves in fattening their horses, heal-
ing their men and recruiting their regiments."[5] And Lee,

---

[3] *Ibid.*, p. 175.

[4] *R. and L.*, p. 138.

[5] *Ibid.*, p. 120.

it is to be remembered, was no Puritan. Only, he saw what was ahead.

His greatest anxiety was over the waning man power. A new conscription bill had been passed by Congress, widening the scope of the draft. During the late winter the conscript officers scoured the hiding-places of the draft evaders. Often they worked at the peril of their lives, for hundreds of those evading the draft had banded together for mutual protection. Many of the recruits were mere boys. The militia in some of the states, notably Georgia, had kept out of the regular service many able-bodied men as home guards. Lincoln was having trouble filling his armies, but Davis was having more.

Yet in spite of this he set his face like flint against the proposal for the employment of negroes in the fighting units. They were, and had been from early in the war, extensively employed in the work battalions. But to ask them to fight Davis knew would mean the doom of slavery, for freedom would have been the necessary price, and this he refused to pay. Doubtless, the mass of southern people would not have stood by the government in so drastic a policy, but could it have been adopted it would have greatly increased the southern man power and prolonged the war.

Lee's own physical condition was the cause of much anxiety to those around him. He had, as usual, refused to occupy a house, and had spent the winter in a tent. A cold contracted during the bad weather had developed into an aggravated condition of sore throat, and then had gone down into the lungs and weakened him greatly. The old army disease, dysentery, attacked him in his weakened condition. Yet he refused to give up, although there were days when it was almost impossible for him to leave his tent. He was now fifty-seven and for the last three years he had had heavy burdens and great responsibilities.

April, however, found him better. During that month Longstreet rejoined him with the corps which had been resting after their disappointing western campaign. Lee signalized their return by a great review. Near Mechanicsburg the ragged regiments were drawn up in two lines. But their guns were shining in the spring sunshine as Lee rode along the lines. He wore a new hat that day, a thing to be remembered, for his old one had served him long. The bands played, and the men cheered, he raised his hat— was gone. It is his last review.

On the morning of May fourth he had the principal commanders to breakfast. His old negro served a better breakfast than was usually eaten in that tent, with real coffee, a rare luxury indeed. The General himself said grace, and then gave them the astonishing news that General Grant had crossed the Rapidan during the night. "In fact he is crossing now. We might even have him in to breakfast with us." With swift strokes he sketched his plan. He would allow Grant to get into the Wilderness and fall upon him. This man was to do this, and this other that. Breakfast was soon over. The bugles sounded, the guns began their rumbling, the quick step of infantry was heard. The last struggle for Richmond had begun.

But a week before the day arrived he had written to a young cousin: "You must sometimes cast your thoughts on the Army of Northern Virginia and never forget it in your prayers. It is preparing for a great struggle, but I pray and trust that the great God, mighty to deliver, will spread over it His almighty arms and drive its enemies before it."[6] One can not wholly understand him without remembering that.

---

[6] *Ibid.*, p. 123.

CHAPTER XXXII

The Wilderness

GRANT knew two things as he crossed the Rapidan. First, that power to stay the war out was Lee's aim, and a campaign like the one of the previous summer resulting only in delay would be of exceeding peril to the North. Second, that the southern man power was waning and what Lee must fear most was heavy casualties. He therefore steadfastly set himself to wear Lee down, to inflict heavy casualties even though he had to suffer heavily in return, and thus compel Lee to immobilize his army behind defenses, at which he would keep up a constant hammering and a further wearing down while Sherman swept on in the great plan. For this men have called him a butcher, just as they called Haig a butcher in that dreadful summer of 1918. But war is butchery, nothing less, and the way to victory is only through blood. The trouble with the romantics is that they have confused a battle-field with a tilt-yard.

This man Grant was a realist, and his critics are emotionalists. His whole effort as soon as he became generalissimo, according to General Badeau of his staff, was to employ every resource to one end:

"This was the primal idea, the cardinal principle with which he began his campaigns as general-in-chief—to employ all the force of all the armies continually and concurrently, so that there should be no recuperation on the part of the rebels, no rest from attack, no opportunity to re-

inforce first one and then another point with the same
troops, at different seasons, no possibility of profiting by
the advantage of interior lines; no chance to furlough
troops, to reorganize armies, to re-create supplies; no
respite of any sort, anywhere, until absolute submission
ended the war."[1]

The absence of that sort of realism had dragged the war
out through three bitter years, and had wasted more lives
than Grant lost.

The Army of the Potomac as it advanced across the
Rapidan to carry out its part in this program numbered
115,000 of all arms "equipped for duty."[2]   Lee had a
little more than half as many, 66,351 present for duty, of
which 61,025 were effectives.[3]   In addition to this difference in numbers, while Grant could choose where and
when to strike, Lee, on the defensive, had to be ready to
resist before the movement was defined.   These facts must
be borne in mind before one can properly estimate the
events of the next weeks, or Lee's part in them.

On the fourth of May the Rapidan was crossed at
Germanna Ford, nine miles east of Lee's position at Mine
Run, and at Ely's Ford four miles farther on.   Grant took
with him supplies for ten days in some four thousand
wagons.   He was prepared for Lee's attack at the fords,
but none was made.   After getting safely over he pushed
south through the Wilderness, hoping through this maneuver to compel Lee to abandon his entrenched position
and to engage him in battle in the open country beyond
the forest.

Only those who have seen the Wilderness can under-

---

[1] Quoted by Fuller, p. 209.

[2] Fuller, p. 223.

[3] *Ibid.*, p. 212.

stand what an inferno it must have been on those spring days that followed. Years before they had mined there for the low-grade ores the little country furnaces used in the production of charcoal iron. The surface is broken with the abandoned pits, and there are numerous little ridges and knolls, and all is covered with a dense undergrowth over which pine and cedar, sweet-gum and oak, lift their tops. There are many little water courses through it and the only roads are winding cow-paths. Except along the main roads that skirt it the artillery could not be employed and cavalry were useless. Regiments stumbled on each other and the enemy by turns, and in the gloomy recesses of the thick forest, as in King Arthur's last great battle in the West, friend fought with friend and foe with foe. To add to the horror the woods took fire. Swinton, the historian of the Army of the Potomac, sums up the awful tale:

"In that horrid thicket there lurked two hundred thousand men and through it lurid fires played: and though no array of battle could be seen, there came out of its depths the crackle and roll of musketry like the noisy boiling of some hell-cauldron that told the dread story of death."[4]

For Lee did not permit Grant to pass safely through and choose his own battle-ground, where his weight of numbers would be compelling. He knew the Wilderness and so did his men. He remembered how Jackson had fallen on Hooker's flank in this same country and almost annihilated him. "He determined, therefore, to co-operate with the country and make use of it to reinforce his weak-

---

[4] Swinton, p. 429.

ness."[5] He had deliberately allowed Grant to pass the Rapidan without attack so that when the immense army and its teams were encountering the difficulties of the forest he could fall upon its flank, pen it up as he had penned up Hooker, and either destroy it or drive it in a tangled rout back to the river. This was his plan as, early on the morning of the fourth, he started out from his lines at Mine Hill. On the morning of the next day Ewell struck at Grant's flank and so began two days of as fierce fighting as the eastern area had ever seen.

By the evening of May sixth both armies were fought to a standstill. Thousands lay in the undergrowth, either dead or wounded, while the fire ran from bank to bank and licked its way up the trees and the smoke choked those who escaped the flame. Neither side could claim victory, yet for the northern army it was a greater prize than Gettysburg. For it was Lee's last great attack on the scale of the earlier days. Henceforth his strategy was purely defensive. His losses were great. Grant's campaign of attrition had begun.

That it did not end in a northern defeat was due to Grant's determination. Had any of the previous commanders of the Army of the Potomac been in his place, with plans foiled and a resolute foe hanging on his flank, retreat across the river would have been the result. But Grant decided to advance. He proposed to continue his march toward Richmond, compelling Lee to follow. The daring that had won at Vicksburg was now moving on Richmond. That, in Sherman's judgment, was the supreme movement in Grant's life. "Undismayed, with a full comprehension of the importance of the work in which he was engaged, feeling as keen a sympathy for the

---

[5]Fuller, p. 231.

dead and wounded as anyone, he gave his orders calmly, specifically and absolutely—'Forward to Spottsylvania.' "[6] The effect on that army that had so often turned back was amazing. They knew they had a leader at last. And Lee knew he had an opponent.

Lee's "eyes" were to serve him again before they were for ever closed soon after. The watchful Stuart saw Grant's wagons starting toward Chancellorsville, and sent the word to Lee who at once guessed Grant's intentions and ordered troops to Spottsylvania. So when Grant's advance reached there they found their way barred with breastworks.

The Bloody Angle of Spottsylvania! That is what many a man in blue and many a man in gray remembered until they sounded taps for him. For three days Grant attempted to find a weak spot in Lee's lines. At length he discovered what he thought was a place which could be carried. In fact it was carried in the first terrific rush of the three divisions that Hancock led. But Lee had his reserves ready and he prepared to lead them himself in place of Gordon. "But these are Virginians and Georgians who have never failed," said Gordon, and turning to the men he cried, "Is it necessary for General Lee to lead this charge?" "No," they answered. "General Lee to the rear. We will drive them back."[7] And drive them back they did. "The sight," said one who was there, "was terrible."[8] Lee had saved the field but at a price he could not afford.

The day before Grant had sent his famous dispatch to Washington: "I propose to fight it out on this line if it

[6] Quoted by Fuller, p. 239.

[7] Fitzhugh Lee, p. 336.

[8] Fuller, p. 253.

takes all summer." And that was not mere heroic madness, though it was bloody. For Lee lost between nine thousand and ten thousand men in the five days' fighting at Spottsylvania. Every man that the Confederacy could gather had to be sent to him. Johnston, with Sherman driving at him, could have no reenforcements. The great plan was succeeding.

But Lee lost more than the men who fell behind the breastworks. At Chancellorsville he had lost his "right arm," Jackson. Now he lost his "eyes," Jeb Stuart. On May ninth Sheridan began one of those brilliant cavalry movements that were to play so large a part in the remainder of the war. With his troopers he started to ride around Lee's flank and rear to Richmond. Stuart threw himself across his road while with a portion of his force he worried Sheridan's rear. Some bitter fighting ensued, but Sheridan was held long enough to allow enough troops to be gathered to man the Richmond defenses. At Yellow Tavern Stuart himself led a charge against the First Michigan regiment. There was a shocking collision, a mêlée of sabers and pistols, and in it Stuart fell. They got him back to Richmond to the home of his sister-in-law, where yellow roses bloomed in the garden behind a low red brick wall.[9] And there he died.

With Grant still hammering at his lines, Lee issued the following order to his army on May 20th:

"Among the gallant soldiers who have fallen in this war, General Stuart was second to none in valor, in zeal, and in unflinching devotion to his country. His achievements form a conspicuous part of the history of this army, with which his name and service will be forever associated. To a military capacity of a high order and to the nobler

---
[9]Thomason, p. 500.

virtues of a soldier he added the brighter graces of a pure life, guided and sustained by the Christian's faith and hope. The mysterious hand of an All-Wise God has removed him from the scene of his usefulness and fame. His grateful countrymen will mourn his loss and cherish his memory. To his comrades in arms he has left the proud recollection of his deeds and the inspiring influence of his example."[10]

The years were bearing heavily on Lee. As one after another of his captains fell his loneliness increased, and the maintenance of the struggle came to rest on him alone. The wonder is he bore it so well and so long.

And back in Richmond they were beginning to see things, and Mrs. Chesnut was writing in her Diary:

"Read today the list of the dead and wounded. One long column was not enough for South Carolina's dead. I see Mr. Federal Secretary Stanton says he can reinforce Suwarrow Grant at his leisure whenever he calls for more. He has just sent him 25,000 veterans. Old Lincoln says in his quaint backwoods way, 'Keep a-peggin'.' Now we can only peg out. What have we left of men, etc., to meet these 'reinforcements as often as reinforcements are called for'? Our fighting men have all gone to the front; only old men and little boys are at home now."[11]

No, there was no one to send twenty-five thousand veterans to Lee and no veterans to send. And he was needing them sorely. Grant's strategy was working better than they yet realized north of Mason and Dixon. But Lee realized—and yet he did not falter.

[10] Fitzhugh Lee, p. 338.
[11] Chesnut, p. 310.

Chapter XXXIII

Petersburg

ALTHOUGH Grant had inflicted heavy losses on Lee he had also suffered heavily himself. So he decided to abandon his attempts on the line at Spottsylvania and to try once more by maneuver to force Lee out of his entrenchments. Again he moved with the utmost secrecy, under the cloak of darkness, only to find Lee with his whole army in front of him. By the twenty-third Lee was in position behind the North Anna ready for any attack that Grant could make. Some of Grant's divisions succeeded in getting across the river, but to no avail. So again Grant withdrew and repeated his march around Lee's right. On June third he made a frontal attack on Lee's position at Cold Harbor, in which he suffered the bloodiest repulse of his career.

On the twelfth he marched off to the James River, and a new phase of the war began. He had covered seventy miles in a month, fighting all the way and, having suffered casualties of 54,929 men, nearly half his effective force at any time, found himself still far from achieving his objective.[1] But he had inflicted heavy casualties. The army with which Lee held the defenses of Petersburg was by no means the army with which he had begun the campaign. Yet in spite of his waning strength the resolution and skill with which Lee addressed himself to his task in that summer of '64 bear testimony to the quality of his generalship. He had forced his opponent time after time

---

[1] Maurice, *Lee*, p. 241.

to accept battle on ground of his choice. He had "co-operated with the country" and through it added materially to his strength. He had foreseen every movement Grant had made and had prepared for it. It was imagination against logic in one of the most astounding struggles this continent has seen.

When Grant started across the Rapidan he had ordered Butler with his Army of the James to move up that river on Richmond. The start was made, but after landing at City Point Butler waited to hear of the results of Grant's advance. At length on the ninth he moved toward Petersburg, but with his usual fatuousness, he refused to listen to the suggestion of his subordinate commanders that he assault at once. Petersburg, before which Grant was to sit for nine months, was but weakly held and could have been taken, but Butler scorned those whom he called "the West Point men" and the assault was not made. Had he carried out his instructions and captured Petersburg, the South Side and Weldon railways would have been at his mercy, materially altering the whole campaign.[2] Instead he made a futile gesture toward Richmond, was repulsed by Beauregard and, falling back, entrenched himself between the James and the Appomattox, where in Grant's phrase, he was "completely bottled up." Butler was one of those liabilities that Lincoln had to carry owing to the exigencies of New England politics. However Lee found his stupidity useful.

Lee seems to have been uncertain as to Grant's movements in the maneuver toward the James. Beauregard was in great danger, and again Petersburg might have fallen. But Smith, whom Grant had sent to attack Petersburg, moved forward cautiously, too cautiously. By the six-

---

[2]Fuller, p. 261.

teenth Lee had discovered Grant's aims and hurried reenforcements to Beauregard and that dashing general kept
up a gallant defense until the main body of Lee's army
came up and things settled down into siege operations.

The struggle of the next nine months was more than
that between armed men, between siege guns and defenses,
between bravery and valor on the one hand and valor and
bravery on the other. It was a struggle between two indomitable wills. There have been comparisons made between Lee as the skilful fencer whose marvelous bladework
and perfect timing were arrayed against Grant's bludgeon
and brutal blind blows. But however the methods of
each may be described, the thing that lay behind the
method was the will that faced the facts and refused to be
beaten. Lee, knowing that the odds were against him,
was playing constantly for time, time to wear out the
North, to defeat Lincoln in the coming election and then
to win peace from the anti-war party. Grant, scorning
the losses, was holding Lee tight while Sherman advanced
toward the sea, and Farragut went forward to Mobile, and
Sheridan swept the valley clean of everything that would
sustain an army. Will against will the struggle went on
for nine long bitter months. When it ended in Lee's
surrender he had only a skeleton of an army to turn over
to the victor and no land left to defend.

That Lee's hopes that through delay he might aid in the
defeat of Lincoln and so make the peace party in the
North dominant were not fatuous may be seen by a glance
at the situation as it existed in that summer of '64. The
people of the North did not know that in the march across
to the James Grant had nearly out-maneuvered Lee, that
but for Butler's stupidity and Smith's later caution he
would have had Petersburg, with Lee's lines of supply en-

THE MILITARY CHIEFTAIN OF THE CONFEDERACY
BRONZE STATUE OF GENERAL R. E. LEE

by Rudolph R. Evans, of Virginia. It is placed in the old
hall of the House of Delegates in Richmond on the exact
spot where Lee received from the Legislature the command
of the Virginia forces.

—Wide World Photo

dangered. All that they seemed to remember was that the lists of casualties were growing larger. Daily before their eyes rose the vision of lives destroyed by bullets and camp diseases, of a vast and ever-growing army of widows and orphans. Lincoln was the "widow-maker" his opponents cried.[3] Many a soldier wrote home, as did Benjamin Sparrow to his Cape Cod cousin from the Petersburg trenches, "Were you to see what this army has to go through you would say God pity the soldier and fortunate are they who die on the field and thereby escape the slow dragging hours of dying by inches."[4] Many distinguished Americans believed and said that the war was a failure. Greeley voiced the growing demand for a peace by understanding. "Peace! Peace!" was the cry that was heard on every hand.

The Democratic National Convention nominated McClellan for president, largely as a bid for the soldier vote, because McClellan was far more popular with the army than Grant, but it permitted Vallandigham, openly known as disloyal, to write the platform declaring the war a failure and demanding peace. Lincoln was the subject of foul abuse and misrepresentation even in his own party. He barely won his renomination and that only through the shrewd political management of the Blairs. And not even his friends dared hope for his reelection. So confident was Davis of the outcome of the campaign against Lincoln and its result for the South that to two unofficial emissaries who came pleading for peace in July he made answer:

"Some weeks ago Grant crossed the Rapidan to whip Lee and take Richmond. Lee drove him back in the

---

[3] *Illinois Centennial History*, Vol. III, p. 326.
[4] Letter in possession of author.

first battle, and then Grant executed what your people call a brilliant flank movement and fought Lee again. Lee drove him a second time, and then Grant made another flank movement and so they kept on, Lee whipping and Grant flanking until Grant got where he is now. And what is the net result? Grant has lost 75,000 or 80,000 men—more than Lee had at the outset—and is no nearer taking Richmond than at first, and Lee, whose front has never been broken, holds him completely in check and has men enough to spare to invade Maryland and threaten Washington. . . . So in a military way I should certainly say that our position was better than yours."[5]

We see things clearly now, but the North saw only in that summer that Lee seemed the master he had so often been before. And had it not been for Sheridan's victories in the Valley and Farragut's at Mobile Bay and Sherman's at Atlanta, Lee's policy of delay might have won. But these victories came in time to swing the North to Lincoln—and then there was to be no peace of surrender by the North. For Grant also had a will such as no northern commander had manifested.

But Lee knew that if the policy of delay failed there was little else for him to do. On July twenty-first he had written Davis:

"I hope your Exc. will put no reliance on what I can do individually, for I feel that will be very little. The enemy has a strong position & is able to deal us more injury than from any other point he has ever taken. Still we must try & defeat them. I fear he will not attack us but advance by regular approaches. He is so situated that I cannot attack him."[6]

---

[5] Rhodes, Vol. IV, p. 515.

[6] *Lee's Confidential Dispatches to Davis*, p. 254.

This is the first admission we find in Lee's dispatches of any doubt as to the outcome through military measures. He could only hold on and hope that the North would beat Lincoln. Grant followed exactly the strategy which he anticipated and advanced "by regular approaches." And so the summer passed on and the winter came. The weapon with which Lee had always won was maneuver, but that weapon had been taken from him.

Chapter XXXIV

The End Draws Near

As THE shadows grew deeper over the Confederacy the thoughts of men turned more and more to Lee. More than any other he stands out in that last dark winter. The failure of Davis grew more apparent with every hour. He was attacked, denounced or ignored. The leaders of the Congress were his active enemies. In December he became desperately ill and the rumor ran that he was dying. Of the military leaders Johnston was in retirement owing to his quarrel with Davis, Bragg had proved a broken reed, and the mad Hood was slowly destroying the Western Army in futile movements. Stuart had fallen at Yellow Tavern and Jackson was long dead. Jones confided to his Diary "the people have no longer any faith in the President, his cabinet, Congress, the commissaries, quartermasters, enrolling officers and most of the generals." [1] But while men were failing everywhere Lee was holding on the Petersburg line. The Army of Northern Virginia was ragged and cold and often very near starvation, but it was still fighting, still confident that it could hold Grant in check and keep him from his goal. The one man who was steadily successful was at its head. Yet he was still subordinate to Davis, Davis who had failed. Why leave him there?

So the talk of a dictator which had been heard before was heard again. Jones, who knew all the back stairs gos-

---

[1] Jones, Vol. II, p. 420.

sip of Richmond, had written on January 2, 1864, "There is talk everywhere on the subject of a dictator and many think a strong government is required to abate the evils we suffer."[2] And again two days later: "On Saturday resolutions were adopted by the senate complimenting General Lee. This is his big opportunity, if he be ambitious, and who can see his heart? What man ever neglected such an opportunity?"[3]

Now the talk began to grow in volume and intensity. A dictator could do things that could not be done by a constitutional government. He could seize private property, particularly foodstuffs and transportation, impress men wherever found, put the negroes into the ranks, in general do everything that was essential, sacrifice everything that was necessary, to get the armies ready for the field by spring. There could be no peace by compromise for Lincoln had been returned to power. European intervention was a dream that was past. Even Gladstone had ceased to compare Davis with Washington. The only hope lay in smashing Sherman and then turning on Grant. To do it a dictator was needed. So they reasoned. And there was only one man who could do it, they reasoned further. That was Lee.

Had Lee been willing there is little question that Davis would have been thrust aside and he given the supreme power. There were many in the Congress who would have welcomed it. It was whispered in Richmond that a group of Congressional leaders had approached him about it. It was a situation that to an ambitious man was pregnant with opportunity. But Lee's ambition did not lie in that direction. He could not bring himself to lift a hand against

[2] *Ibid.*, p. 123.
[3] *Ibid.*, p. 124.

the authority that had been set up by constitutional method. If the cause could not succeed under that authority, then it must fail. He could not do otherwise.

But he would do everything to keep that army fit for the task that lay before it when the grass would spring again. Even though Lincoln had won, another year's delay might raise the courage of those in the North who wanted peace. He became more solicitous than ever for the welfare of his men. No detail seemed too small for him. An old Carolina colonel tells of how on one winter night, with a cold rain falling, as he was making the rounds near Petersburg, he suddenly met Lee on foot accompanied by an aide. "I just wanted to see, Colonel, what shelter your men had tonight."[4]   And his dispatches to Davis are full of demands for the things the men needed. "The soap ration for this Army has become a serious question. . . . The great want of cleanliness which is a necessary consequence of these very limited issues is now producing sickness among the men in the trenches and must effect their self-respect and morale."[5] "Neither meat nor corn are coming over the Southern Roads."[6] So it runs through the winter. Nor was his concern unwarranted. Butler testified that he examined the haversacks of prisoners taken by his men "and found therein, as their rations for three days, scarcely more than a pint of kernels of corn, none of which were broken but only parched to blackness by the fire, and a piece of meat, most frequently raw bacon, some three inches long by an inch and a half wide and less than half an inch thick." And he adds "the lank, emaciated condi-

---

[4]Told to author by his son, Archibald Rutledge.

[5]*Confidential Dispatches*, p. 288.

[6]*Ibid.*, p. 308.

tion of the prisoner fully testified to the meagreness of his means of sustenance."[7]

On the day after "the most inclement day of winter" Lee wrote to the Secretary of War that his troops "were greatly exposed in line of battle two days, had been without meat for three days and in scant clothing took the cold hail and sleet." He reported that there was not a pound of meat at his disposal. And he added: "The physical strength of the men, if their courage survives, must fail under this treatment . . . with these facts, taken in connection with paucity of numbers, you must not be surprised if calamity befalls us."[8] America has more than one Valley Forge. Petersburg is the second.

He was not content with bombarding Davis with dispatches. His wagons scoured the country round for extra supplies. Mrs. Lee, in her invalid chair at Richmond, kept busy knitting socks and sending them to him. He writes her on November thirtieth: "If two or three hundred would send an equal number we should have a sufficiency."[9] It is little wonder that when the South thinks of the war it thinks of Lee, as the North thinks of Lincoln. It was he and he alone that kept that army in the Petersburg lines, that kept the cause alive through that winter. He would not be dictator but he would do what he had been set to do when he drew his sword in defense of Virginia. And all the while Grant's guns kept roaring and his lines crept farther in toward that railroad line that was vital to Lee's very life.

A letter from Mrs. Davis tells of what was in the mind of many: "We are in a sad and anxious state here now.

[7] *Butler's Book*, p. 610.
[8] Fitzhugh Lee, pp. 368-69.
[9] *Ibid.*, p. 365.

The dead come in, but the living do not go out so fast."[10]
Not to Lee's army. Nor were they all dead who left it. Desertion, which began seriously after Gettysburg, now became more than ever a problem. Men can not starve for ever. Lee found it necessary to insist that the death penalty be inflicted. "I think," he wrote to Davis, "a rigid execution of the law is mercy in the end." On the sixth of February, 1865, he was given the empty title of commander-in-chief of all the Confederate armies. Had the appointment come two years earlier it might have meant something, but Davis would not hear of it then. He was still thinking of himself as another Washington. Now there was little for Lee to command save his own army.

About the same time the Confederate Commissioners returned to Richmond from the Hampton Roads Conference with the word that they had failed. The news that Lincoln had refused any terms but surrender aroused a storm of indignation. Then was the time that Davis should have abandoned the thinly held Richmond defenses and allowed Lee to take the field, and draw Grant high up into the country among the hills and mountain spurs, "whose friendly aid he knew so well how to apply."[11] Had he done so the war might have been considerably prolonged. Lee could have been joined by Johnston, and have drawn to him all the detachments in West Virginia, North and South Carolina. He had his plans made for the movement, but Davis would not permit him to carry them out. The Confederacy would live or die with Richmond. Whom the gods would destroy! . . .

Had there been any possibility of his being reenforced sufficiently Lee might have driven Grant into the swamps

---

[10] Chesnut, p. 331.
[11] Long, p. 403.

of the Chickahominy as he had driven McClellan. But Davis knew there was no possibility. His force was slipping away. Night after night more deserters slipped through to the rear. Politics, not strategy, was dictating the end of the war as it had dictated its beginning. Lee had to sit still and watch his army melt away. Some at least in Richmond knew what was happening. Wrote Mrs. Chesnut on March thirtieth, "I pass my days and nights partly at this window. I am sure our army is silently dispersing. Men are moving the wrong way, all the time. They slip by with no songs and no shouts now. They have given the thing up."[12] A week later: "They say General Lee is utterly despondent and has no plan if Richmond goes, as go it must."[13] It was another of those times in which Lord Wolseley said he was "too subservient to the civil authority," and he adds, "it was a great strategic error."[14]

The spring came, the roads were drying out and Sherman was moving north. Late in March Lee learned from one of his spies that Grant was preparing to hold his entrenchments with a skeleton force and move with his main army around the Confederate right flank. He proposed to meet this by a surprise attack on Grant's center at Fort Stedman. General Walker, who shared in the assault on the fort, states that Lee's object was to open the way for a force of cavalry through to City Point and capture Grant himself.[15] Surely no more daring move was planned during the war.

The assault was made, the works were carried, the

---

[12] Chesnut, p. 374.
[13] Ibid., p. 377.
[14] MacMillan's Magazine, Vol. 55, p. 331.
[15] Fuller, p. 344.

surprised garrison made prisoners. Had the supporting column now advanced and seized the hill in the rear of Fort Stedman Grant's army would have been cut in two. But some one failed, and Lee's daring stroke ended in disaster. There ensued a week of fierce fighting in which his forces were still further decimated. Sheridan took forty-five hundred prisoners from Pickett at Five Forks, and the South Side Railroad was now at Grant's mercy. A. P. Hill fell the next day before Petersburg, Hill on whom Lee had relied so often. There was nothing to do but to retreat.

CHAPTER XXXV

The Last March

IT WAS Sunday the second of April, and Jefferson Davis had gone to church as was his custom. It was Communion Sunday, and he had planned to take the Sacrament from the hands of his friend, the Reverend Charles Minnegerode, rector of St. Paul's. The congregation was listening to the sermon when the sexton tiptoed softly up the aisle, his brass buttons gleaming on his faded old blue coat, and handed the President a message. He read it, reached for his hat, and followed the sexton out of the church.

It was a message from General Lee that Richmond must be evacuated that day. He could hold on no longer. He had ordered his trains to Amelia Court House where he meant to reassemble his army and from there move on to Danville, so that he might join Johnston. He telegraphed the Secretary of War: "It will be a difficult operation, but I hope not impractical."[1] Truly difficult, for the enemy were pressing hard, feeling that the end was near at last. That night his troops slipped out of their lines, leaving behind everything that could not be swiftly moved, and the morning found them heading south along the roads to Appomattox.

They were pleasant country roads, those country roads of Virginia, crossing many a little river, passing many a pleasant field where the spring flowers were blooming, by many a tangled wood where the spring birds sang. But

[1] Schaff, p. 37.

they were not thinking of the beauty of them that day, that harried, hurried host pressing on to escape the blue horsemen that followed after. Harried yes, but not afraid. One who helped to lead them as they began that retreat declared they were "buoyant in spirit, brave in heart, and of undoubted morale . . . and they followed Lee with an almost childlike faith, which set no bounds to his genius and power of achievement."[2]

All day long they pressed on, and Tuesday morning found them at Amelia Court House, where Lee had ordered that supplies be sent from Richmond. But no supplies were there, and as Lee wrote to Davis in reporting the surrender six days later: "Not finding the supplies ordered to be placed at Amelia Court House, nearly twenty-four hours were lost in endeavoring to collect in the country subsistence for men and horses. The delay was fatal and could not be retrieved."[3] Some one had blundered at Richmond in the excitement of getting away from that doomed city. And Sheridan had time to come up and join Ord.

But it was not only twenty-four hours that were lost. A drizzling rain fell all the day, and the men were wet and hungry. That night they began to slip away. "At morning roll-call," says the historian of a Richmond battery, "a number of men did not answer their names."[4] And an officer of cavalry says that on reaching his regiment on Wednesday morning, "I beheld the first signs of dissolution of that grand army which had endured every hardship of march and camp with unshaken fortitude, when looking over the hills I saw swarms of stragglers moving in every

---

[2]Fitzhugh Lee, p. 381.
[3]*Ibid.*, p. 383.
[4]Schaff, p. 76.

direction."⁵ Not even morale can stand against the inevitable.

Speed was now a vital necessity, but the rain continued to fall, and the streams rose and had to be bridged. The mud, that heavy Virginia mud, grew deeper, so that the wheels sank to the hubs, and it was almost impossible to move the trains. The horses, thin and almost exhausted, floundered along in the mud, and the men plodded beside them. It is no wonder that so many deserted. It is rather a wonder that any persisted. We have no record of what Lee thought as he found Sheridan in front of him and turned back to bivouac at Amelia Springs. No rations at Amelia Court House, his enemy across his way! Did he see the doom of his hopes as he sat that night looking into the fire and planned the movement for the coming day?

The next morning he arose early and wrote a dispatch to Gordon: "I hope the rear will get out of harm's way, and I rely greatly upon your exertions and good judgment for its safety."⁶ There were few left on whom he could rely. And Gordon did not fail him that day. Then he took the road toward Farmville, for the last march of the Army of Northern Virginia. On that road "as the sun was going down, the Confederacy, under Sheridan's mortal wounds sighed out its last hope."⁷ For Ewell, after desperate fighting, was forced to surrender. The news came to Lee as with Mahone he rode off to find why Ewell had not come up. They ran into a disordered mass of men fleeing before the northern cavalry, hurrying teamsters with teams and no wagons, retreating infantry without their guns, men without hats. "Lee at the sight of the spectacle," says Mahone, "straightened himself in

⁵ *Ibid.*, p. 77.
⁶ *Ibid.*, p. 77.
⁷ *Ibid.*, p. 94.

the saddle and exclaimed as if talking to himself, 'My God! has the army dissolved!' "[8]

Yet he would not give up although events were forcing him. The next morning early General Wise, one of the little band that had forced Virginia into the war, came to his quarters, demanding as vehemently that he end the struggle as once he had urged its beginning.

"Ah, General, do not talk so wildly," answered Lee. "My burdens are heavy enough. What would the country think of me if I did what you suggest?" "Country be damned!" was the quick reply. "There has been no country, General, for a year or more. You are the country to these men. They have fought for you. They have shivered through a long winter for you. Without pay or clothes, or care of any sort, their devotion to you and faith in you have been the only things that held this army together. If you demand the sacrifice, there are still left thousands of us who will die for you. You know the game is desperate beyond redemption, and that if you so announce, no man or government or people will gainsay your decision. That is why I repeat the blood of any man killed hereafter is upon your head."[9]

Still he pushed on. He would not yield yet. The sun came out at noon and the wet bedraggled men were warm again. They marched, then stopped to fight as their determined pursuers came up, stopped long enough to get the wagons ahead, and then followed. It is an epic tale, heroic resistance, dogged pursuit, on until the night brought rest. His staff noticed that Lee exposed himself unsparingly to fire. He sat on Traveller on the brow of a hill watching the foe as he attacked. He rebuked a staff officer for un-

---

[8] *Ibid.*, p. 112.
[9] Wise, pp. 434-35.

necessarily exposing himself. When the officer reminded him that he was exposed he answered a bit sharply, "It is mv duty to be here. I must see."[10]

During the afternoon Grant had talked to some of his officers about the propriety of sending a note to Lee suggesting surrender. That evening when he knew from Sheridan that he would soon be across Lee's path, he sent him the following.

"Headquarters, Armies of the United States
"April 7, 1865—5 P.M.
"General R. E. Lee, Commanding C. S. Army:

"General: The results of the last week must convince you of the hopelessness of further resistance on the part of the Army of Northern Virginia in this struggle. I feel that this is so, and regard it as my duty to shift from myself the responsibility of any further effusion of blood, by asking of you the surrender of that portion of the Confederate Southern army known as the Army of Northern Virginia.

"Very respectfully,
"Your obedient servant,
"U. S. GRANT,
"Lieutenant-general, Commanding
"Armies of the United States."[11]

Before Lee received this note a group of his own officers approached him with the word that in their opinion further resistance was useless. He answered:

"Oh no, I trust it has not come to that. We have yet too many bold men to think of laying down our arms. . . . Besides, if I were to say a word to the Federal Commander

---

[10] Long, p. 415.
[11] *Ibid.*, p. 418.

he would regard it as such a confession of weakness as to make it the condition of demanding unconditional surrender—a proposal to which I will never listen."[12]

When Grant's note reached him he replied that he did not entertain the opinion therein expressed as to the hopelessness of the situation, and "therefore before considering your proposition ask the terms you will offer on condition of its surrender." Grant's reply was most conciliatory, yet Lee still hoped to be able to cut through. On the evening of the eighth he held his last council of war. It met in the woods near his headquarters. There were no camp chairs left and the men sat on blankets or saddles about the fire. There were present Longstreet and Gordon, commanding what was left of that immortal infantry, Fitzhugh Lee of the cavalry, and Pendleton, chief of artillery. The letters of Grant and the replies were read. The situation was discussed from every angle. "If all that was said and felt at that meeting could be given it would make a volume of measureless pathos. In no hour of the great War did General Lee's masterful characteristics appear to me so conspicuous as they did in that last council."[13]

It was decided to make another attempt to cut through Grant's lines at daybreak. Gordon tells how, as he rode away from the meeting, he directed one of his staff to return and ask Lee as to where he should halt for the night if he got away. His answer was, "Tell General Gordon that I shall be glad for him to halt just beyond the Tennessee line." And the gray eyes must have twinkled as he said it, weary as he was. "His purpose," says Gordon, "was to let me infer that there was little hope for our escape . . . but

---

[12] Ibid., p. 417.
[13] Gordon, p. 435.

that if we should succeed he expected me to press toward the goal in the mountains."[14]

The audacious movement began at dawn. Gordon afterward was to say, "I take great pride in recording the fact that the last charge of the war was made by the footsore and starving men of my command with a spirit worthy the best days of Lee's army."[15] They even captured two pieces of artillery. But it was all in vain. They carried the word to Lee, and when he received the message he said, "Then there is nothing for me to do but to go and see General Grant, and I would rather die a thousand deaths."[16] Let his aide tell the rest of the story.

"Convulsed with passionate grief, many were the wild words which we spoke as we stood around him. Said one, 'Oh, General, what will history say of the surrender of the army in the field?' He replied, 'Yes, I know they will say hard things of us; they will not understand how we were overwhelmed by numbers. But that is not the question, Colonel: the question is, Is it right to surrender this army? If it is right, then I will take all the responsibility.' "[17]

But he was not yet sure. He wanted the word of Longstreet, who had dared so often to disagree with him. So Longstreet came, and noticed that his chief's "brave bearing failed to conceal his profound depression."[18] Lee told him of the situation in which the army was and asked for his view. "I asked," writes Longstreet, "if the bloody sacrifice of his army could in any way help the cause in

---

[14] *Ibid.*, p. 436.
[15] *Ibid.*, p. 436.
[16] Long, p. 421.
[17] *Ibid.*, p. 422.
[18] Longstreet, p. 624.

other quarters. He thought not. 'Then,' I said, 'your situation speaks for itself.' "[19]

In spite of all this it was not easy for Lee to yield. Remember how with proud defiance after that tragic day at Antietam he had held his ground among the dead as though he dared his adversary to strike again. And also after Gettysburg, as though no matter how great his losses, he would defy Meade to attack. Men who do so such things do not yield easily. But now there was nothing else to do.

[19] *Ibid.,* p. 625.

Chapter XXXVI

Appomattox

WHEN the Army of Northern Virginia marched out of the Petersburg lines it numbered approximately twenty-six thousand men. When, a week later, it stood surrounded by the northern forces at Appomattox Court House it totaled only a little more than ten thousand effectives. Lee's report to Davis announcing the surrender declares, "There were 7,892 organized infantry with arms, with seventy-five rounds of ammunition per man. I have no accurate report of the cavalry, but believe it did not exceed 2100 effective men."[1] "That ghost of an Army," the correspondent of a Richmond paper called it in his account of that eventful Sunday. Death, hunger and desertion had done their worst.

America, young as it is, has witnessed some dramatic moments. But few are more dramatic than the one that took place on that Sunday morning, April 9, 1865. The scene was the simple brick house of a Virginia farmer in a sleepy little Virginia village. The principals were the leaders of the greatest armies that had ever fought upon this continent in the bitterest struggle the land had ever known. There was no display of pomp, no pride of victory. Could some one from a land afar suddenly have been called on to witness the scene he would have thought the victor the conquered and he who was laying down his arms the leader of the successful host. It was a scene of

[1] Long, p. 424.

strange contrasts, and whatever Robert Lee may have thought he bore himself with a greater calm than he to whom he surrendered. He dressed himself with the greatest care that Sunday morning, putting on a new gray uniform, snowy linen, and a handsome sword and sash that a blockade runner had brought in, the gift of some English ladies who sympathized with his cause. His high boots also were new and "stitched with red silk" and his spurs were large and gleaming. When General Pendleton rode up to his headquarters and expressed his surprise at his appearance he answered, "I have probably to be General Grant's prisoner and I thought I must make my best appearance."[2] One of his aides told General Porter that they had been forced to abandon their baggage and those who had more than one suit of clothes put on the best and destroyed the rest.[3]

Grant met him dressed, as he had been through the pursuit, in a private's blouse with nothing to indicate his rank but the shoulder straps. He wore no sword, and his trousers were tucked in ordinary boots, well-covered with mud. When he left camp that morning he had not expected the end so soon. He declares in his *Memoirs*:[4] "I must have contrasted very strangely with a man so handsomely dressed," and adds, "that was not a matter that I thought of till afterward." Yet in a conversation that he had with Dr. Fordyce Barker after the war, he confessed that he was afraid that Lee might imagine that he intended a discourtesy to him because of the incident in Mexico when Lee at headquarters had rebuked him for his appearance. This incident, said the General, suddenly flashed across his

[2]Lee, *Pendleton*, p. 404.
[3]Porter, p. 474.
[4]Grant, Vol. II, p. 490.

mind and "made him uncomfortable lest General Lee should recall it also and imagine that he intended to affront him."[5] It is not likely that Lee thought this, but it is also unlikely that he failed to remember that earlier meeting.

They met in a house belonging to Wilmer McLean. The first great battle of the war had opened near his former home beside Bull Run. The owner had left it to get away from the movements of armies. And now his home was the scene of the last great act in the tragedy whose beginning he had witnessed. The time was noon. Lee and his aides were the first to arrive, and Grant shortly followed. He extended his hand saying, "General Lee," and they shook hands, and began to talk about old army times. "Our conversation," wrote Grant, "grew so pleasant that I almost forgot the object of our meeting."[6] Lee had to call his attention to that object. Whereupon Grant stated the terms he had in mind, that the Army of Northern Virginia should lay down its arms, not to take them up again unless properly exchanged.

Again the talk wandered off into other fields, and again Lee had to interrupt with the suggestion that Grant write out the terms he proposed. When Lee had read them over he remarked with some feeling that this would have a happy effect on his army. He asked for rations for his men and rode away. There was no mention of the handing over of his sword, nor any offer of it. As one reads the stories of those who witnessed it Lee seems the one unruffled person in the room, with Grant so solicitous to soften the blow by every possible means that his usual calmness had left him. And when one turns to the tale of the horrid years that followed, when those who had been safe behind

---

[5] Page, *Lee*, p. 250.
[6] Grant, Vol. II, p. 490.

the lines carried on a contemptible war on a helpless people, it is good to think of that scene in Wilmer McLean's parlor, and of the considerateness that made that difficult hour easier than it might have been had a lesser man controlled it.

When the word reached Grant's troops of the ending of it all the batteries began to fire salutes. Immediately an orderly was sent to order the guns to cease firing, Grant saying as he sent him: "The war is over, the rebels are our countrymen again; and the best sign of rejoicing after the victory will be to abstain from all demonstrations in the field."[7]   But not even Grant could stop the cheering. They had been anxious too long to keep them quiet then. And Cyrus Harper wrote to his mother back in West Virginia, "We cheered and the Johnnies cheered at a desperate rate, they were as well pleased as we were."[8]   Perhaps that sturdy soldier missed the meaning of the Johnnies' cheers. As Lee, after his meeting with Grant, rode along his lines, so runs a yellowing newspaper story, "there arose and ran along its length the same old familiar huzzas, not sonorous and deep as when poured from tens of thousands of manly throats, but still breathed from hearts that were stout and true, and the hills and woodlands of Appomattox caught up and reechoed the last huzzas of that army, shouted forth in its last hours, in recognition of its beloved commander, revered in adversity as he was revered in victory."[9]   Well might they cheer him. Under his leadership, as the *London Times* declared, "they were victorious until victory could no longer be achieved by human valor and then they fell with honor."[10]

That night he wrote his last order, taking leave of his

---

[7] Porter, p. 486.
[8] Letter in possession of author.
[9] Old Scrap-Book.
[10] *London Times*, April 24, 1865.

army. And in the morning he rode off to Richmond with some half-dozen of his staff. He entered the city without display and took the shortest route to his house, trying to avoid all public demonstrations. But the word spread that he was coming. The sidewalks filled with people and cheers followed his passing. Except for an occasional bow he gave no sign or token of the things that were passing in his mind. He raised his hat as he ascended the steps of his rented house, bade his staff good-by and passed within. The days of his warring were done.

And these are his last words to his army:

"Headquarters Army of Northern Virginia,
"April 10, 1865.

"After four years of arduous service, marked by unsurpassed courage and fortitude, the Army of Northern Virginia has been compelled to yield to overwhelming numbers and resources. I need not tell the survivors of so many hard-fought battles, who have remained steadfast to the last, that I have consented to this result from no distrust of them; but feeling that valor and devotion could accomplish nothing that could compensate for the loss that would have attended the continuation of the contest, I have determined to avoid the useless sacrifice of those whose past services have endeared them to their countrymen. By the terms of agreement, officers and men can return to their homes and remain there until exchanged. You will take with you the satisfaction that proceeds from the consciousness of duty faithfully performed; and I earnestly pray that a merciful God will extend to you his blessing and protection. With an unceasing admiration of your constancy and devotion to your country, and a grateful remembrance of your kind and generous consideration of myself, I bid you an affectionate farewell.
"R. E. LEE, General."[11]

---

[11] Fitzhugh Lee, p. 396.

PART THREE

THE YEARS OF REBUILDING

CHAPTER XXXVII

The New Struggle

WHEN Robert E. Lee rode away from Appomattox, where he had surrendered the remnants of his once invincible army, life seemed to have little left for him. He was a beaten soldier. The laurels he had won in the Seven Days, at Fredericksburg, and at Chancellorsville had withered since the Wilderness. Men were not calmly weighing then the splendor of that last defense. That was to come later. Now the door to preferment in his profession was closed— and for ever. He was bankrupt. He who had known affluence was to know it no more. Everything he possessed had been confiscated or destroyed. Arlington was already the shrine of the nation's warrior dead, and the White House on the Pamunkey was in ruins. And he was denied the right to seek that political preferment to which many less able soldiers turned. He died disfranchised, a prisoner on parole.

Only one thing remained for him, to toil with all his power in the rebuilding of Virginia. In this he had to deal with a discouraged and impoverished people who, not having the vision he had, could not understand what he was trying to do or why he was trying to do it. And he had a body which had suffered from the rigors of the war years and that weakened further under the strain. But the same spirit which had compelled him to resign his commission in the old army because Virginia demanded it, caused him to do the thing which was to occupy his remaining years, and which was to open for him what is in many ways the most glorious phase of his career.

There is every evidence that his obligation in this matter had been carefully thought out before the surrender, when in those last months in Petersburg he saw the inevitable draw near. He had told Grant the day after Appomattox that "he should devote his whole efforts to pacifying the country and bringing the people back to the Union."[1] Grant had urged him at that time to suggest to Davis that armed resistance should be ended on all fronts,[2] and while he felt that he could not go that far there is no question that his surrender had the same effect. With that surrender he became at once in his own mind a citizen of the United States. In one of the few interviews he ever gave, that given to a correspondent of the *New York Herald* on April twenty-sixth, the interviewer notes: "It was a most noticeable feature of the conversation that General Lee, strange as it may appear, talked throughout as a citizen of the United States. He seemed to plant himself on the national platform and take his observations from that standpoint."[3] It was not strange to him. Virginia had led him out of the Union. Now Virginia was back. So was he. His task was to spend the remainder of his life and all of his powers in aiding Virginia to fit herself anew, after the weariness and waste of war, for that place.

It need hardly be said that it was a difficult task, perhaps more difficult than that he had faced as commander of the Army of Northern Virginia. And there was no romance in it, no blare of bugles, no battle flags fluttering in the

---

[1] O. R., Vol. XCVII, p. 716.
[2] Porter, p. 491.
[3] *New York Herald,* April 29, 1865.

breeze. But it was conflict, just as real as in the battle years, against foes not easily overthrown, against conditions difficult to face, against deeply implanted hatreds, against the misunderstanding of old comrades, against all the dreadful aftermath of war. Never was he more the soldier than in those days of peace, as the clouds thickened over the South-land and the malice of old Stevens of the twisted foot and his followers vented itself in shameful deeds, darker than slavery itself. He did not live to see the end of the fighting, but this was a war that he helped to win.

It is almost impossible for those who have never seen a land over which armies have passed and where battles have been fought to understand the condition of Virginia in that spring of '65. Everything that he had feared for his land in those weeks of indecision had happened. The great houses by the slow rivers lay in ruins, the fields were weed-grown and brush-covered, the slave cabins in large measure deserted, their late occupants scattered as wind-blown leaves. The mills had known Sheridan's torch. There were no mails, no public conveyances, no banks, no money.[4] The whole economic structure was destroyed and the people knew not where to turn. Virginia and the whole South was full of the prophets of despair. They had staked their all on a dream and the dream was done. "Our hopes have fled," wrote one editor, "and we sit in darkness. The nemesis of God has indeed involved us in a frightful vortex." And from almost every home at least one had gone never to come back and often he was the breadwinner.

And the hatreds he had to meet! They of the South were a proud people. Such do not lightly bear defeat.

[4] Lee, *Pendleton*, p. 408.

And armies are not gentle things. They who had suffered from them did not forget easily. While the men were fighting, the women had to sit still and endure. One of them had written in her Diary in '64:

"These plunderers have nearly ruined Cousin Mann. They have taken his corn, killed his hogs and sheep, driven off his horses and cattle, leaving him only six hundred acres of bare ground—literally and truly bare, for they have trampled and killed the very grass. I think the prophet Joel had the Yankees in mind when he said: 'The land is as the garden of Eden before them and behind them a desolate wilderness, yea, and nothing shall escape them.' "[5]

It is not to be wondered at that they did not forget these things in '65. And it is not to be wondered at that one of them should begin his will with the following:

"1st. I give and bequeath to my children and grand-children and their descendants throughout all future generations, the bitter hatred and everlasting malignity of my heart and soul, against the Yankees, including all the people north of Mason and Dixon's line, and I do hereby exhort and entreat my children and grandchildren, if they have any love or veneration for me, to instil into the hearts of their children and grandchildren and all their future descendants from their childhood, this bitter hatred and this malignant feeling against the aforesaid people and their descendants throughout all future time and generations."[6]

Extreme, of course, but there were enough who felt that way to make Lee's task difficult.

[5] *Magazine of Lees of Virginia*, September, 1928, p. 49.
[6] Will of J. G. B. Brown, November 22, 1866. On file Hanover Court House, Virginia.

ARLINGTON

From a water-color sketch made by Benson F. Lossing in 1856

LEE AND JACKSON

From Stone Mountain Memorial

Hardest to bear was the misunderstanding of his old comrades. Beauregard wrote him a sharp criticism of his course. He answered:

"I need not tell you that true patriotism sometimes requires a man to act exactly contrary at one period to that which he does at another, and the motive which impels them, the desire to do right, is precisely the same. The circumstances which govern their actions change, and their conduct must conform to the new order of things. History is full of illustrations of this: Washington himself is an example of this. At one time he fought against the French, under Braddock, in the service of the King of Great Britain; at another, he fought with the French at Yorktown, under the orders of the Continental Congress of America, against him. He has not been branded by the world with reproach for this, but his course has been applauded." [7]

But in spite of all these things he kept to the course he had laid down. He tells Commodore Maury: "The thought of abandoning the country and all that must be left in it is abhorrent to my feelings and I prefer to struggle for its restoration and share its fate rather than to give up all as lost, and Virginia has need for all her sons." [8] When Jubal Early planned his book on his campaigns Lee wrote: "I would recommend, however, that while giving facts which you think necessary for your own vindication, you omit all epithets or remarks calculated to excite bitterness or animosity between different sections of the country." [9] But he was not content with urging the end of bitterness. He advised his soldiers "to qualify themselves

---

[7] Long, p. 457.
[8] Page, *Lee*, 264.
[9] Long, p. 458.

to vote and elect wise and patriotic men who will devote
their abilities to the interests of the country and the heal-
ing of all dissensions."[10] When young Captain Wise took
the oath before the Provost-Marshal his father, the ex-
Governor, burst out: "You have disgraced the family!"
"But General Lee advised me to do it." "Oh, that alters
the case. Whatever General Lee says is all right, I don't
care what it is."[11]

Imagination staggers when we think what might have
happened had he followed another course, had he fanned
the flames of hatred. The South suffered terribly as it
was in those dreadful days of Reconstruction. But had
the war degenerated into guerrilla fighting, as it might
easily have done, the South would have been swept with
fire and sword and the North covered with everlasting
dishonor. More than any other factor in the prevention
of this was the influence of Robert E. Lee, because he was
the one leader of the South who could exercise decisive influence. In those days, just after his flight, Davis's influence was gone. Lee stood supreme.

What an ally he would have found had Lincoln lived!
For the darkest hour of the South was not when Richmond
was evacuated or when Lee surrendered at Appomattox.
The darkest hour was when Lincoln fell. And the mad-
dest deed that ever was done in this America was when
that addled actor thought to strike a blow for the South
and instead struck at her. Well might Davis call it "the
last crowning calamity of a despairing and defeated though
righteous cause."[12] For Lincoln had he lived would have

---

[10] *R. and L.*, p. 163.

[11] Avary, p. 70.

[12] *Prison Life of Jefferson Davis* (Diary, August 20, 1865), Carleton Co., N. Y.,
1866.

rendered Stevens impotent and held back the flood of malignant hatred of the Radicals who had never fired a gun in battle. Lincoln knew the South. While he had fought it with all his power he would have saved it from much that it had afterward to suffer.

On the night after Lee's surrender something happened that showed the drift of Lincoln's mind. Washington was ablaze with excitement. Throngs surrounded the White House madly calling for a speech. When at length Lincoln appeared he said he had no speech ready, but he added, " 'I have always thought "Dixie" one of the best tunes I ever heard. I insisted yesterday that we had fairly captured it. I presented the question to the Attorney-General and he gave his opinion that it is our lawful prize. I ask the band to give us a good turn upon it.' In that little speech he claimed of the South by right of conquest a song—nothing more."[13]

His last speech to his Cabinet on the morning of the day of his assassination made it very plain that he meant what he said in his Second Inaugural, that his task should be "to bind up the wounds of the nation." He told them, "I hope there will be no persecution, no bloody work, after the war is over. No one need expect me to take any part in hanging or killing these men. Enough lives have been sacrificed; we must extinguish our resentments if we expect harmony and union."[14]

Had Lincoln lived to carry out his plans the man who had outwitted him in his quest for Richmond those long years would have been the man who would have aided most in the shaping of the new day and the new order. But Booth's bullet made that impossible. Lee had to plow

---

[13] Avary, p. 43.
[14] Nicolay and Hay, Vol. X, p. 283.

his furrow alone. How well he plowed let one of Lincoln's successors tell:

"He stood the hardest of all strains, the strain of bearing himself well through the gray evening of failure, and therefore out of what seemed failure he helped build the wonderful and mighty triumph of our national life, in which all his countrymen, North and South, share."[15]

[15] Roosevelt, in the *Sewanee Review*, 1907.

Chapter XXXVIII

The Weeks of Waiting

LEE on his return to Richmond continued to occupy the rented house on Franklin Street where his family had lived during the war. It now became the Mecca of many. They came to view the Capital of the Confederacy and the famous soldier who had so long defended it. Among these were many Union officers, impelled by a genuine admiration for his professional skill. With them came Meade. "The years are telling on you, Meade," Lee said, "your hair is getting gray." "No it is not the years, General. You are responsible for my gray hairs."[1]

An old sergeant, plainly Irish and plainly also a "regular," appeared one day followed by a negro bearing a huge basket of provisions saying that he had been with "the Colonel" in the old Second Cavalry, that he heard he was in want and that as long as he had a cent his Colonel should not suffer. It was difficult to persuade him that "the Colonel" was not in want, but he submitted reluctantly to the compromise suggestion that the basket should go to the hospital.[2]

One deputation came following the report that Lee was to be indicted for treason. Two tattered Confederates knocked at his door with the word that they represented "sixty other fellows around the corner who are too ragged to come themselves." They offered him a house and a

---

[1] Young, p. 326.
[2] R. and L., p. 159.

farm in the mountains of Virginia with a defile near by
"where he could defy the whole Northern army." He
had to decline the offer, but the loyalty behind it moved
him deeply.[3]

But he could not stay in Richmond. His wife's declining health caused him deep anxiety. He felt that he had
to get her away from the city to some quiet place, to get
away himself where he would not be the center of so much
attention. He wrote General Long, "I am looking for
some little quiet house in the woods where I can procure
shelter and my daily bread."[4] Early in June he mounted
Traveller and went for a visit to his kinsman, Colonel
Carter, at his plantation on the Pamunkey River. With
true Virginia hospitality the neighbors entertained him
with the accustomed groaning tables. Driving home from
such a feast he said to his host, "Thomas, there was enough
dinner today for twenty people. All this will now have
to be changed; you cannot afford it; we shall have to
practice economy."[5]

Late in June he moved his family by canal boat to Cumberland County to a small cottage which with the land
attached had been placed at his disposal by Mrs. Edmund
Randolph Cocke. That night on the boat the captain
offered him the most comfortable bed he had, but he preferred to sleep on deck with his military cloak covering
him. That was the last night, doubtless, that he ever spent
under the open sky.[6] Settled in the country, he had some
weeks of quiet, riding Traveller daily, sometimes taking
long trips and renewing old friendships, on Sunday wor-

---

[3] Long, p. 439.
[4] *Ibid.*, p. 439.
[5] *R. and L.*, p. 168.
[6] *Ibid.*, p. 171.

shiping in the little country church, and resting. It was a haven of delight after the urgent years.

But he was not allowed to be alone and quiet for long. An English nobleman offered him a mansion and an estate "commensurate with his individual merits and the greatness of an historic family."[7] Offers of land, of corporation stock in return for his endorsement, of positions in the business world that would have made his situation easy, poured upon him. The latter he would not take because he felt he was not fitted to perform their duties. The former—gratuities of any sort—he simply could not receive.

His father had written his record of the earlier war in which he had borne a part. Now he planned to do the same thing. He wrote to many of his old officers asking for any documents in their possession that would help him. He also made a request of the War Department in Washington for permission to copy such documents as might help him in this work, but Stanton was not Lincoln and the request was refused. The obstacles in the way proved insurmountable, and he gradually gave up the idea.

President Johnson issued in June a proclamation of a limited amnesty to the leaders of the Confederacy. Acting under this proclamation Lee made application for amnesty, and sending it through General Grant he reminded the latter that under the terms of the surrender his former soldiers were "protected by the United States Government from molestation so long as they conformed to its conditions."[8] In spite of this he had been indicted for treason along with Davis by a Norfolk grand jury.

[7] Long, p. 439.

[8] R. and L., p. 164.

Grant forwarded his letter to Stanton with a rather sharp endorsement:

"In my opinion the officers and men paroled at Appomattox Court House and since, upon the same terms given to Lee, cannot be tried for treason so long as they observe the terms of their parole. This is my understanding. Good faith, as well as true policy, dictates that we should observe the conditions of that convention. Bad faith on the part of the Government, or a construction of that convention subjecting the officers to a trial for treason, would produce a feeling of insecurity in the minds of all the paroled officers and men. If so disposed they might even regard such an infraction of terms by the Government as an entire release from all obligations on their part. I will state further that the terms granted by me met with the hearty approval of the President at the time, and of the country generally."

Such plain speaking had its effect. Not even Stanton dared stand out against the sturdy soldier. The indictment was quashed, but the recommendation Grant added, that amnesty be granted his great opponent, was never acted upon. Yet in 1869 we find Lee urging "all our young men to qualify as citizens," and vote at the elections, "although I am denied that privilege."

So the summer passed. Then in August came Judge Brockenbrough, in a borrowed suit of clothes, because he had none of his own that were fit to wear, to offer him the chance to do the thing he had been waiting for. This was the Presidency of Washington College.

Chapter XXXIX

Washington College

WASHINGTON COLLEGE was the outgrowth of one of those log colleges which we find wherever the Scotch-Irish Presbyterian stock settled and made their homes. It was begun in 1749 under the shadow of the Blue Ridge in the Valley of Virginia among a people who were to be among the first to espouse the cause of independence, and its founder was Robert Alexander, an Edinburgh University man. In 1776 it received a new name, typical of the time, Liberty Hall. Its head for twenty years was the Reverend William Graham, a classmate of Light Horse Harry Lee in Princeton. Year after year Graham sent out into the service of the rising commonwealths beyond the mountains and into the towns of the Valley men who, as theologians, statesmen, lawyers and teachers, shaped the thought and life of their time. The school steadily grew until it attracted the attention of George Washington.

In 1785 the legislature of Virginia tendered to Washington, as a testimonial to the service he had rendered, certain shares in two canal companies. He accepted these shares only on condition that he be permitted "to turn the destination of the fund invested in me from my private emoluments to objects of a public nature." To this school in the West he transferred this gift, writing the Trustees at the same time that "to promote literature in this rising empire and to encourage the arts have been ever among the warmest wishes of my heart." This gift added fifty thousand dollars to the school's endowment, and its name was changed to Washington College.

The outbreak of the Civil War found this college in a flourishing condition. But the war years were sad years for Washington College as for everything else in Virginia. Its students were in the armies and its exercises were suspended. The crowning calamity came with General Hunter's occupation of Lexington in June, 1864. The minutes of the Board of Trustees contain the following report written on August 4, 1864, by Professor Campbell, then clerk of the faculty:

"We regret that we are compelled to report the buildings in a very dilapidated condition. This has arisen, in part, from their having been, to so great an extent, unoccupied, and consequently exposed more than usual to the depredations of mischievous boys. But the damage previously done was greatly increased by the conduct of Hunter's Army while they occupied the town. By them all closed doors were broken open, window glass and sash were smashed to pieces, and preparations were made for burning the buildings, which is said to have been prevented by the timely intervention of Capt. David A. Moore, a member of your board. A large part of the fencing was destroyed, but the damage done by the invaders to the fencing and to the external parts of the buildings, is trifling compared with what was done within. . . . The doors of the Laboratory were broken open and every article it contained either broken or carried off. Not only were bottles of Chemicals and apparatus generally broken to pieces and strewn on the floor, but the glass and sash of all the cases arranged around the rooms, were entirely demolished: while the windows to some extent shared the same fate. The whole presents a scene of desolation and destruction which could not easily be surpassed."[1]

---

[1] Minute Book, Trustees Washington College, pp. 374-75.

In addition to all this its invested funds were gone. A bankrupt institution, with shattered equipment, it seemed as though its future was behind it, that is to every one except the Board of Trustees who with indomitable Scotch-Irish pluck met on August 4, 1865, four months after the surrender, to consider ways in which they might reestablish it. Several names were discussed for the presidency, and the Board seemed ready to take a vote.

But before the vote could be taken, Colonel Christian said that he wanted to make a statement. A friend of his who was also a friend of Miss Mary Lee had recently told him that Miss Lee had said that while the southern people seemed willing and eager to give her father everything he needed, no offer had yet been made by which he could do the thing he wanted most, earn a living for himself and his family. One after another of the Board members declared that it would be a great thing if General Lee could be secured to head the college, but that it seemed presumption to think he would take the place. At length Colonel Christian after repeated urging made the nomination and immediately all other names were withdrawn and the election was unanimous.[2]

Even then the Board was afraid that it had acted rashly. "How could they announce to the world that they had elected to the presidency of a broken-down college the greatest man in the South?" they asked one another. After further discussion Judge Brockenbrough, the rector, was chosen to represent the Board and to present the case in person. But the Judge declared, as he glanced down at his well-worn clothes, that he could not enter General Lee's presence dressed as he was, that those were the best clothes he had, and that he had no money to buy others.

---

[2] *Lee after Appomattox*, pp. 1-2.

Another member offered the Judge a suit of broadcloth that had been sent him by one of his sons who lived in the North, the Board borrowed the money for his journey from a lady who had just sold her tobacco crop, and thus equipped he set out.

The offer was a complete surprise to General Lee. He had already declined the vice-chancellorship of the University of the South at Sewanee in Tennessee, but this would keep him in Virginia. After several days spent in consideration of the matter he wrote the following letter to the college authorities.

"Powhatan Co. 24 Aug. '65.

"Gentlemen:

"I have delayed for some days, replying to your letter of the 5 inst. informing me of my election by the Board of Trustees to the Presidency of Washington College, from a desire to give the subject due consideration. Fully impressed with the responsibilities of the office I have feared that I should be unable to discharge its duties to the satisfaction of the Trustees or to the benefit of the Country. The proper education of youth requires not only great ability but, I fear, more strength than I now possess, for I do not feel able to undergo the labour of conducting classes in regular courses of instruction. I could not therefore undertake more than the general administrative supervision of the institution. There is another subject which had caused me serious reflection and is, I think, worthy of the consideration of the Board. Being excluded from the terms of amnesty in the proclamation of the President of the U. S. of the 29th of May last, I am an object of censure to a portion of the Country. I have thought it probable that my occupation of the position of President might draw upon the College a feeling of hostility. I should therefore cause injury to an institution which it would be my highest desire to advance. I think it is the duty of every citizen, in the present condition of the country, to do all in his power to aid in the restoration of peace and harmony, and in no way to oppose the policy of the state or general government directed to that object. It is particularly incumbent with those charged with the instruction of the young to set them an example of submission to authority and I could not consent to be the cause of animadversion upon the college.

"Should you however take a different view & think that my services in the position tendered me by the Board will be advantageous to the college and country, I will yield to your judgment and accept it. Otherwise I must most respectfully decline the office.

"Begging you to express to the trustees of the college my heartfelt gratitude for the honors conferred upon me and requesting you to accept my cordial thanks for the kind manner in which you have communicated its decision,

"I am, Gentlemen, with great respect,

"Your most obedient servant,

"R. E. LEE."[3]

That General Lee had been thinking of the part that education must play in the rebuilding of the South can be seen from another letter which he wrote about this time to the Reverend G. W. Leyburn:

"So greatly have those interests [educational] been disturbed at the South, and so much does its future condition depend upon the rising generation, that I consider the proper education of its youth one of the most important objects now to be attained, and one from which the greatest benefits may be expected. Nothing will compensate us for the depression of the standard of our moral and intellectual culture, and each State should take the most ener-

---

[3]Library of Congress Manuscripts.

getic measures to revise the schools and colleges, and, if possible, to increase the facilities for instruction, and to elevate the standard of learning."[4]

So at the age of fifty-eight, when most men are beginning to think of quiet, General Lee rode into Lexington to begin a work which was wholly new to him at the munificent salary of fifteen hundred dollars a year.

There was Spartan simplicity in the ceremony of his inauguration. A recitation room of the college was the scene. The audience was composed of the faculty and students, the pastors of the town churches, and two county officials. The Board entered with the President-elect. Prayer was offered by Doctor White, of the Lexington Presbyterian Church, and a New York newspaper man noticed that "he prayed for the President of the United States." Judge Brockenbrough stated the object of their coming together. "He felt," he said, "the serious dignity of the occasion, but it was a seriousness and a dignity that should be mingled with heartfelt joy and gladness." General Lee remained standing, his arms quietly folded as the Judge went on to congratulate them on having obtained one so loved and great to preside over the college. The oath of the President was then administered by Justice William White. It is as follows: "I do swear that I will, to the best of my skill and judgment, faithfully and truly discharge the duties required of me by an act entitled 'An act for incorporating the rector and trustees of Liberty Hall Academy,' without favor affection or partiality. So help me God."

General Lee affixed his signature to this oath and it was handed to the county clerk "for safe and perpetual guar-

[4] R. and L., p. 210.

dianship," whereupon the new President received the keys
of the college. The ceremonies ended with a round of
congratulations.[5]

The physical condition of the college occupied him first.
The repair of the buildings had begun before his arrival
but he at once gave this his personal attention. The
grounds needed much work, the fences were down and the
walks were ankle deep in mud. As a first step to the im-
provement of the latter, General Lee had a quantity of
broken limestone spread over them. As there were no
rollers available to smooth down the rough broken surface,
both horsemen and footmen took to the grass. One morning he met Colonel Preston riding in this way and putting
his arm affectionately around the horse's neck and petting
him, he said, " 'Colonel, this is a beautiful horse; I am sorry
he is so tenderfooted that he avoids our new road.' Afterwards Colonel Preston always rode on the stoneway!"[6]

A young lawyer, who had been in his army and who was
afterward to be a distinguished figure in Virginia, the
Honorable William A. Anderson, remembers that the first
case he had was when General Lee retained him soon after
his arrival from law school to establish the boundaries of
the college property. After having a surveyor run the
lines according to the old deeds, he found that some of
the foremost citizens of Lexington, whose grounds ad-
joined the campus, including the War Governor, John
Letcher, were encroaching upon the college property and
had to be warned to remove their fences back to the right
place.

In the archives of the college is to be found his letter-
book of this period. Everything is written in his own

[5] *New York World*, October 2, 1865.
[6] *Lee after Appomattox*, p. 21.

hand. It is a transcript of those busy days. Here is an order for shingles to repair some building, and there one for stoves for the students' rooms. Or he is arranging for the delivery of wood for the college wood-yard while the roads were open, so as to save the boys the heavier cost of the winter haul. Or he is writing an almost daily report to a father in Texas whose son is sick, or frequently and very tactfully to many fathers about their sons' failure to meet his expectations for them. As one studies these old flimsy pages with their fading ink one realizes the infinite care for detail that characterized the man. It was a small job, this presidency of a little country college with insufficient funds, a job that many of his proud captains would have scorned, that no other soldier of like fame in the world's history would have attempted, but it was his chance to rebuild Virginia and nothing about the task was alien to him. With infinite toil and meager help he went ahead.

Although General Lee's experience in educational matters was limited to his three years of service as Superintendent of West Point he had some very definite ideas as to the education that the times demanded, and he proceeded to put these into practise. He believed firmly in a broad background of a classical and literary culture. One of his faculty quotes him as saying that it had been his lifelong regret that he had not completed his classical education (in which, however, he had a respectable scholarship) before going to West Point. Yet he was also a strong advocate of practical, even technical, education as can be seen by a study of the plans formulated for the college. He did not, however, believe in separate technical schools but thought, to quote his own words, "that scientific and professional studies can best be taught when surrounded by the liberalizing influence of a literary institution." Especially was he opposed to a military education for other than army officers. "Military education," he used to say, "is an unfortunate necessity for the soldier but the worst possible preparation for civil life. For many years I have observed the failure in business pursuits of men who have resigned from the army, it is very rare that any one of them has achieved success." This aversion to military usages found its way into his administration of discipline, which was in marked contrast to what might have been expected of one who had exercised military authority for so many years. Another member of his faculty records an incident as typical of the extent to which he carried this aversion to military usages.

"It sometimes happened that the faculties of the college and Virginia Military Institute followed by the students and cadets marched in a joint procession. On such occasions General Lee and General Smith (superintendent of V. M. I.) marched side by side. General Smith always held himself in exact military posture and brought his feet, especially the left one, down firmly in perfect time, whereas not even the beating of the bass drum could make General Lee keep step. He simply walked along in a natural manner, but although this manner appeared so natural, it seemed to me that he consciously avoided keeping step, so uniformily did he fail to plant his foot simultaneously with General Smith or at the beat of the drum."[7]

There followed quickly some changes in curriculum to meet the demands of the time as the President saw them. It is not to be thought that all these changes originated in his own mind. He had the wisdom to surround himself

---

[7] *Ibid.*, p. 33.

with the best men he could get and to seek council from them. But having taken their thought he made it his own. At a Board meeting in October, three months after General Lee assumed the presidency, a plan was adopted for establishing additional professorships in Practical Chemistry, "including Metallurgy and the application of the principles of chemistry to agriculture, mining, manufacturing and the mechanic arts, together with vegetable and animal physiology;" in "Experimental Philosophy and Practical Mechanics"; in "Applied Mathematics including the science of Civil Engineering"; in Modern Languages, and in History.[8] The old classical college was reaching out to the needs of the new day in the shaping of men who would be fitted for leadership in its new tasks. The old aristocratic life was gone. A new democracy brought new tasks. A new South was having its beginning as he led it on.

The changes in curriculum did not end here. As rapidly as funds permitted the following were added. In 1867 a school of Law and Equity to provide trained lawyers and legislators. In 1868 a School of Civil and Mining Engineering to train the leaders required for that industrial development of the South that could no longer depend on slave labor for its bread. In 1869 a School of Journalism, and in 1870 a School of Commerce and Business Administration. These last two were the first collegiate schools of this type in America. In June, 1869, another radical departure was had in the setting up of a summer term where the work done was of college standard.

The School of Journalism is typical of the far view that President Lee took in planning the development of his college and meeting, through it, the need of the times.

---

[8] Minute Book Trustees, pp. 389-90.

The blackness of darkness of Reconstruction was all over the South. The newspapers suffered with the rest, and false opinions, lying propaganda, unworthy rumors, found a place in their pages. Lee saw clearly the need of a new leadership in editorial chairs, a trained and an informed leadership, and on March 30, 1869, he sent this recommendation to the Trustees: "I beg leave, to submit for your consideration, several propositions from the faculty. . . . The proposition recommending the institution of 50 scholarships for young men proposing to make printing and journalism their life work and profession."

The catalogue for 1869 announced that "The Board of Trustees have authorized the faculty to appoint to scholarships a number of men intending to make practical printing and journalism their business in life. These scholarships are to be free from tuition and college fees, on condition that when required by the faculty they shall perform such disciplinary duties as may be assigned to them in a printing office or in other positions in the line of their profession for a time equal to one hour in each working day." The idea of the President behind the new move was that men must understand the world in which they lived before they could report it for others, and that character and vision must be planted in men before they dared assume the responsibility of the Fourth Estate. Thus it was in keeping with the idea that was fundamental to him in the whole matter of education. Education was to him far more than the making of merely informed men. The man must also be a man of character, and the teaching and discipline were primarily to that end. The boy that came to his college was an individual. He must be shaped to be an individual in relations, able to take his place as a wise man and a good man in human society and to per-

form his part in the forward movement of that society.
And character to him meant Christian character. To a
venerable minister of Lexington he said: "I shall be disappointed, sir, if I fail in the leading object that brought
me here, unless these young men all become consistent
Christians."[9] This rings out in the letters to parents one
finds in the old letter-book. It also underlay all his deal-
ings with students, all his plans for the development of
the college. It is the reason why he insisted on the building of the College Chapel before he would consent to
spending any money on a house for himself.

That he was not a mere pietist, idly dreaming of the
impossible, will be seen in this testimony as to how wide-
spread was his influence on all phases of the college life.
The words quoted are those of Professor Joynes, of the
Department of Modern Languages during his presidency,
but they are repeated by many others, teachers and
students.

"Nor was it a moral influence alone that he exerted in
the college. He was equally careful of the intellectual interests. He watched the progress of every class, attended
all the examinations, and strove constantly to stimulate
both professors and students to the highest attainments.
The whole college, in a word, felt his influence as an ever-
present motive, and his character was quietly but irresis-
tibly impressed upon it, not only in the general working
of all its departments, but in all the details of each. Of
this influence General Lee, modest as he was, was perfectly
aware, and, like a prudent ruler, he husbanded it with wise
economy. He preferred to confine his direct interposition
to purely personal acts, and rarely—and then only on
critical occasions—did he step forward to present himself

[9] *Lee after Appomattox*, p. 19.

before the whole body of students in the full dignity of his presidential office. On these occasions, which in the latter years hardly ever occurred, he would quietly post an address to the students, in which, appealing only to the highest principles of conduct, he sought to dissuade them from threatened evil. The addresses which the boys designated as his 'general orders,' were always of immediate efficacy. No single case ever occurred in which they failed of instant and complete effect; and no student would have been tolerated by his fellow-students who would have dared to disregard such an appeal from General Lee."[10]

One is amazed as one reads the testimony of those who were associated with him during these days at the extent to which he carried his interest in the work of the individual student. He made a weekly examination of the records of absences and failures in recitations, and with that retentive memory which had ever distinguished him, he kept this record clearly in his mind. One day as the faculty were discussing the standing of students, the President remarked of one, "I am sorry to see that he has fallen back so far in his mathematics." "You are mistaken, General," said the Professor, "he is one of the best men in my department." "He only got fifty-four last month," was the reply. On looking at the record it was found that there had been a mistake in copying and that the President was correct as it stood. There were times when the gift of satire that he could use on occasion was employed to stir up the lagging students, as when inquiry was made by a father as to his son's standing: "He is a quiet orderly young man, but seems very careful not to injure the health of his father's son. He got last month only forty on his Greek, thirty-five on mathematics, forty-seven on his

---

[10] R. and L., p. 301.

Latin and fifty in his English, which is a very low standing. Now I do not wish our young men to really injure their health, but I wish them to come near it as possible."[11]

The enrolment grew more rapidly than the facilities of the college for taking care of it. The first year it was eighty-seven in the college and fifty-nine in the preparatory department. The standards were steadily raised and the preparatory department abolished. Yet four years later, the last year of which President Lee was able to make a report to the Board, there were three hundred and forty-eight in the college alone and it stood among the first in the South, drawing its students from every state in the old Confederacy and from many outside of it.

---

[11] Long, p. 448.

Chapter XL

The Years at Lexington

ALTHOUGH those years at Lexington were busy years, busy with the problems that any college brings to its executive, yet there was also in them time for the simple pleasures of life. These centered largely about his family and his home. His favorite seat in the house was in a deep window from which he could see the rolling fields of grass and grain that swept on to the tree-covered mountains. The Valley of Virginia is a fair valley, good to look upon, good also to live in. Perhaps as he sat at the window looking out over it he did not think alone of its beauty, but of the days when it was the key to his strategy, and when, with Stonewall leading, his tattered regiments moved in swift and amazing fashion along its metaled roads. Over those same roads and up into those mountains he rode on Traveller at the ending of the day. Perhaps there were times when he drew rein and waited as though he listened for far-off bugles. He writes to his daughter of "my solitary evening rides, which give me abundant opportunity for quiet thought."[1] What those thoughts were he kept to himself. At least if they were bitter he told no one of them. There is no more vivid contrast in all the pages of history than the story of these Lexington days and those Napoleon spent at St. Helena. "Dignified, patient, useful, sweet in domesticity, they in all things com-

---

[1] *R. and L.*, p. 305.

manded respect,"[2] wrote a former enemy about them.

The day began with attendance at Chapel. This he expected of his associates on the faculty, and this he never failed in himself when he was at home. Nor was it a pose, a thing that was done because it was the thing to do. Coming out of the Chapel one day it was noticed that he was visibly affected. Some one ventured to ask the reason. He answered, "I was thinking of my responsibility to Almighty God for these hundreds of young men."[3] His letters and the accounts that remain of his family life bear every evidence of a vital faith in the Christian religion. He was throughout his life a very devout man, as devout as Stonewall Jackson, with an added note of sweetness and light. Perhaps this more than any other thing accounts for him. It is not only blood that gives a man steadiness. So one of his old chaplains who had followed him all those years of war and who was his friend and counselor after the war was done, has this to say about it:

"As I was watching alone by his body the day after his death I picked up from the table a well-used pocket Bible, on the fly-leaf of which was written in his well-known and characteristic chirography 'R. E. Lee, Lieutenant Colonel, U. S. A.' As I turned its leaves and saw how he had marked many passages . . . I thought of how, with simple faith, he took this blessed book as the man of his counsel and the light of his pathway; how its precious promises cheered him amid the afflictions and trials of his eventful life and how its glorious hopes illumined for him the valley and shadow of death."[4]

---

[2] C. F. Adams, Address Lee Centennial.

[3] *Lee after Appomattox*, p. 107.

[4] *Ibid.*, p. 189.

Place beside this the words he wrote just after Gettysburg to the dying wife of his wounded son, then a prisoner of the northern army: "In His own good time He will relieve us, and make all things work together for our good, if we will give Him our love and place in Him our trust."[5] This explains much about those latter years and their serenity. And on the day he died his wife wrote to a friend that his was "a course of righteousness that never wavered from the path of duty at any sacrifice of ease or pleasure and long too has the will of God been the guiding star of his actions."[6]

After Chapel followed the routine duties of the day. There were letters to be written, examinations to be attended—he was present regularly at these—discipline to be dealt out. He was disposed to be lenient with students who were reported to him as being derelict. He would say to the faculty, when it was proposed to send a student home, "Don't you think it would be better to bear with him a little longer? Perhaps we can do him good."[7] A member of that faculty tells of a piece of advice he gave him as to his treatment of poor students: "Always observe the stage driver's rule." "What is that, General?" "Always take care of the poor horses."[8] But he could send home his point! An old student of his remembers the morning when, crossing the campus, he met another coming from the President's office. "I would rather go through hell than face Marse Robert again."

Then when the day's work was done came the ride on Traveller. That iron-gray horse was a privileged charac-

---

[5] Adams address.
[6] *Virginia Magazine of History and Biography*, January, 1927.
[7] *R. and L.*, p. 331.
[8] *Lee after Appomattox*, p. 28.

ter. He was allowed to roam at will about the grounds of the President's house, wherever the grass was greenest and freshest. Toward this old companion in battle Lee was more demonstrative than he was with men. Usually when he entered the gate he would leave the walk, and caress Traveller's head for a moment before passing on to the house. He permitted no one but himself to take him to the blacksmith's to be shod, and on these occasions he would say to the smith, "Have patience with Traveller; he was made nervous by the bursting of bombs around him during the war."[9]

The evening usually found him at home. Mrs. Lee's rheumatism grew steadily worse and she was forced to spend much of her time in a wheel-chair. There were often guests in the evening. Two rooms, opening on each other, were devoted to their entertainment. In one the General and Mrs. Lee sat, the General reading, while Mrs. Lee did the family mending. For there was little for new clothes in those days and they had to be made to last as long as possible. The other was occupied by the younger people. One of his students has left this account of these evenings.

"When ten o'clock came, if the guests were not disposed to leave, the General would come into the front room, and sit down by the side of a man who was enjoying a tête-à-tête with one of the young ladies. In a moment or two she would join Mrs. Lee in the dining-room. The young man had not come for the purpose of monopolizing the General and so found it convenient to make his bow and depart. The General then proceeded to the same plan with another man until it was evident to all that the

---

[9] *Ibid.*, p. 68.

President thought it was time for all sensible people to be in bed."[10]

Commencement time the house would be full, usually with young girls, the friends of his daughters, who had come for the final festivities of the college year. No one enjoyed those days more than the General, and his son records the fact that "the girls enjoyed his society more than they did that of their college adorers."[11] One evening at an entertainment in his house, he found one dashing belle surrounded by many admirers, some of whom had been in his army. He stopped and began to rally her upon her conquests, saying, "You can do as you please with these other young gentlemen, but you must not treat my 'old soldiers' badly."[12]

His friends on the faculty speak of him as an agreeable companion, with a great deal of bonhomie and pleasantry in his conversation, not exactly witty, but able to give a light turn to table talk, and enjoying greatly any joke. He could also be slightly caustic at times. There are traces of this to be found in his letters, as in that to the spiritualist who wrote asking his opinion of von Moltke. He wrote that "the question was one about which military critics might differ, that his own judgments were poor at best, and that inasmuch as they had the power to consult through their mediums Cæsar, Alexander, Napoleon, Wellington and all of the other great captains who had ever lived, he could not think of obtruding his opinion in such a company."[13] The same trait is manifest in his answer

---

[10] *Ibid.,* p. 91.
[11] *R. and L.,* p. 314.
[12] *Ibid.,* p. 315.
[13] *Ibid.,* p. 316.

to the woman friend who complained that she could not get anything in Lexington suitable for a Lenten diet—no fish, no oysters, nothing of the sort. He gravely assured her: "I would not trouble myself so about special dishes; I suppose if we try to abstain from special sins that is all that will be required of us."[14] How his eyes must have twinkled as he said it!

His letters to his children reveal the fact that they were never out of his thoughts. They are full of intimate tenderness and sage wisdom. His sons were seeking to rebuild their ruined plantations. He tells them about the crops that should be planted, of the labor that should be employed, of the sort of cattle to raise, of the necessity of making the plantations self-supporting in regard to food. "Shad are good in their way but they do not run up the Pamunkey all the year."[15] To his daughter-in-law he sends the news of the doings of the family:

"Mildred, you know, is the only one of the girls who has been with us this winter. She has consequently had her hands full, and considers herself now a great character. She rules her brothers with an iron rod, and scatters her advice broadcast among the young men of the college. I hope that it may yield an abundant harvest. The young mothers of Lexington ought to be extremely grateful to her for her suggestions to them as to the proper mode of rearing their children, and though she finds many unable to appreciate her system, she is nothing daunted by their obtuseness of vision, but takes advantage of every opportunity to enlighten them as to its benefits."[16]

The children of the faculty and of the neighbors were

[14] *Ibid.*, p. 317.
[15] *Ibid.*, p. 510.
[16] *Ibid.*, p. 304.

his special delight. The small son of his neighbor, Professor Campbell, used to watch in the evening for Traveller so that he might run to open the gate. And the General would reach down and gather him up on the saddle behind him to ride to the stable. And one morning the small daughter of another neighbor stood watching a picnic party of college boys and town girls loading themselves into a coach for a trip to the Natural Bridge, when he came along. "Would you like to go with them?" he asked her. "Oh, yes, General!" And picking her up he swung her into their astonished midst with the injunction to see that she was taken care of, and then dispatched a servant to tell the child's mother what had happened. The coming of John Robinson's circus was a great day for the campus children. For the showman was an old Confederate who thought General Lee was the greatest man on earth and he always sent the choicest block of seats to him with his compliments. Then he would gather every child around, big and little, and the President's office would be shut that afternoon, while he sat with his adoring host about him to watch the clowns and the elephants and all the mimic splendor.

While he avoided all publicity and refused to be paraded as a hero he found great delight in visiting among his friends on the old Virginia plantations. Oftentimes he went on these journeys alone, for Mrs. Lee was not equal to much traveling over the rough roads. On these occasions he usually rode Traveller. Coming back from one such visit he found himself in a strange country at nightfall, and sought shelter for the night at a crossroads tavern. The tavern-keeper, who did not recognize him, showed him to his room, and when his son, an ex-Confederate, came in, he told him that a man was spending the night 'with them whose face was familiar but whom he could not place. The son answered, "I do not know who you have in the house, but that's Marse Bob's horse in the barn. I've seen it often enough to know." When the General was leaving in the morning he asked for his bill. The host told him there was no charge. Lee insisted that he could not permit that, that the host had to make his living and that he was able to pay. With simple directness the man answered: "If ever me or mine take anything from you or yours I hope we'll end in the poorhouse."

Two letters show his unwillingness to embarrass those who were in difficult political situations. One was written when the Radicals in Congress were moving heaven and earth to punish President Johnson for carrying out, as he thought, the policies of Lincoln. No restitution had ever been made by the national government for the seizure of Arlington. Lee was the executor of the Custis estate and this was among the properties of that estate and had been willed to his children. Reverdy Johnson, the Senator from Maryland, wrote offering to intercede with the President to secure the return of this property or to procure adequate restitution. In answer to this generous offer Lee wrote:

"I had hoped when passion had subsided and reason resumed her sway that the people of the country would prefer, from former associations, seeing Arlington in possession of Mr. Custis's descendants than appropriated to its present use. But that day seems to me now as distant as at the beginning. I may never see it. Knowing how the President's time is occupied in public matters and how his acts are turned by his opponents to operate against him, I have been unwilling to intrude upon him my private affairs, preferring to wait for some general action of his, in which they might be embraced."[17]

---

[17] Reverdy Johnson papers, Library of Congress.

Not even for his own advantage, poor as he and the family were, would he add one difficulty to those already faced by the hard-driven man in the White House.

Three years later when Grant had become president and when the vindictiveness of the Radicals was at the flood a suggestion was made that he should invite the President to visit Washington College. His reply reveals his fear of embarrassing him who was being driven in turn by the Radicals to actions that were inconsistent with his former attitude. "I should be glad if General Grant would visit Washington College, and I should endeavor to treat him with the courtesy and respect due to the President of the United States; but if I were to invite him to do so, it might not be agreeable to him, and I fear my motives might be misunderstood at this time, both by himself and others, and that evil would result instead of good."[18] It was all part of the same plan that he had formed when he went back to Richmond to do nothing that would hinder and everything that might help to a better understanding.

He steadfastly declined the use of his name for political office. The Democrats sought to nominate him for governor of Virginia, but he would have none of it, fearing that he would only add to the bitterness of the time. In the presidential campaign of 1868 the loyalty of the South to the federal government and its attitude toward the negroes became a vital issue. General Rosecrans, who was one of the active managers of the Democratic party, sought from him an expression of the attitude of the South on these questions. He looked on this as an opportunity to assure the people of the North and West that the South had accepted the changes wrought by the war and intended to abide the result in good faith. The following paper was

[18] *R. and L.*, p. 334.

prepared and his name headed the list of those who signed it.

"Whatever opinions may have prevailed in the past with regard to African slavery or the right of a State to secede from the Union, we believe we express the almost unanimous judgment of the Southern people when we declare that they consider these questions were decided by the war, and that it is their intention in good faith to abide by the decision. At the close of the war, the Southern people laid down their arms and sought to resume their former relations to the government of the United States. Through their State Conventions, they abolished slavery and annulled their ordinances of secession; and they returned to their peaceful pursuits with a sincere purpose to fulfil all their duties under the Constitution of the United States which they had sworn to support. If their action in these particulars had been met in a spirit of frankness and cordiality, we believe that, ere this, old irritations would have passed away, and the wounds inflicted by the war would have been, in a great measure, healed. As far as we are advised, the people of the South entertain no unfriendly feeling toward the government of the United States, but they complain that their rights under the Constitution are withheld from them in the administration thereof. The idea that the Southern people are hostile to the negroes and would oppress them, if it were in their power to do so, is entirely unfounded. They have grown up in our midst, and we have been accustomed from childhood to look upon them with kindness. The change in the relations of the two races has wrought no change in our feelings toward them. They still constitute an important part of our laboring population. Without the labor the lands of the South would be comparatively unproductive; without the employment which Southern agriculture affords, they would be destitute of the means of subsistence and become paupers, dependent upon public bounty.

Self-interest, if there were no higher motive, would therefore prompt the whites of the South to extend to the negro care and protection. The important fact that the two races are, under existing circumstances, necessary to each other is gradually becoming apparent to both, and we believe that but for influence exerted to stir up the passions of the negroes, the relations of the two races would soon adjust themselves on a basis of mutual kindness and advantage.

"It is true that the people of the South, in common with a large majority of the people of the North and West, are, for obvious reasons, inflexibly opposed to any system of laws which would place the political power of the country in the hands of the negro race. But this opposition springs from no feeling of enmity, but from a deep-seated conviction that, at present, the negroes have neither the intelligence nor the other qualifications which are necessary to make them safe depositories of political power. They would inevitably become the victims of demagogues, who, for selfish purposes, would mislead them to the serious injury of the public.

"The great want of the South is peace. The people earnestly desire tranquillity and restoration of the Union. They deprecate disorder and excitement as the most serious obstacles to their prosperity. They ask a restoration of their rights under the Constitution. They desire relief from oppressive misrule. Above all, they would appeal to their countrymen for the re-establishment in the Southern States of that which has been justly regarded as the birth-right of every American, the right of self-government. Establish these on a firm basis, and we can safely promise, on behalf of the Southern people, that they will faithfully obey the Constitution and laws of the United States, treat the negro population with kindness and humanity, and fulfil every duty incumbent on peaceful citizens, loyal to the Constitution of their country."[19]

---

[19]Robertson, pp. 261-62.

The letter was widely circulated and had a profound effect on the campaign. Grant's majority in the election that followed was only 336,301. Had Mississippi, Texas and Virginia been allowed to vote the result would have been otherwise.

When summer came and the college duties were at an end for a while he was accustomed to take Mrs. Lee to the White Sulphur Springs to drink the waters. They had a cottage on "Baltimore Row." Whenever he was present he himself pushed her wheeled chair about, into the dining-room and out on the verandas or wherever she wished to go. There was one custom peculiar to the "Old White" of a promenade up and down the long parlor after a meal. There those who had been guests before aided in the introduction of newcomers. It was a gay informal scene. General Lee, who had been coming there for many years before the war and after, was always prominent on these occasions and took time to dispense those courtesies which made things easier for many. In the evenings the great dining-room was transformed into a ballroom and the negro waiters became the orchestra.

Northerners had begun to come back to the Springs and the General was especially solicitous for their comfort. It was not always an easy task to make them feel at home. One evening a group of recent arrivals, bearing a name celebrated in the war, stood apart with no one to bid them welcome. General Lee inquired of a group of young people whether they had sought to show these northern strangers the hospitality of which Virginia boasted. Getting no response he finally declared his intention of introducing himself and asked for any of the young women who would go with him. "I will go, General Lee, under your orders," said one. "Not under my orders," he corrected, "but it will gratify me to have your assistance." As they crossed the room he stopped to tell his young companion "of the grief with which he found a spirit of increasing resentment and bitterness in the young people of the South, of the sinfulness of hatred and social revenge, of the duty of kindness, helpfulness and consideration for others." "But, General Lee, did you never feel resentment toward the North?" The answer came in quiet tones: "I believe I may say, looking into my own heart, and speaking as in the presence of God, that I have never known one moment of bitterness or resentment."[20]

The summer of 1870 was the last time White Sulphur saw him. To a young girl who had been asked to visit the family that summer and had sent a message of regret with the hope that she might come the next summer, he sent this word: "Tell her that she should have come now, next summer will be too late, I shall not be here." And in answer to the remonstrance of the one to whom he spoke he added, "My child, I think I am the very oldest man you have ever seen."[21]

---

[20]Bond, pp. 31-32.
[21]*Ibid.*, p. 51.

CHAPTER XLI

The End

NEXT summer he was not there. The end came suddenly
on October 12, 1870. In October of the previous year
he had contracted a severe cold which he had great difficulty in shaking off, and it left him greatly weakened. It
grew apparent as the winter wore on that there was a
serious trouble with his heart, an inflammation of the
heart-sac brought on by the rheumatism from which he
had suffered since the closing years of the war.[1] No more
could he put Traveller into a gallop on the evening rides.
In fact those rides became few. His doctors ordered him
to go South in order to escape the rigors and the storms
of winter's end in Lexington. He writes to his daughter
Mildred:

"I think I should do better here, and am very reluctant
to leave home in my present condition: but they seem
so interested in my recovery and so persuasive in their un-
easiness that I should appear obstinate, if not perverse, if
I resisted longer. I therefore consented to go and will take
Agnes to Savannah, as she seems anxious to visit that city,
or perhaps, she will take me. I wish also to visit my dear
Annie's grave before I die. I have always desired to do so
since the cessation of active hostilities, but have never been
able."[2]

---

[1] Long, p. 471.
[2] *R. and L.,* p. 385.

He found the journey trying, and was a little dismayed with the outpouring of the people to see him when his train stopped. His daughter writes: "At Raleigh and another place the people crowded to the depot and called 'Lee! Lee!' and cheered vociferously but we were locked up and 'mum.'" He found the winter cold and raw, but his letters to his wife tell as they had from the beginning of his joy in the flowers he saw as his train passed: "the yellow jasmine covering all the trees."[3] His old soldiers crowded on him everywhere, and he was compelled to endure a round of receptions that must have been trying to a sick man. It is little wonder that he writes, "I wish I were back."[4]

May found him back in Virginia, visiting the friends in whom he delighted. One of these houses was Shirley where his mother had been born and where he often went as a boy. A daughter of the house tells of that visit: "We regarded him with the greatest veneration. We had heard of God, but here was General Lee!"[5] The legend was already beginning to take form! At another house one of his young cousins, in talking with him wondered "what fate was in store for us poor Virginians." This was his answer—and it is the philosophy behind all those last years—"You can work for Virginia, to build her up again, to make her great again. You can teach your children to love and cherish her."[6] Until the last he was Lee of Virginia.

He returned to Lexington in time for the final examinations at the college, and attended as usual to his duties

[3]*Ibid.*, p. 390.
[4]*Ibid.*, p. 395.
[5]*Ibid.*, p. 405.
[6]*Ibid.*, p. 410.

during that period. Early in July he went to Baltimore to consult a specialist. This journey gave him an opportunity to visit again that cousin to whom he had turned in the days when he was making his great decision, and who was his constant adviser, Cassius Lee, of Alexandria. This was one of the few times when he talked unreservedly about the war. "He told of the delay of Jackson in getting on McClellan's flank, causing the fight at Mechanicsville, which fight he said was unexpected, but was necessary to prevent McClellan from entering Richmond, from the front of which most of the troops had been moved. He thought that if Jackson had been at Gettysburg they would have gained a victory 'for Jackson would have held the heights which Ewell took on the first day.' He said that Ewell was a fine officer, but would never take the responsibility of exceeding his orders and having been ordered to Gettysburg he would not go further and hold the heights beyond the town."[7]

That summer he was again at White Sulphur, returning as he thought in better health. On September twenty-eighth, after a busy day in the college he went at four o'clock to a vestry meeting at Grace Church. The afternoon was wet and cold, and a rain had set in which lasted several days and ended in the worst flood that section ever saw. The church was cold and damp and he sat with his military cloak about him. The meeting lasted until after seven o'clock as plans were being discussed for the building of a new church. Just as the meeting closed the treasurer announced that a deficit existed in the minister's salary and General Lee said, "I will give that sum."[8] Let

[7] *Ibid.*, p. 415.
[8] Long, p. 472.

WHEN ENEMY CIVIL WAR GENERALS SAT DOWN IN PEACE

A rare photo, taken sixty-two years ago at White Sulphur Springs. Va. Seated, left to right: Blacque Bey, General Lee, George Peabody of Massachusetts and W. W. Corcoran of Washington, noted philanthropists of their day; James Lyons. Standing: Generals John W. Geary, John B. Magruder, Robert D. Lilly, Lew Wallace, P. G. T. Beauregard, Henry A. Wise, Joseph L. Brent and James Connor.

—Wide World Photo

his wife tell the rest of the story, as she wrote it on that October day when he died:

"On the evening of the 29th the same time when that terrible storm commenced, was our regular church evening and after it was over a very protracted vestry meeting of rather an exciting nature. The Gen'l had been unusually occupied all day so much so as not to have had any time for recreation except a little snooze after dinner in his arm chair. When I went into tea at seven he had not returned and I sat down to my sewing waiting for him. About half past seven we heard him come in, put his hat and coat as usual in his room and then as he entered the dining room, I said, 'You have kept us waiting a long time. What have you been doing.' He stood up at the foot of the table to say grace but did not utter a sound and sank back on a chair. I said 'You look very tired. Let me pour you out a cup of tea,' but finding he made no reply and seeing an expression on his face that alarmed me, I called Custis who asked him if he wanted anything and on his failing to make any reply we sent off immediately for the Dr. who had been at the same vestry meeting and he sent for the other one too, in the course of fifteen minutes we had both here and they applied cold cloths to his head and hot applications to his feet and got him undressed and put to bed, while undressing he seemed perfectly conscious and helped pull off his things but didn't speak and slept almost continuously for 2 days and nights the Drs. thinking that his attack proceeded from overstrained nerves and only required rest but finding he did not improve as they had hoped they cupped him and gave him medicine which roused him somewhat and they confidently expected his recovery. He did not speak except a few words occasionally, but always greeted me with an outstretched hand and kindly pressure, took his food with some pleasure and we vainly thought was getting on comfortably, but on Sunday night he suddenly became almost insensible and lay in the condition until Tuesday night when all hope was relinquished indeed. Thursday morning they had none. We all sat up all night, every moment almost expecting to be his last. He lay breathing most heavily and the Dr. said entirely unconscious of pain. I sat with his hand in mine all moist with heavy perspiration and early in the morning came into my room to change my clothes and get a cup of tea, when I went back he lay in much the same condition, only there were some more severe struggles for breath—these became more frequent and intense and after two very severe ones, his breath seemed to pass away gently and he so loved and admired now lies cold and insensible. . . ."[9]

Lexington knew he had gone by the tolling of the bells. All business was suspended and the college closed. The whole South mourned. His old chief of artillery, now the rector of Grace Church, read the service. They buried him in the vault beneath the Chapel he had built. His grave bears only this inscription.

General Robert Edward Lee.

He needs no other. There he sleeps, "his fame the common property and his greatness the common boast of a proud, jealous and exultant people."[10]

---

[9] *Virginia Magazine of History and Biography,* January, 1927.
[10] Editorial in *Baltimore Sunday Telegram,* October 16, 1870.

BIBLIOGRAPHY

BIBLIOGRAPHY

AMBLER, CHARLES HENRY, *Sectionalism in Virginia from 1776 to 1861*, University of Chicago Press, 1910.

AVARY, MYRTA LOCKETT, *Dixie after the War*, Doubleday Doran & Co., New York, 1906.

BARTON, W. E., *The Lineage of Lincoln*, The Bobbs-Merrill Company, Indianapolis, 1929.

BARTON, W. E., *Lincoln at Gettysburg*, The Bobbs-Merrill Company, 1930.

BOND, CHRISTIANA, *Memories of General Robert E. Lee*, The Norman, Remington Co., Baltimore, 1926.

BOYD, THOMAS, *Light-horse Harry Lee*, Charles Scribner's Sons, New York, 1931.

BRADFORD, GAMALIEL, *Lee the American*, Houghton, Mifflin Co., Boston, 1927.

BRUCE, PHILIP A., *Robert E. Lee*, Macrae, Smith Co., Philadelphia, 1907.

BURGESS, JOHN W., *The Civil War and the Constitution*, Charles Scribner's Sons, 1901.

BUTLER, BENJAMIN F., *Autobiography and Personal Reminiscences of Major General Benj. F. Butler; Butler's Book*, A. M. Thayer & Co., Boston, 1892.

CHESNUT, MARY B., *A Diary from Dixie*, Peter Smith, New York, 1929.

CONGER, A. L., *The Rise of U. S. Grant*, The Century Co., New York, 1931.

COOKE, JOHN ESTEN, *The Life of General Robert E. Lee*, D. Appleton & Co., New York, 1871.

COOKE, JOHN ESTEN, *The Life of Stonewall Jackson*, Ayres and Wade, Richmond, 1863.

COOKE, JOHN ESTEN, *Surry of Eagle's-Nest*, F. J. Huntingdon & Co., New York, 1866.

COOKE, JOHN ESTEN, *Hammer and Rapier*, G. W. Carleton, New York, 1871.

DAVIS, JEFFERSON, *The Rise and Fall of the Confederate Government*, D. Appleton & Co., 1881.

DODD, WILLIAM E., *Jefferson Davis*, Macrae, Smith Co., 1907.

DODD, WILLIAM E., *Statesmen of the Old South*, The Macmillan Company, New York, 1921.

DODD, WILLIAM E., *Lincoln or Lee*, The Century Co., 1928.

EARLY, JUBAL A., *Autobiographical Sketch and Narrative of the War between the States*, J. B. Lippincott Company, Philadelphia, 1912.

ECKENRODE, HAMILTON J., *Jefferson Davis, President of the South*, The Macmillan Co., 1923.

FULLER, J. F. C., *The Generalship of Ulysses S. Grant*, Dodd, Mead & Co., New York, 1929.

GIBBON, JOHN, *Personal Recollections of the Civil War*, G. P. Putnam's Sons, New York, 1928.

GORDON, JOHN B., *Reminiscences of the Civil War*, Charles Scribner's Sons, 1903.

GRANT, U. S., *Personal Memoirs of U. S. Grant*, Charles L. Webster & Co., New York, 1885.

HAGUE, PARTHENIA A., *A Blockaded Family*, Houghton, Mifflin Co., 1888.

HAY, JOHN, *Unpublished Diary*, Library of Congress.

HENDERSON, G. F. R., *Stonewall Jackson and the American Civil War*, Longmans, Green & Co., New York, 1898.

HENDERSON, G. F. R., *The Science of War*, Longmans, Green & Co., 1905.

HUNTER, ALEXANDER, *Johnny Reb and Billy Yank*, Neale Publishing Co., Washington, 1905.

JAMES, MARQUIS, *The Raven*, The Bobbs-Merrill Company, 1930.

JONES, J. B., *A Rebel War Clerk's Diary*, J. B. Lippincott Company, 1866.

JONES, J. WILLIAM, *Personal Reminiscences of General Robert E. Lee*, D. Appleton & Co., 1876.

JONES, J. WILLIAM, *Life and Letters of Robert Edward Lee*, Neale Publishing Co., 1906.

KNOWLES, DAVID, *The American Civil War*, Oxford Press, 1926.

Lee's Dispatches, 1862-1865, G. P. Putnam's Sons, 1915.

LEE, FITZHUGH, *General R. E. Lee*, D. Appleton & Co., 1894.

LEE, (MRS.) SUSAN (PENDLETON), *Memoirs of William Nelson Pendleton*, J. B. Lippincott Company, 1893.

LEECH, SAMUEL V., *The Raid of John Brown at Harper's Ferry as I Saw It*, Published by Author, 1909.

LONG, ARONISTEAD L., *Memoirs of Robert E. Lee*, J. M. Stoddart & Co., New York, 1886.

LONGSTREET, JAMES, *From Manassas to Appomattox*, J. B. Lippincott Company, 1903.

LONN, ELLA, *Desertion during the Civil War*, The Century Co., 1928.

MAURICE, FREDERICK, *An Aide-de-Camp of Lee*, Little Brown & Co., Boston, 1927.

MAURICE, FREDERICK, *Statesmen and Soldiers of the Civil War*, Little Brown & Co., 1926.

MAURICE, FREDERICK, *Robert E. Lee, the Soldier*, Houghton, Mifflin Co., 1925.

MCCALL, SAMUEL W., *Thaddeus Stevens*, Houghton, Mifflin Co., 1899.

MCKIM, RANDOLPH H., *The Soul of Lee*, Longmans, Green & Co., 1918.

MCMASTER, JOHN B., *A History of the People of the United States during Lincoln's Administration*, D. Appleton & Co., 1927.

MOORE, ALBERT B., *Conscription and Conflict in the Confederacy*, The Macmillan Company, 1924.

MORSE, ANSON DANIEL, *Parties and Party Leaders*, Marshall Jones Company, Boston, 1923.

NICOLAY AND HAY, *Abraham Lincoln, A History*, The Century Co., 1890.

O. R., *Official Records of the War of the Rebellion*.

PAGE, THOMAS NELSON, *Robert E. Lee, the Southerner*, Charles Scribner's Sons, 1908.

PAXTON, *Elisha Franklin Paxton*, by his son. Privately printed, 1905.

PORTER, HORACE, *Campaigning with Grant*, The Century Co., 1897.

R. AND L. *Recollections and Letters of General Robert E. Lee*, by Captain Robert E. Lee. Copyright, 1904, 1924, by Doubleday, Doran & Co.

RHODES, JAMES F., *A History of the United States from the Compromise of 1850 to the McKinley-Bryan Campaign of 1896*, The Macmillan Company, 1892-1919.

RILEY, FRANKLIN L., *General Robert E. Lee after Appomattox,* The Macmillan Company, 1922.

ROBERTSON, ALEXANDER F., *Alexander Hugh Holmes Stuart,* The William Byrd Press, Richmond, Va., 1925.

SCHAFF, MORRIS, *The Sunset of the Confederacy,* J. W. Luce and Co., Boston, 1912.

SMITH, EDWARD C., *The Borderland in the Civil War,* The Macmillan Company, 1927.

SNOW, WILLIAM, *Lee and His Generals,* Richardson and Co., New York, 1867.

STEPHENS, ALEXANDER H., *A Constitutional View of the Late War between the States,* National Publishing Co., 1868-70.

SWINTON, WILLIAM, *Campaigns of the Army of the Potomac,* Charles Scribner's Sons, 1882.

TAYLOR, WALTER H., *Four Years with General Lee,* D. Appleton & Co., 1877.

THOMASON, JOHN WILLIAM, *Jeb Stuart,* Charles Scribner's Sons, 1930.

VON HOLST, HERMAN E., *John C. Calhoun,* Houghton, Mifflin Co., 1882.

WHITE, HENRY A., *Robert E. Lee and the Southern Confederacy,* G. P. Putnam's Sons, 1897.

WILSON, WOODROW, *Division and Reunion, 1829-1889,* Longmans, Green & Co., Boston, 1893.

WISE, JOHN S., *The End of an Era,* Houghton, Mifflin Co., 1899.

WORSHAM, J. H., *One of Jackson's Foot-Cavalry,* Neale Publishing Co., Washington, 1912.

YOUNG, JAMES C., *Marse Robert, Knight of the Confederacy,* Rae D. Henkle Co., N. Y., 1929.

INDEX

INDEX